VANCOUVER
AFTER DARK

VANCOUVER AFTER DARK

The Wild History of a City's Nightlife

AARON CHAPMAN

ARSENAL
PULP PRESS
VANCOUVER

ARSENAL PULP PRESS
Suite 202 – 211 East Georgia St.
Vancouver, BC V6A 1Z6
Canada
arsenalpulp.com

The publisher gratefully acknowledges the support of the Canada Council for the Arts
and the British Columbia Arts Council for its publishing program, and the Government
of Canada, and the Government of British Columbia (through the Book Publishing Tax
Credit Program), for its publishing activities.

Arsenal Pulp Press acknowledges the xʷməθkʷəy̓əm (Musqueam), Sḵwx̱wú7mesh
(Squamish), and səl̓ilwətaʔɬ (Tsleil-Waututh) Nations, speakers of Hul'q'umi'num'/
Halq'eméylem/hən̓q̓əmin̓əm̓ and custodians of the traditional, ancestral, and unceded
territories where our office is located. We pay respect to their histories, traditions, and
continuous living cultures and commit to accountability, respectful relations, and friendship.

Cover design by Oliver McPartlin
Text design by Electra Design Group
Front cover photo: Granville Street, 1959. Ken Oakes, *Vancouver Sun*
Edited by Derek Fairbridge
Copy edited by Shirarose Wilensky
Proofread by Alison Strobel

Printed and bound in Canada

Library and Archives Canada Cataloguing Publication:
Title: Vancouver after dark : the wild history of a city's nightlife / Aaron Chapman
Names: Chapman, Aaron, 1971– author.
Identifiers: Canadiana 20190130156 | ISBN 9781551527833 (softcover)
Subjects: LCSH: Popular music—British Columbia—Vancouver—History and criticism.
  LCSH: Nightclubs—British Columbia—Vancouver—History.
Classification: LCC ML3484.8 V22 C46 2019 | LCC ML3484.8* | DDC
782.421640971133—dc23

CONTENTS

West Hastings Street at night in the 1920s. *Credit: Dominion Photo company c/o the VPL Special Collections #22253*

INTRODUCTION

"... I'm on the guest list. What's the cover charge? Good to see you again! I thought I told you you weren't allowed in here anymore? What time do you open? What time is the band on? What time do you close? Can you work for me tonight? Is it last call? Can I get your number? What are you doing now? What are you doing later? Can your friend come along? Can your friend stay home? Can we leave the gear here overnight? What do you mean you gave the money to the drummer? What was the name of that place again? I'll never forget that night ..."

The nocturnal language found in nightclubs is perhaps the same the world over. But if you check out any travel guide, tourist brochure, or promotional film about Vancouver over the decades, you'll notice they rarely showcase the city's nightlife. Aside from a few nondescript photos of twinkling city lights at night—shown to reassure visitors that nighttime does indeed exist here—Vancouver after dark is not usually presented to visitors as the main attraction.

Instead, Vancouver tends to value its picturesque daytime beauty above all else. The imagery of the city that is sold to the outside world depicts bright bustling neighbourhoods full of boutique shops, set against a backdrop of photogenic beaches and mountains, both of which can be visited in the same afternoon. When they are shown at all, images of the city's nightlife delve no deeper than a few suggestions of smiling couples dining at a nameless bistro or a group of friends cheering in an arena for a sports event—almost as if to caution those who do step out for the night not to stray too far or stay out too late. Don't sleep in, don't miss getting up early to sip a designer coffee on some waterfront patio with an Instagram-worthy view. But there is more to Vancouver than sunny English Bay beaches or sophisticated Yaletown gastropubs that is worthy of being celebrated.

Perhaps it's not surprising that Vancouver's nightlife has never been honoured as much as its daytime equivalent, because those who ran the city over the decades have done their best to suppress its nocturnal side, monitoring not only the kinds of nightspots its citizens might escape to but also what they did there. There were cafés that were allowed to serve food but not offer entertainment. There were cabarets that presented musical acts, but patrons were not allowed to get up and dance. And there were supper clubs that both offered entertainment and served food but could not sell alcohol. Perhaps no single industry in the history of Vancouver has been as regulated and constricted over the years as its nightclubs. In the 1950s and '60s, the Vancouver Police Department (VPD) spent their time conducting dry squad raids to ensure nightclub patrons were not

Granville Street, 1966. *Credit: Aaron Chapman Archives*

imbibing alcohol. Pious government officials viewed alcohol consumption with suspicion and regarded those who frequented nightclubs with disdain. God forbid an evening's entertainment involve seeing a show, having a dance, and enjoying a drink or two. The fear about alcohol—the blood that ran through the nightclubs' veins—was that it would reduce good upstanding citizens to desperate vampires who would surely forget their daytime responsibilities to their families, their country, and their faith if booze were ever freely available to them at night.

But despite all the city's efforts to make the lives of both those who managed and went to nightclubs difficult, the ballrooms, the lounges, the dives, and the discos have always been here, even if those places haven't always boldly advertised themselves.

Vancouver is overdue to proudly showcase the history of the unique nightlife that developed here. The city benefitted from being on Canada's western frontier. In the 1950s and '60s, many visiting Ameri-

can entertainers, following established touring routes that went back to the days of vaudeville, came north to Vancouver to perform, and then simply turned around and headed back down the Pacific coast once their engagements finished, instead of continuing eastward through the rest of Canada. Vancouver got to see performers that the rest of the country often missed out on.

In the 1970s, when original music by Vancouver-based artists took on greater prominence, some of Canada's most defiant rock 'n' roll poured out of the city's nightclubs. Vancouver's nightclub owners prospered humbly, often in downbeat locations, where they fostered world-class musicians who could compete with any New York or Hollywood session player. And one of those most downtrodden skid row clubs incubated the biggest comedy duo of the decade. In the 1980s, a litany of some of the biggest rock bands began to camp out in one of the city's legendary recording studios and were seen regularly blowing off steam at downtown nightclubs. In the 1990s, as modern DJs emerged in the local underground dance clubs, their playlists got noticed globally. What is it about the rainy mists of Vancouver that has inspired such world-renowned musicians, singers, DJs, and club impresarios over the decades?

It seems like there has been something more at play in Vancouver than in other cities, but the city has changed so quickly and so dramatically over the last thirty years that there is a sense that we have lost too many of our fabled nightspots in that time. Many Vancouverites of a certain age reminisce about the good times they had at the Cave or Isy's Supper Club. The Smilin' Buddha Cabaret has taken on a deep mythology in the city's early punk rock lore. And other nightspots, from the Town Pump to Richard's on Richards, evoke similar feelings of nostalgia. In 2018, the online publication *Vancouver Is Awesome* released a series of T-shirts that featured the logos of local companies and establishments of the past, and the best-selling shirt depicted the logo for the iconic Luv-a-Fair nightclub. Nostalgia expresses a wish to return not only to a certain era but to the very places where those special memories were forged.

There is a sentiment that good times come and go; therefore, no nightclub is meant to last forever. And Vancouver isn't the exception to that rule. But I have not included every lost tavern or watering hole in *Vancouver after Dark*—that would be impossible! Instead, I have chosen to shine a spotlight on the clubs that had live entertainment and where some pivotal changes or trends occurred—nightspots that provide a glimpse into the cultural history of Vancouver at the time. Any complete history of the city's nightlife needs to include the remarkable evolution of Vancouver restaurants, or its after-hours spaces—a murky collection of back doors to knock on at half-remembered addresses that in their clandestine hearts might hold the best stories never told.

As well, I have only briefly mentioned some of Vancouver's fascinating untamed early gay nightspots that surely deserve a modern history of their own.

I have decided to exclude some famous clubs, such as the Railway and the Yale, because even though they have changed their format or ownership, they are still operational, and their stories aren't over. Likewise, I mention only briefly clubs that remain landmarks in the Vancouver entertainment scene, like the Penthouse and the Commodore. I invite you to explore my earlier books *Liquor, Lust, and the Law* and *Live at the Commodore*, which are dedicated completely to those venues.

Vancouver after Dark travels behind the scenes into some of the city's legendary nightspots to reveal not only the kind of entertainment that was found in them but also the stars, has-beens, and never-wases who lived and worked in them. Although the music and entertainment offered in the city's nightclubs changed over the years, the sort of person who operated these establishments remained remarkably the same. The job of nightclub proprietor attracted business geniuses who might otherwise have excelled at running Fortune 500 companies, as well as gamblers, liars, and cheats—sometimes all the same person. Along with them, the clubs hosted a wild cast of characters of musicians, dancers, dealers, comedians, waitresses, bouncers, bootleggers, rounders, and hangers-on whose only commonality was the belief that the nighttime was the right time. Not everyone makes it out alive. There is plenty of wreckage along the highway in the lives of those who lived and worked in the Vancouver nightclub industry. But they, and others more successful, are just some of the unsung heroes who have made Vancouver more exciting after dark. It was the people who made these places legendary, who proved that Vancouver has never been "No Fun City." You just needed one of them to show you where the party was.

And it all began 100 years ago.

Granville and Dunsmuir at night in 1947. *Credit: City of Vancouver Archives CVA 586-10173*

CHAPTER ONE

THE CITY AFTER SUNDOWN

The Rex Theatre at 25 West Hastings
Street, 1914. *Credit: City of Vancouver Archives
CVA 99-240*

The history of Vancouver's nightlife goes back much further than the first appearance of twentieth-century nightclubs and dance halls. The people of the Musqueam, Squamish, and Tsleil-Waututh nations have inhabited the area that is today considered Vancouver and the Lower Mainland for about 10,000 years. There is a mistaken conventional wisdom that the Indigenous people of hundreds of years ago lived in such harmony with nature that they remained busy during daylight hours and did not have significant nocturnal activities. This assumption ignores the traditions that ran for centuries when First Nations people of the region lived communally in longhouses, where elders and senior members would often gather and tell stories into the night. There were also the potlatch traditions in which other communities would be invited to witness ceremonies that celebrated or honoured events such as births, weddings, and funerals.

"Generally, Indigenous people [of the Pacific Northwest] didn't go out too much at night outside of their houses, for fear of spirits, ghosts, or the unknown—it wasn't dogmatic, just cautious," notes University of British Columbia professor Chris Arnett. "But it largely depended on the activities and time of year. During the winter season it was believed that guardian spirits revisited the villages and people held all-night dances where people 'danced who they were,' that is, their guardian spirits possessed them and they 'danced' them in the longhouse—every spirit had its own characteristics and style which the dancer *alluded* to, but it was never overt."

The ceremonies of local Indigenous cultures are complex and sensitive traditions. To compare them to such whimsical modern activities as nightclubbing is brusque, reductive, and distinctly flippant. But it is still worth observing that these different cultures that have called this region home have each sought their own evening rituals and nocturnal lives. Over the centuries people who have lived under this same Lower Mainland sky, regardless of their individual cultures, have shared an idea—an impulse—that the nighttime could be a time for celebration, or enjoyment of songs, stories, and dance.

The wild history of Vancouver after dark, and the history of its gathering places, is a winding timeline formed in great part by the simultaneous combative attempt by the ruling class to quash them. The provincial government outlawed First Nations potlatching and dancing from 1884 to 1951, at the same time that it was wrestling with the mere concept of the city's nightspots. The restriction of business hours, the prohibition of alcohol, the promotion of concepts that the city's nocturnal hideaways were hedonistic dens of iniquity that "good people" simply didn't go to—these were all tools used again and again to suppress the region's nightlife.

Vancouver's dance halls, clubs, ballrooms, and cabarets didn't appear all at once or overnight. Perhaps the first thing that resembled anything close to the modern urban nightclub was the saloon.

One could argue that the municipality of Vancouver itself was built around a saloon. The genesis of the city was centred in what is now the neighbourhood of Gastown, which was named for bar owner "Gassy Jack" Deighton, who in 1867 opened the Globe Saloon at what is today Maple Tree Square. Saloons were predominantly rustic, blue-collar, male-only establishments that served beer or whisky. They generally did well in Vancouver in the years after the city was incorporated in 1886, benefitting in part from the Gold Rush, when travellers and prospectors would stop in the city for a drink or two before heading north.

By the early 1890s, more conservative citizens regarded saloons as merely places where men drank to excess and recklessly spent their income that might otherwise be used to support their families. Some establishments were perhaps more refined than

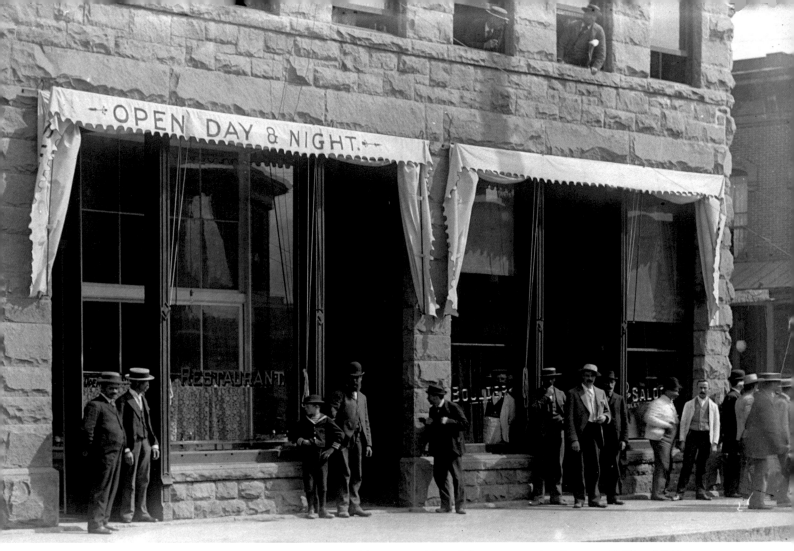

The Boulder Saloon and Barbershop at the corner of Cordova and Carrall Streets, sometime between 1900 and 1910. The building still stands in Gastown and currently operates as a restaurant. *Credit: City of Vancouver Archives CVA SGN 36*

what these teetotallers would have suggested, but, certainly, most of them were pretty rough around the edges. To attract business some saloons offered customers free food, which was often salty so as to encourage more drink purchases. And the revelry could go on all night, since saloons were allowed to stay open twenty-four hours a day. The legal drinking age was sixteen.

What the saloons usually didn't provide was entertainment. Some patrons were prone to break out in song among friends while imbibing, but there is little evidence that the saloons of the time had scheduled performers, or stages on which to properly present them. Our modern-day concepts of saloons having a ragtime piano player in a corner are likely inspired by the American westerns of film and television. There is little evidence that saloons along the coast of British Columbia featured formal, promoted acts or house entertainers. That didn't mean entertainment didn't take place—or at least crude forms of it didn't break out in the occasional impromptu passing of the hat, or a beer bought for a performer stopping in. In Victoria in 1901, a juggler named Murphy entertained a small crowd of onlookers at the Albion Saloon by swallowing a spoon, and after that a two-inch iron bolt. "The next feat was the most difficult one," reported the *Victoria Daily Times*. "Murphy tried and tried in vain to reproduce the articles. He was ultimately obliged to go to the hospital." The story reported that, a week later, Murphy was "rapidly improving in health."

Anything akin to what we might recognize today as a nightclub was considered to be evil by some city fathers in Vancouver's early days. On April 20, 1897, a local licensing board called a meeting in front of Mayor William Templeton, where a businessman and would-be impresario named Edward Gold sought to open a music hall called Theatre Comique in a brick-and-iron building he owned on Water Street. His plan was to charge admission for entertainment, showcasing "good, salaried performers" that would be "respectable, proper, and a credit to the city."[1] He also wanted to sell alcohol in the theatre. Music halls were then uncommon in the province, because licences for them were very difficult to obtain, mostly because they gave the bearer clearance to sell alcohol.

Those speaking to the licensing board that evening were not a group of Vancouver musicians or performers, or intrigued members of the public who wished to support local theatre. On the contrary, the presenters were two local religious leaders weighing in on the dangers of inviting such an establishment into the city's precincts.

Reverend Eby, a Methodist, was adamant that a music hall that sold liquor should not be allowed. Assuring members of the board that he was not attending the hearing as a clergyman but as a citizen, the reverend said that the good people "and electors of Vancouver were not puritanical," but they wanted to see "amusement carried out with purity." Eby stressed that "the seductive influences of the saloons" were greater in Vancouver than anywhere else in Canada. Vancouver, with a population then of about 18,000, was home to sixty hotels and saloons. By comparison, Winnipeg, with a population of 40,000, had only forty. Eby even protested the free food and lunches given out by saloons and summarized what he considered to be a typical evening: "These sandwiches create a thirst like the devil. Then girls are brought in to wait serving beer ... This is only a decoy to buy drinks."[2] He also shared vague anecdotes about a music hall that had just opened in the small Kootenay town of Rossland, BC—more than 600 kilometres away—and created nightmarish morality problems for the town.

Reverend W. Meikle, a Presbyterian evangelist, added to Eby's objections, urging that all saloons should disappear from the block where the proposed theatre would be. He also proposed that every other saloon in the city close at nine o'clock on Saturday evenings, leaving one to wonder if the reverend was more irked that saloons were compromising attendance at his Sunday sermons, with too many of his church's congregation showing up the next morning hungover, or not showing up at all. The music hall licence was denied.

Pressure from other local Christian temperance league supporters and sympathetic conservative politicians across the province further impeded the development of other performance spaces where patrons might legally enjoy alcohol. In truth, even some of the more liberal citizens viewed the saloons as dens of excess and immoral behaviour. In 1905, Vancouver City Council voted to abolish saloons that were not connected to a hotel, and only those hotels that had bedrooms for twenty-five or more guests and a restaurant were permitted to have a bar. The province also raised the legal drinking age from sixteen to eighteen.

[1] "The Concert Hall," *Vancouver Daily World*, April 13, 1897, 3.
[2] "Music Hall Question," *Vancouver Daily World*, April 20, 1897, 5.

The interior of the Balmoral Saloon at 2 West Cordova in 1904. *Credit: City of Vancouver Archives CVA 677-166*

Despite opposition and regulation, British Columbia remained a rough-and-tumble outpost compared to the rest of Canada. "The temperance movement was weaker in BC than in other parts of the country," notes Vancouver historian Lani Russwurm. "The majority of residents in the early twentieth century hailed from England and Scotland, where alcohol was a well-established part of 'civilized' culture. And even though Vancouver's population was ballooning in this period, it was still culturally a frontier town that tolerated things like drunkenness and prostitution more than cities east of the Rockies, largely because of the disproportionate number of young male workers. Not surprisingly, the loud demands of the prohibitionists did not translate into political will in a provincial government making a killing on liquor taxes."[3]

The hotel bars continued to operate without interruption—but still without entertainment. Patrons who wanted to see musical acts *and* have a drink were forced to visit establishments that catered to only one activity or the other. But soon the hotels faced another hurdle: outright prohibition.

Although many Canadians regard prohibition as a distinctly American kind of morality enforcement, it was indeed briefly enacted in British Columbia. During World War I, popular notions that temperance was patriotic and that alcohol fuels were needed for the war effort meant that prohibition was voted into law in British Columbia in 1917.

Oddly, it was prohibition that kick-started the appearance of cabarets in Vancouver. Some bars went out of business, others converted to cafés and sold

[3] Lani Russwurm, "A Boozy History of Prohibition in Vancouver," Forbidden Vancouver Walking Tours, https://forbiddenvancouver.ca/2017/04/27/boozy-history-prohibition-vancouver/.

"near beer" that had an innocently low alcohol content of one percent. But other bars, hoping to make money and attract customers, despite being unable to sell alcohol, converted to cabarets by offering live music and dancing.

"You see the word 'cabarets' mentioned in North America as early as 1912 and 1913, beginning in New York," says Vancouver theatre historian Tom Carter. "But it spreads quickly. Soon you have waves of veterans coming back from the First World War who had seen the cabarets of Europe before they were sent home, where people could eat, drink, and dance, and there would be entertainment all night long—and that helped the idea travel."

Although Vancouver City Hall viewed cabarets suspiciously as representative of the same kind of free-for-all as saloons, general public support helped make these establishments a reality—regardless of prohibition. This marked the beginning of nightclubs in the city.

"Around 1919 and 1920, Vancouver nightspots really begin to change," says Carter. "The cabaret licences start to happen. Many of the old cafés change to cabarets. All the new places opening up in Vancouver in the 1920s are cabarets. Prior to that, it was segregated. You went to a restaurant to eat and a bar to drink and a theatre for your entertainment. Now people could bring their date and see a floor show while they're eating dinner, then have the tables clear, and you could dance—that just left you to sneak your own alcohol in."

With the arrival of cabarets in Vancouver but no liquor licences, thus began the era of the bottle club. These businesses effectively ran as restaurants, serving food and beverages no stronger than pop, with ice, which customers might add their own alcohol to under the table. Or some establishments allowed customers to bring in their own bottles, and then the staff would hide them behind the bar or elsewhere in the building and pour on their behalf. These kinds of tactics made them targets for inspections and raids by the VPD dry squad.

Prohibition in BC ended in 1921, and until then the cabarets tended to be small. But Vancouver nightspots were changing rapidly. By this time, ballrooms had come to dominate Vancouver nightlife. Although they didn't have kitchens to serve food, and might only have a table off to the side to sell soft drinks, that didn't mean there wasn't any fun to be had in them.

CHAPTER TWO

BALLROOMS AND BANDSTANDS

Danceland in May 1965. Originally the Alexandra Ballroom, it was renamed in the 1950s. *Credit: City of Vancouver Archives CVA 447-351*

THE ALEXANDRA BALLROOM / DANCELAND

Today, the corner of Robson and Hornby Streets, with its food-truck promenades and glossy boutique entrances, doesn't exactly evoke the sense that this was once a place to dance everything from the waltz to the jitterbug. But the venerable Alexandra Ballroom once stood at the southeast corner. Later renamed Danceland, it was once known as one of the city's top dance halls, with a dance floor that curiously survived long after the building itself was demolished.

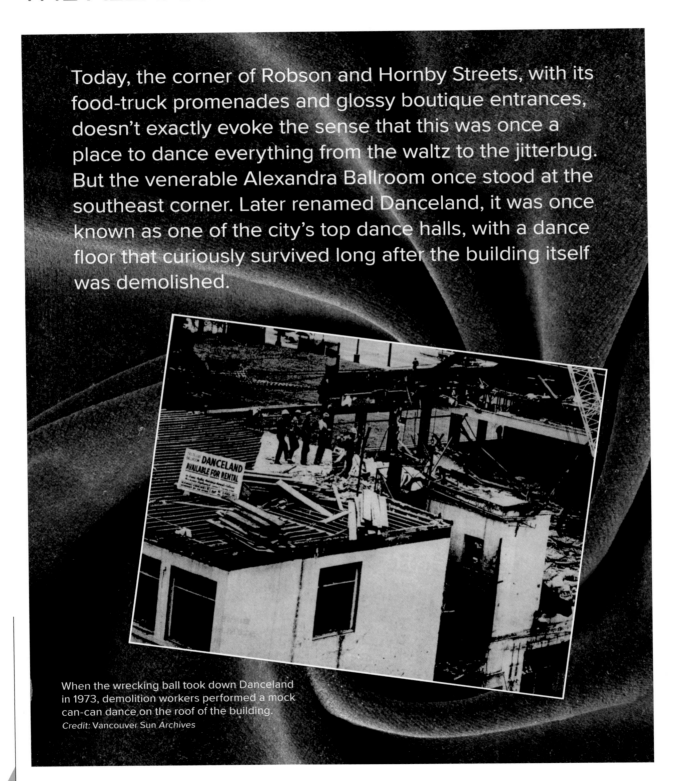

When the wrecking ball took down Danceland in 1973, demolition workers performed a mock can-can dance on the roof of the building.
Credit: Vancouver Sun Archives

The Alexandra Ballroom—known simply as the Alex to many Vancouverites at the time—opened in 1922 on the second floor of the Clements Building at 804 Hornby Street and featured local dance orchestras led by some of the city's best-known bandleaders. In the 1920s, Leo Smuntan (nicknamed Leo Suntan) played every Tuesday, Thursday, and Saturday night, with Charlie Cawdell and His Cariboo Cowboys filling in on the other evenings.[4]

Orchestra Leader Leo Smuntan was better known by his name Leo Suntan to Vancouver music audiences in the 1920s. *Credit: Neptoon Records Archives*

In the 1930s, bandleaders such as Eric Gee and Trevor Page would headline with their own orchestras, playing favourites of the day such as "A String of Pearls," "Little Brown Jug," and "Jersey Bounce." And although the band name might not have had the stinging handle typical of rock groups that play clubs today, it was local group Len Chamberlain and His Twinkletoes that pulled the wallflowers onto the dance floor.

The late legendary Vancouver bandleader Dal Richards recalled playing the Alex in his youth with the Kitsilano Boys' Band: "We used to sit on the floor cross-legged and do radio broadcasts from the Alex, and I dreamed of someday conducting my own orchestra from the bandstand. It was the goal of every bandleader to play there, but as a kid I never thought I'd make it."[5] Richards, of course, eventually performed there and in almost every dance hall and hotel ballroom in town during his decades-long career as a local bandleader.

In the late 1940s and '50s, Vancouverites were hardly limited in their choices for an evening out. The Alexandra Ballroom was just one of a host of venues that dotted the city. Younger crowds in particular flocked to cut a rug at now mostly forgotten downtown dance halls such as the Embassy Ballroom on Davie Street or the Trianon Ballroom at Drake and Granville.

"When we were single and young, we went to the White Rose Ballroom," ninety-two-year-old Mildred Henderson recalled in 2015. "It wasn't a fancy place— just a floor and a bandstand—but we really liked to dance there. The boys would stand on one side, and the girls on the other, and they'd come over and ask you to dance. My friends and I were good dancers and popular wherever we went. And we knew the guys who were the good dancers or not—that's all that mattered to us."

Born in Manitoba but raised in Vancouver since she was five, Henderson recalled the days when she would leave her family's home on Pendrell Street and join friends hopping streetcars to take in a number of local venues in one evening—and the Alexandra was always one of them. "At one point a few places had closed, and it was the only place you could go. It was open late, and they always had a great band," she remembered.

The Alexandra Ballroom wasn't without its rougher nights, though, especially during World War II, when there were occasional fights between youth and the police. The Alexandra acquired enough of a reputation that it was one of three places officially deemed "out of bounds" for Canadian soldiers stationed at the Point Grey Battery to operate the heavy artillery and searchlights in case of a Japanese coastal invasion.[6]

[4] Barney Potts, "Pots and Pans," *Province*, May 29, 1965, 63.
[5] Dal Richards with Jim Taylor, *One More Time!: The Dal Richards Story* (Madeira Park, BC: Harbour Publishing, 2009).
[6] Public Archives Canada, 15th (Vancouver) Coast Brigade Headquarters, Folder 1, file 6, Orders.

The late city councillor Don Bellamy recalled that in the early 1940s the Alexandra was referred to as the Gonorrhea Race Track by many young local dance hall patrons. The other two places forbidden to these soldiers were the Club New Orleans at 699 Drake Street, which was notorious for fights and robberies, and a mysterious private residence at 303 Union Street in the Strathcona neighbourhood that was thought to be a brothel.

In the 1950s, the office of CKNW radio moved into the top floor of the building above the Alexander Ballroom—by then renamed Danceland—and was home to DJ Jack Cullen's collection of more than 100,000 records.

In 1960, Mildred Henderson and her husband bought a home in Burnaby for $15,000. As she got older and busier with her family, she had less time for the dance halls, and when she did go out with her husband and friends, they tended to visit clubs like the Cave and the Commodore Ballroom—the only ballroom of that era that remains. But Danceland would remain a popular spot for a whole new generation of young people as new sounds continued to blare out of its second-storey windows. Club owner and businessman Jim Wisbey took over the venue in its later years, and touring musicians like Del Shannon and early rock 'n' roll and R&B groups such as the Electras and Howie Vickers and the Viscounts performed there regularly.

"It was a great place to play," recalls Gary Taylor, drummer for the Classics, who later managed his own clubs. Taylor played the room in the early 1960s: "At the time, there wasn't so many places to play for local groups. Danceland was one of the only places in town then. It had a good stage and lights—it felt like it was the big time to us!"

By the early to mid-1960s, R&B had begun to take over in Vancouver, and Danceland stuck around long enough to catch the initial wave. On Saturday, September 7, 1963, the Ike & Tina Turner Revue took to the stage at Danceland in one of the last notable shows to ever play there.

In June 1965, the building was demolished. As significant as its decades-long history was, there was no rallying cry for its preservation. The old Alexandra Ballroom had perhaps seen enough wear and tear that it was considered to be past its prime, and what stood for heritage preservation in Vancouver then did not yet extend to the city's nightclubs, dance halls, or theatres. Two years later, the magnificent Pantages Theatre building on Hastings Street was demolished for a parking lot. It wasn't until 1973, when public protest and a "Save the Orpheum" campaign helped rescue the landmark theatre from transformation into a multiplex cinema, that Vancouver seemed to start taking a serious interest in the importance of preserving its historic performance venues.

While Danceland may have been less ornate and dramatically appointed than either the Pantages or the Orpheum, its demolition did feature some theatrical flair. As the club interior was being torn out, demolition workers in hard hats mugged for newspaper photographers, kicking their legs out in a mock chorus line. "We are getting far more in salvage out of the place than we expected," foreman Hugh Glendinning told the *Vancouver Sun*. "We even got a bottle of whiskey, which had fallen down behind the bandstand and was forgotten by some merry-maker. Old vintage, too!"[7]

If anything meaningful was to be preserved from Danceland, it was left to the private citizens who had a personal connection to the old ballroom. And for her part, Mildred Henderson never forgot those nights she spent dancing on that floor. When the opportunity came to save a piece of Danceland for herself, she couldn't pass it up.

"My brother-in-law worked near there at a gas station, and he heard it was closing," she said. "So he went by and they were pulling up the wooden dance

Mildred Henderson on her Danceland dance floor. *Photo: Dan Toulgoet/*Vancouver Courier

floor in long slats and going to throw it all out. He bought all of it. He took some of it for his cabin in Point Roberts, and we got the rest of it for thirty-five dollars. We did our whole basement floor with it."

Prior to demolition, the Danceland floor had supported the dancing feet of legions of Vancouverites. For the next five decades, it survived happy wear and tear from dancing shoes and the occasional spilled drink at more than a few Henderson house parties. The feet of the Hendersons' children, and grandchildren, would stomp on the floor that was

for Mildred a pleasant reminder of her youthful days of swing dancing and jitterbugging in Vancouver's dance halls.

Mildred Henderson passed away in 2019, and her home is likely to be sold and replaced with a new modern one, as with so many old houses in the Lower Mainland. But her family hopes that an interested party might remove the floor and transplant it to a new location. Whoever gets it will have some considerable history under their feet.

[7] Nadine Asante, "And Down Comes Finishing School," *Vancouver Sun,* June 18, 1965, 78.

THE WHITE ROSE BALLROOM

The White Rose Ballroom can be seen as just one of the many Vancouver dance halls that are forgotten today. But the White Rose and many venues like it remained for years—just under different names. The White Rose opened in 1929 at 1236 West Broadway and featured a variety of social events, such as the old-time dance social hosted by the Yorkshire Society in 1935 that showcased music by the Lumberjacks Orchestra. It remained the White Rose until 1956,

White Rose Ballroom announcement, June 1, 1935.
Credit: Vancouver Sun *Archives*

when it was renamed the Arlington Ballroom, and became known as the Arlington Hall in the 1960s, and then the Arlington Cabaret in the '70s. In the '90s, it was rechristened with the name Vancouverites best remember it by: the Big Bamboo nightclub, opened by Stan Fiddis, who began working in nightclubs as a doorman at Richard's on Richards. The club was then renamed Daddyo's in its final incarnation, before the building was demolished in the early 2000s.

THE TRIANON / HOWDEN BALLROOM

On December 29, 1934, the Trianon Ballroom opened its doors at 1313 Granville Street near Drake Street, with Len Chamberlain and His Twinkletoes as the orchestra that provided the night's entertainment. Chamberlain was one of the regular bandleaders who also performed at the Commodore Ballroom in the 1930s. Admission to the Trianon that night was thirty-five cents for gentlemen and twenty-five cents for ladies.

As a 12,000-square-foot building with a sizeable dance floor, it provided enough space for the ballroom's conversion in 1938 into a roller rink. A new

Trianon Ballroom set up shop in a building at 43rd Avenue and Fraser Street. The fun for roller skating Vancouverites ended, though, when W.H. Howden bought the rink for $25,000 and reopened it as the Howden Ballroom in November 1942. For the next twenty years, manager J.D. Rousseau ran it as a hall for society dances and functions.

Although Dixieland and some big band jazz could occasionally be heard at the Howden, it no longer had a house orchestra like the fancier clubs did. The Howden also didn't have a kitchen and was never turned into a supper club to compete with other

Advertisement for the opening night of the Trianon Ballroom at Granville and Drake.
Credit: Vancouver Sun *Archives*

One of Vancouver's first all-female bands, the 6 Rhythm Larks (here performing at the 1953 Pacific National Exhibition opening-day parade) performed regularly at the Trianon Ballroom along with local old-time music star Fred Knight. *Credit: City of Vancouver Archives CVA 180-2256*

Square dance caller Fred Knight. *Credit: Vancouver Sun Archives*

Road construction outside the Howden Ballroom in 1954. *Credit: Tom Carter Archives*

nightclubs at the time. But it did become the local home for less formal crowds and square dancing enthusiasts, with Fred Knight and His Old Time Band as the regular featured entertainment. Knight was a competition-winning local square dance caller, perhaps one of the best known callers in Vancouver in the 1950s and '60s, who'd gotten his start at the Pender Ballroom with the 6 Rhythm Larks in the 1940s.

In 1968, the Howden changed hands and became an Elks Lodge, hosting functions and bingo nights over the next two decades. Bingo, however, proved to be too low-stakes a game for Terry Neuenfeldt. In the late 1990s, Neuenfeldt was Grand Exalted Ruler of Elks of Canada, the fraternal organization's highest position. He'd been involved in the organization for nearly forty years while he'd worked as pressman at

Pacific Press, which published both the *Vancouver Sun* and the *Province* newspapers. But Neuenfeldt would make headlines of his own. In 1999, after his retirement, he developed a considerable gambling addiction. To pay for his casino losses, Neuenfeldt regularly transferred sums as large as $60,000 from the Elks Lodge investment account into his personal bank account. Over a two-year period, he stole more than $1.2 million—most of it lost at the tables of the Nooksack Casino just across the border in Washington State. To make matters worse, most of those embezzled funds had been earmarked by the Elks to help build a centre for hearing-impaired children.

When Neuenfeldt's fraud was discovered in 2001, he was expelled and sued by the local Elks, who were forced to sell off their properties to settle Neuenfeldt's debts. In court, he blamed "mind-altering drugs" that he was prescribed for his diabetes and hypertension and begged forgiveness, adding that the crime had broken his marriage and forced him to declare bankruptcy. He was convicted of fraud and sentenced to three years in prison.

The old Howden Ballroom did make one last musical splash in its final years when, in 1994, a local concert promoter booked the venue for a few all-ages shows featuring a roster of what were then up-and-coming alternative rock acts: Green Day, Gwar, Beck, and Sloan. For marketing purposes, promoter Peter McCulloch revived the old name of the Howden

Ballroom (Elks Lodge did not have the same ring to it). These final concerts were the Howden's last stand before it was torn down and replaced by a Best Western hotel and White Spot restaurant—both of which remain to this day.

Those all-ages audiences packed into the old ballroom to mosh and slam dance no doubt sweated as much as Neuenfeldt did over the million dollars he embezzled from the Elks. But Gwar, Green Day, Beck, and Sloan were certainly a long way from the old days of square dancing at the Howden, and one can only imagine what Fred Knight and His Old Time Band would have thought of alternative music.

Peter McCulloch brought the Howden Ballroom name back for a series of all-ages concerts he promoted, like Beck, on July 2, 1994.
Credit: Neptoon Records Archives

CHAPTER THREE

An Evening with Your Genial Host
Sandy
De SANTIS
At his PALOMAR Supper Club
VANCOUVER CANADA

THE SUPPER CLUBS

Palomar Ballroom Orchestra leader
Sandy DeSantis.
Credit: Neptoon Records Archives

THE CAVE AND THE PALOMAR

If there is one name on the list of all the night-clubs that have come and gone over the decades in Vancouver, the Cave is the one whose loss is perhaps most lamented.

YOUR EXECUTIVE CREDIT CARD
THE CAVE
theatre restaurant - 626 hornby street, vancouver, b.c. - 682-3677
name
signature
1967
credit number ___ C61
YOUR *LULU BELLE* CREDIT CARD ON REVERSE SIDE

COMING MON. FEB. 28th

THAT SAUCY NAUGHTY SINGING COMEDIENNE OF SCREEN & RADIO

MARTHA RAYE *with her own*
ALL STAR REVUE
including the ever-popular
VIKINGS

Cave nightclub staff, February 1949.
Credit: Neptoon Records Archives

Cave swizzle stick, 1960s.

There are even those who never went there who regret its demise, longing for the magic and excitement of a lost era. The Cave was the city's premier venue during the height of the nightclub show era—the early 1960s, when nightlife was stylish and sophisticated. Many Vancouverites even remember its kitschy faux-cavern interior of papier-mâché stalactites and stalagmites with fondness, wishing the club were still here.

Gordon King opened the Cave at 626 Hornby Street in 1938. King had come to town from Winnipeg, where he'd opened the first Cave nightclub in 1935. He later opened another one in Edmonton.

The Vancouver Cave lasted the longest, though, and was the most famous, attracting many big-name American acts that toured along the Pacific coast.

In addition to its subterranean decor, the club featured a special sprung dance floor and a large forty-foot-wide stage. In the early years, the venue hosted performers from the vaudeville era and veteran stars who'd made their names in radio and cinema, like dancers Winston and Lolette, and Kenneth Milton, billed as "the Heifetz of the Harmonica," who played "all sizes and shapes of harmonicas, his numbers ranging from the hottest swing to standard classics."[8]

Served from 5:30 p.m. to 7:30 p.m.
Absolutely No Service During Floor Show

$1.75
Crab Meat Cocktail
or Fruit Cocktail

Daily Soup
or Tomato Juice

ENTREE
Fried Filet of Sole, Tartar Sauce,
Slice Lemon

Roast Sirloin of Beef, Mushroom Sauce

Grilled Pork Chops, Apple Sauce

Vegetable

$2.25
Crab Meat Cocktail
or Fruit Cocktail

Daily Soup
or Tomato Juice

ENTREE
Grilled Filet Mignon with Mushrooms

Fried Half Spring Chicken

Roast Duckling, Celery Dressing,
Apple Sauce

Vegetable
Carrots and Peas
...ed or Mashed Potatoes

Jello, Whipped Cream
Milk

AN APOLOGY . . .
We sincerely regret the inconvenience caused to hundreds of our patrons by not being able to obtain admittance to the Cave during the recent engagement of MISS LENA HORNE. The splendid response to bringing a really "Big Name" attraction was beyond all expectations and we hope that in the very near future we shall again be able to present other great personalities of the movie and entertainment world, at which time we hasten to assure you that we shall be better prepared to take care of you in the proper manner.
CAVE SUPPER CLUB

The Lena Horne appearance at the Cave in April 1948 was one of the biggest shows the Cave, or the city for that matter, had ever seen, with Horne allegedly being paid $7,500 a week. A souvenir menu was printed in honour of the event. Each night sold out to standing room only, resulting in the Cave printing an apology to those unable to get a ticket. *Credit: Neptoon Records Archives*

[8] "Cave Will Present Another Fine Show," *Vancouver Sun*, October 14, 1939, 7.

Local dancers and performers also appeared, along with comedian emcees and even the odd magician.

The Cave changed management and ownership frequently during its history. After World War II, Gordon King's son Max returned from service in the Royal Canadian Air Force to run the club until Isy Walters, who bought it in 1952, sold it in 1958 and then opened Isy's Supper Club a year later.

Before they bought the Cave from Walters, Ken Stauffer and Bob Mitten had both worked at the Arctic Club, one of several members-only cocktail and supper clubs that were popular in Vancouver in the late 1940s and '50s. The two had the sort of good gamblers' instincts that are crucial for being an effective nightclub owner. For instance, they often took chances on booking unknown acts, and most of the time, their intuition was proved right.

Since vaudeville days, Vancouver had been known as Tune-Up City, where performers could rehearse a show in front of a live audience before taking the act down the Pacific coast, through Seattle, Portland, San Francisco, and on to Los Angeles. The same routes exist today in modern concert touring.

In the 1960s, the Cave's main competition was the Palomar Supper Club at 713 Burrard Street. Operated by theatre manager Charlie Nelson and promoter Hymie Singer, the club was named for the Palomar Observatory in California—since that's where people came to look at the stars. This more terrestrial Palomar opened a year before the Cave, on May 22, 1937.[9] Admission was seventy-five cents for men and fifty cents for women. It was an impressive establishment, decorated throughout with art deco white panels and smooth lighting that made it a welcoming place where patrons came dressed up for a night on the town.

The club didn't get off to a smooth start, though. Initially, the congregation of a nearby church protested

Cave wine list menu, circa 1950s.
Credit: Neptoon Records Archives

against the Palomar securing a dance hall licence. The club owners also struggled with cash flow when they were first setting up the business.

"It was a skin-of-the-teeth thing as to whether it would be finished on time," recalls bandleader Dal Richards in his memoir. "Money was tight. Carpenters would work until the weekend, then threaten not to come back if they didn't get their money. Hymie would do things like pull off his expensive wristwatch, hand it to one of them and say, 'Here. This is yours. Bring it back Monday and I'll have your money for you.'"[10]

---

[9] The opening date of the Palomar has been stated incorrectly in other publications and online. Page 11 of the *Vancouver Sun* of May 25, 1937, correctly reports the grand opening of the Palomar to have been on May 22 of that year.

[10] Dal Richards with Jim Taylor, *One More Time!: The Dal Richards Story* (Madeira Park, BC: Harbour Publishing, 2009), 51.

Right: Jazz concert with the Fraser MacPherson band, March 29, 1953. *Credit: Guy MacPherson Archives*
Above: The front door of the Palomar at 713 Burrard, July 1942. *Credit: Tom Carter Archives*

Streetcar poster advertisement for Bob Hope sidekick Jerry Colonna at the Palomar in 1948. *Credit: Tom Carter Archives*

The Mills Brothers were favourites of both the Palomar and the Cave. *Credit: Tom Carter Archives*

Advertisement for the Ink Spots at the Palomar, April 12, 1948. *Credit: Tom Carter Archives*

Sandy DeSantis, who had been the orchestra leader at the Venice Cafe, signed on as bandleader at the Palomar. A good trumpet player and leader, DeSantis was better known in nightclub circles as an inveterate gambler. One night, while lamenting a poor turnout at the club, Nelson, Singer, and DeSantis attended a craps game on Seymour Street. All three lost their money so quickly that they we forced to return to the Palomar to scrounge for cash from the till. They returned to the game and DeSantis got a hot hand, making twelve straight passes, and walked away with $7,000. Nelson went back the next night and lost his share of the win.

The height of the Palomar's success was during World War II, when servicemen on leave would bring their dates to the club. The establishment did not have a liquor licence, so it remained a bottle club, where patrons hid a bottle in their coats or under their tables and bought ice and mix. If they didn't bring a bottle, a bootlegger at a back corner table who worked for the club could supply one.

In the 1940s, the Palomar featured performances by some of the biggest names in the entertainment industry, including Nat King Cole, the Ink Spots, Peggy Lee, Frankie Laine, Louis Jordan, Billie Holiday, and even Louis Armstrong, in a particularly memorable appearance where he brought local act the Crump Twins onstage with him. Even a young Yvonne De Carlo (then called Peggy Middleton) appeared as a dancer in a Palomar floor show long before she moved to Hollywood and became a famous actress and singer.

DeSantis eventually became a part owner of the Palomar. His gambling winnings often helped pay the rent during slow months, but by the late 1940s, his luck, and the club's, was changing. DeSantis began to accrue significant gambling debts—enough to make some of his debtors impatient.

In November 1949, four armed men with silk stockings on their heads forced their way into DeSantis's home at 15th Avenue and Balsam Street, tied up

Louis Jordan at the Palomar in January 1949.
Credit: Neptoon Records Archives

Sandy and his wife and robbed them. While the goons threatened to kill the couple's cocker spaniel, who whined in fear while the DeSantises were restrained on the floor, the ringleader ordered Sandy at gunpoint to produce whatever money he had in the house. The thieves made off with $360 in cash and Mrs DeSantis's $500 wedding ring. The couple managed to free themselves, but when they tried to call the police, they found their phone lines had been cut. When the police were finally summoned, DeSantis told them that he had never seen the gunmen before and had no idea who they were.

In the early 1950s, Joe and Ross Filippone, owners of the Penthouse Nightclub, bought fifty percent of the Palomar from DeSantis in an effort to help him pay off his gambling debts, but DeSantis had back taxes to deal with as well. The Palomar closed in 1955. In the end, the property owner sold the land to a Utah development firm, and the Palomar was demolished. At Burrard and Georgia Streets, an

PRESENTING
APRIL 20 - 30
THE
FIRST
VANCOUVER
APPEARANCE OF

MARVIN GAYE

also . . . AMERICA'S MOST
UNUSUAL PICKPOCKET
RAVEL

and . . . THE DANCING DEBS

Singing in the CAVE

Marvin GAYE

COMING SOON to the CAVE ▷ THE Sensational **SUPREMES** MAY 4 - 14 ▷ Zany . . . Hilarious **HOMER & JETHRO** MAY 16 - 21 ▷ The Exciting **KIM SISTERS** MAY 24 - JUNE 4

JAN. 30 thru FEB. 11   IN PERSON

"Mister Excitement"

WAYNE NEWTON

also

The Fresh & Funny Comedy of —
JACKIE KAHANE
& . . . the Dancing of BONNIE & DARLENE

WAYNE NEWTON

OPENING WED. FEB. 15th FOR 10 DAYS ONLY **RICKY NELSON**   OPENING WED. MAR. 8th - 18th England's foremost Singing Star **MATT MONRO**

Left: Marvin Gaye at the Cave, April 1966. Right: Wayne Newton at the Cave, Jan./Feb. 1967. *Credit: Neptoon Records Archives*

office tower with ground-floor retail outlets now stands in its place.

The Palomar closed, but the Cave was doing well. The Palomar's dance floor had been bigger and its stage small. The Cave's larger stage was better suited to the new style of nightclub shows emerging in the 1950s. A key to the club's success had much to do with the popular Cave orchestra, led by reed player Fraser MacPherson and featuring some of the top players in the city.

As far as club gigs went for local musicians, there were few better regular jobs than the Cave. The orchestra positions that paid union scale were coveted ones that most musicians in Vancouver did their best to keep. However, a few recent histories of the Cave suggest there was a colour barrier that kept black musicians from becoming orchestra members there. Harlem Nocturne proprietor and trombonist Ernie King stated, "I was qualified enough to play in The

Cave, but they didn't want a guy like me, they wanted an all-white band, not a coloured band with me sitting there. There were never any black musicians, unless it was a black band from the States."[11]

Veteran Vancouver saxophonist Gavin Walker agrees race was a factor for musicians seeking entry into some Vancouver nightclub orchestras at the time and notes that the Cave orchestra in particular presented other challenges. "The guys that got the orchestra positions at the Cave—'The Downtowners' was their unofficial name—were very protective of their union scale work, and it was a bit of a closed circle. You had to have the ability to play but also be a top-notch sight-reader. The Downtowners also got a lot of CBC work, and when the jazz shows came up on the CBC, these were the guys the CBC hired, not the hard-core jazz players who were mostly white that played other venues like the Jazz Cellar."

[11] Becki Ross, *Burlesque West: Showgirls, Sex, and Sin in Postwar Vancouver* (Toronto: University of Toronto Press, 2009), 66.

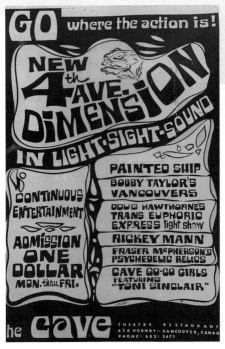

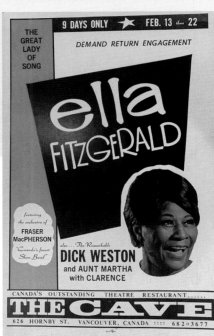

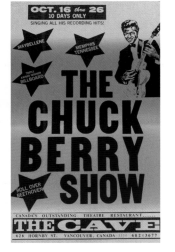

A selection of posters from the Cave. *Credit: Neptoon Records Archives*

One musician who did make the cut was Blaine Tringham, who began playing at the Cave as a junior orchestra member in his early twenties. "A freelance horn player could make a pretty good living just by answering the phone and saying, 'yes,'" Tringham says with a laugh. "At the Cave, initially you'd be the third or fourth call, but eventually you'd work your way up to the first if you were any good. But in those days, the protocol was that whoever called you first got the gig, and I'd take any gig I could. So sometimes you'd take a gig at some other place like Isy's, then the Cave might call you and you'd have to tell them you were already booked, even if you preferred to play there."

Louis Prima at the Cave, May 1969.
Credit: Neptoon Records Archives

Trumpeter Blaine Tringham recording at Little Mountain Sound Studios. *Credit: Blaine Tringham*

Tringham recalls that pay at the Cave was $160 a week and $120 a week at Isy's, because the hours were shorter. "That doesn't sound like a lot today, of course, but you have to remember this was the early 1960s. The rent in my furnished apartment was $65 a month, so you could make a good living as a club musician then."

And with the number of nightclub acts that came through town at the Cave in the 1960s, Tringham stayed busy, but the schedule left little turnaround time to rehearse new acts. In the daytime, there were three-hour rehearsals for two ninety-minute shows. The constant flow of stars required a regular team of skilled musicians with seasoned chops on the Cave bandstand. In suits and ties, heads down in the charts on their music stands, Fraser MacPherson's band appeared completely focused and reserved from an audience perspective, but Tringham confesses things were not always what they seemed.

"The guys at the Cave could drink," he says. "They had a capacity you couldn't believe. I was just a kid and didn't drink at the shows because I was too nervous to screw up a part or miss a cue. But the regular Cave musicians bought Beefeater gin by the case and kept it backstage in these lockers that were supposed to be for clothes. They'd always have a cup of it at their feet, sipping it, and gin looked just like water. Every night those guys got loaded. Sometimes they'd send the busboy to the liquor store to get more. The amazing thing was they never screwed up."

Tringham continues, "There was a guy named Stew Barnett—he was the king of the trumpet at the Cave. As many drinks as he sipped away at, he never made a mistake through the whole show. It was only at the very end of the night he'd run out of gas. The curtain would close and he couldn't get out of the chair. It was like a marathon runner who'd hit the finish line. He was a great guy and a great musician. Everybody smoked and drank there while they played, taking a quick puff of a cigarette between parts. It was like that in the recording studios, too. That's just what you did then!"

The Cave orchestra had their favourite performers to work with. Mitzi Gaynor rehearsed her entire nightclub show in Vancouver before taking it to Las Vegas, and came back year after year. Tringham recalls that although Mel Tormé had a reputation for being difficult, the band enjoyed playing with him and he was a complete professional. Anthony Newley, meanwhile, "confessed to us he was really nervous with this debut at the Cave because it was a new nightclub show he was trying out. But he was a lot of fun. Just one of the guys." Another favourite was singer and actress Jaye P. Morgan, who might be best remembered as a TV game show panellist during the 1970s. "She was very outspoken about—how shall I put this?—who she liked. There was a guy in the band she kept hitting on in front of us, saying that she was going to take him to bed. She was teasing him like crazy, even during the shows. It was very funny. One night his wife came down to see the show and he sweated through the whole night hoping Jaye wouldn't say anything."

Over the years, the Cave featured many touring nightclub acts: older ones like the Mills Brothers

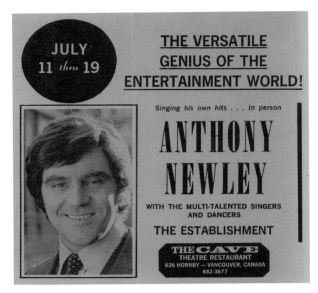

Anthony Newley at the Cave, July 1969.
Credit: Neptoon Records Archives

and Roy Orbison appeared along with more modern performers like Diana Ross and the Supremes, James Brown, the Righteous Brothers, Sonny & Cher, and Bette Midler.

Danny Baceda, who operated Oil Can Harry's jazz club, bought the Cave for $100,000 in 1971. A month later, he bought Isy's Supper Club, making him the biggest nightclub owner in Vancouver at the time. But the expansion happened too quickly, and by 1972, Baceda went into receivership. Ken Stauffer bought back the Cave in 1973, running it briefly before selling it to Stan Grozina.

Originally from Slovenia, Grozina spent his early years in a series of German labour camps during World War II. He immigrated to Canada with twenty dollars in his pocket and soon became involved in the construction business in Winnipeg. He retired in Vancouver and bought the Cave, sinking $75,000 into renovations. But when the Cave reopened, Grozina's bookings were hit and miss. The club had success with rock bands like the Animals, Canned Heat, Trooper, and Doug and the Slugs, and Grozina occasionally booked some exciting emerging underground bands as well,

Even Elvis got into the act for the Cave's final bow: the demolition of the nightclub, July 25, 1981. *Photo: Deborah Cameron*

like the local new wave band Pointed Sticks in 1979. The musicals he booked weren't as successful, however, and with disco taking off in some downtown clubs, and punk rock emerging in others, the Cave was suddenly a horribly old-fashioned place to go. At that point, Grozina began booking wet T-shirt contests—things were going downhill fast.

They had, in fact, been heading that way for a while. The golden era of nightclub acts was over, and nightclub culture itself was changing. In many ways, the clubs had become victims of the performers' success. The acts the nightclubs had nurtured had now become too successful to stay there, and the top performers who had once booked ten-day or two-week club engagements now came for one- or two-night stops at the Queen Elizabeth Theatre or, if they were big enough, the Pacific Coliseum.

The Cave was unable to make the transition the Commodore Ballroom did. The Commodore had once seen an older generation of entertainment but had made the jump to a modern concert space, thanks to owner Drew Burns, whose policy of renting the room to outside promoters ultimately gave the club its future.

Stan Grozina was no Drew Burns. He mistakenly hoped the old nightclub-style acts would live to see another day, and he could not imagine the Cave as any other kind of establishment. A disastrous booking in 1978 of an aged Ginger Rogers resulted in a $40,000 loss that doomed the club financially.

"You could really feel that things were changing by the early 1970s," recalls Tringham. For him, and other musicians like him, the very music they were being called to play was changing. While the calls for live shows dried up, recording sessions for jingles were taking off. Tringham eventually moved to Burbank, California, where he became an in-demand player for television recording sessions, though he continued to play live, including, notably, in orchestras backing Frank Sinatra in Las Vegas.

"I feel lucky to have been at the Cave when I did. It was the right place at the right time," he says.

The Cave closed in 1981, and there was no "Save the Cave" grassroots effort to keep it alive. Aside from a few expressions of nostalgia, there seemed to be little public outcry that the Cave would be no more. It was demolished that summer. Some of the club's old stalactites and stalagmites were saved and auctioned off. The Hong Kong Bank of Canada Tower was built in its place, marking the end of an era when the Hornby Street strip of nightclubs thrived.

Jack Wasserman
Credit: Vancouver Sun Archives

These days, little remains of that street's nightlife glory days, aside from the small iron plaque honouring the legendary talk-of-the-town *Vancouver Sun* columnist Jack Wasserman. The plaque forever marks that stretch of Hornby as "Wasserman's Beat." And it was from this beat that he mythologized Vancouver. Although Wasserman described himself simply as a "saloon writer," his gossip column frequently included hard news. He spent years covering what was happening in the clubs—interviewing performers, overhearing loose talk between club managers, and catching tips from neighbourhood bartenders. Readers of his column often felt like

Memorial plaque commemorating Jack Wasserman and "Wasserman's Beat" on Hornby Street. *Photo: Aaron Chapman*

they'd been out for a night on the town with him. In 1977, at the age of fifty, after more than twenty-five years as an overall gadabout on his beat along Hornby Street, Wasserman died while giving a speech at the Hotel Vancouver.

But Hornby is a different street now in a different city. On a late evening any night of the week, a few patrons might be seen at the corner of Hornby and Dunsmuir, stepping out for a cigarette from the Blackbird Public House or Brandi's Show Lounge, but otherwise, the sidewalks of Hornby between Georgia and Pender at night are quiet. Hy's Steakhouse is the only business left from the old days, but only two flickering fake candles twinkle outside its door past its eleven p.m. closing time. There are no enticing neon signs or doormen on the street ushering you into the pleasures of the nightclubs inside. Only a few lonely taxi cabs glide by, heading to and from more exciting destinations. There is nothing to indicate this short stretch was were the city came to be entertained at the Cave and other thriving clubs. The sights and sounds of Vancouver's nightlife have moved elsewhere. And late at night, on its lonely sidewalk, Jack Wasserman stares out on a quiet Hornby Street with no one to talk to.

ISY'S SUPPER CLUB

Left: Isy Walters holds court with friends at the club, 1960s. *Credit: Vancouver Sun Archives.* Right: Postcard of the interior of Isy's Supper Club, which stood at 1136 West Georgia. *Credit: Author's personal collection*

If the Cave was the premier showroom of all the old clubs in town, Isy's Supper Club was perhaps always its slightly roguish younger sibling. In the 1960s, Isy's quickly rose to become one of the most prominent nightclubs in Vancouver. Some of the top R&B, Motown, jazz, and comedy performers of the period played its stage, but there was always something raffish about Isy's that separated it from the Cave. And of all the old clubs, none ended more tragically than what was originally Isy's Supper Club.

Isadore Waltuck was born in Russia in 1906. After he arrived in Vancouver, he got his start in show business in the 1920s as a teenager, selling popcorn at the Empress Theatre that was at Hastings and Gore Streets. Young Isy was even occasionally tossed a part in one of the stage plays as a newsie or messenger boy. At fourteen, he ran away from home and joined the circus as a carny and travelled across North America. By the 1930s, he'd settled back in Vancouver, where he continued to hone his promotional abilities selling potatoes door to door. He then got involved in the scrap metal business and, on the side, became a booking agent for local entertainment everywhere from the Pacific National Exhibition to parties and events at the Mandarin Gardens restaurant.

In the early 1950s, Isy legally changed his last name to Walters and met Hymie Singer, owner of the Palomar club. Walters sank some of his scrap metal profits into converting the old Pantages Theatre into the State Theatre, but the burlesque shows Singer and

Walters produced there failed to catch on with anybody except the Vancouver police morality squad, who deemed some of them too risqué. Somehow, between his burgeoning career as an unlikely theatre impresario and his day job at the scrap metal company where he answered the phone as a booking agent, Walters opened the Club Sirocco in Victoria in 1950.

On July 14, 1952, Walters bought the Cave nightclub and ran it until 1958, when he claimed he wanted to retire. Those years were good for the Cave, and Walters came along when a steady hand was needed most. The Cave's previous manager, Max King, had never taken much serious responsibility for the club, and it was common knowledge that he spent most of his time there alone, getting horribly drunk and shooting a BB gun at targets set up around his office.

But after less than a decade steering the ship, even Isy'd had enough. The ulcer-inducing nature of running a club, spending long hours playing a never-ending guessing game to anticipate how to meet fickle public tastes to sell tickets—on top of all the usual worries of a business owner—had got to him. "I have spent more than a million dollars on entertainment and I've never seen a bad show," Walters said in an interview with Jack Wasserman in the *Vancouver Sun* in 1963. "Some are just better than others. Of course, that's my way of looking at it—because no operator in his right mind wants to put on a bad show. Believe me, we get sicker than the audience when a show stinks."[12]

Surprisingly, almost as soon as Walters was out of show business, he got back in, claiming the "the bug"

Isy and son Richard "Richie" Walters onstage at Isy's.
Credit: Richard Walters

was too much to stay away from. In 1959, Walters opened Isy's Supper Club at 1136 West Georgia, this time partnering with his twenty-seven-year-old son, Richard.

Richard Walters certainly wasn't new to the nightclub world. He had worked under his father at the Cave and was now ready to jump deeper into the business. "My dad was really talented at booking. Isy deserves a lot of credit for what he brought to the entertainment and nightclub scene in Vancouver," recalls the eighty-eight-year-old. "The Cave and Isy's

[12] "Jack Wasserman Tells Us about Club Men," *Vancouver Sun*, April 5, 1963, 5.

Everly Brothers at Isy's, 1968.
Credit: Neptoon Records Archives

Buddy Rich at Isy's, 1967.
Credit: Neptoon Records Archives

became the two big clubs in town in the sixties, and we were a part of both of them," he says proudly.

Richard was perhaps destined for the entertainment business from the beginning. He attended General Gordon Elementary School in Kitsilano and, later, Prince of Wales Secondary School, but after school, he could be found hanging around the State Theatre, where he became friends with Sammy Davis Jr., who was performing there with his father and uncle in the Will Mastin Trio. "Sammy Davis Jr. was at our house for dinner many times," Richard says. "One night after dinner, I remember we went down to the theatre and we were horsing around and turned the fire extinguisher on the burlesque dancers there. Isy got so mad at me for

that. There was a lot of poker playing at the theatre back then, too. I remember [singer] Mimi Hines was a terrible player, and she'd always lose money and be running across to this Chinese restaurant across the street to borrow money from the guys who ran the place."

Isy's Supper Club was designed in the style of a Las Vegas casino show lounge, but capacity quickly became a concern if they were going to compete against the Cave—Isy's was only a third the size. "Early on, Isy called me into his office and said we needed to think bigger. We had all these plush chairs and big tables in there at first, so we took them all out and just put in two-by-two tables, and overnight we doubled the capacity of the room to six hundred," Richard

Stevie Wonder at Isy's, 1967.
Credit: Neptoon Records Archives

Sarah Vaughan at Isy's, 1969.
Credit: Neptoon Records Archives

recalls. And Isy's found other ways to compete with the Cave. "While the Cave had a bigger budget, our room was better, because none of the seats were bad," Richard explains. "If you were in the balcony of the Cave, unless you were at the front row, those seats were lousy. So because we set things up like that early, it made a big difference."

Carl Logan was the first house bandleader at Isy's, but he was replaced by Carl DeSantis, brother of Sandy DeSantis, the bandleader at the Palomar. Eventually, Bobby Hales, who would become one of the city's best-known bandleaders, got the job leading Isy's house orchestra, with a bandstand composed of some of the top local musicians who rotated between calls from the Cave and the Marco Polo.

"I worked at Isy's a lot," recalls trumpeter Blaine Tringham. "Like the Cave, the acts would come in with a book of sheet music, and you'd rehearse with them in the day for a couple of hours. But there were a lot of Motown acts there at Isy's, so it was usually different and a younger crowd. While an act like Mitzi Gaynor might be appearing at the Cave, Isy's would have an act like Sam & Dave. There was always something wild going on. I remember one night a couple of showgirls got into a fight, and one of them fell on Bobby Hales's horn that was sitting on its stand!"

Richard Walters was not only a co-owner but also the club emcee, a central role that had him meeting many of the acts. He says, "Stevie Wonder was amazing—what a talent—but he kind of kept to himself and his handlers. Little Richard and I hit it off, maybe because we had the same name!"

As a lifelong jazz fan, Richard was fortunate to meet some of his favourite musicians. "Sarah Vaughan was wonderful. But we booked her the same night as the Cave had Ella Fitzgerald. That was tough. We needed to compete with the Cave, but we never wanted to go head-to-head like that. Sarah was great, though. Her friends nicknamed her Sailor because she could be very rough, but I didn't think so. When I met her, she said, 'Richard, my friends call me Sassy ... call me that,' and I can't say anything bad about her. Another was Buddy Rich—he loved dirty jokes. When he found out that Dusty Springfield was to appear a few weeks later, he warned me she was going to be a handful, but I had no idea how bad," Richard recalls solemnly, foreshadowing what would be one of the most notorious shows in the history of Isy's Supper Club.

Richard remembers driving to the airport to pick Springfield up on the day of her arrival and bring her into town. Their drive into the city went very pleasantly, but things took a turn that night.

"The first night, there were a lot of sound problems, the sound was horrible. A lot of feedback from the club's sound system, and it ruined the show," recalls Tringham, who was playing that night in the band that rounded out her own drummer, bassist, and pianist who travelled with her. "Afterward, she was livid, and I remember she went up to Richie and said, 'I can't have this, I'm not going to put up with this!' and Richie really apologized profusely. The second night, the same thing happened. She got through the show, but there were more squawks and sound problems. When the curtains closed, Richie came running up to apologize and she cold-cocked him. When she hit him, she ran off upstairs. He chased after her backstage into the band room, and her band guys held him back. It was a real mess. To be honest, Richie wasn't really a popular guy with musicians in

Dusty Springfield at Isy's in 1968.
Credit: Neptoon Records Archives

the house band because he could be a bit bossy, so some on the bandstand might have applauded, or at least certainly admired, her for it!"

Richard says the difficulties actually started with Springfield's piano player, who was being "a handful," and the pianist's own attempts to move mikes around caused the sound problems on the second night. Either way, by the third night, everything was fixed and the rest of the shows went smoothly.

"When things settled down, I asked Dusty why she hit me," Richard recalls. "She joked, 'You're the only one here that I like!'"

Dusty Springfield had been problematic, but Lenny Bruce was another story altogether. In August 1962, Lenny Bruce appeared at Isy's and was banned by

'A Show I Wouldn't Want My Sister to Hear'

By BOB SMITH

Not since July, 1962, when the late Lenny Bruce nearly turned Isy's Supper Club into an instant parking lot in two nights, have I heard such strong language in the name of comedy from a cabaret stage.

Richard Pryor's plane arrived about an hour late Wednesday night so his first show, to which I refer, did not start until 10:30 p.m.

If I am any judge of my old friend Isy Walters' attitude after Pryor's funky performance, I would have to say that Isy wished the plane had been delayed even longer.

According to Isy, who talked to Pryor after this first set, some of the words and expressions Pryor used to embellish his sketches are heard every day on the ghetto streets of any major American city.

And I don't doubt Pryor one bit. He is black and has lived there. I am white and have passed through some of these areas casually.

Several times during the evening, Pryor's ironic stream-of-consciousness wit got to me, as it had previously. This is his fourth visit here in the past three years.

COMEDIAN PRYOR
. . . heard on the ghetto streets

I must confess that when I go to hear Pryor I try to be ready for, well, almost anything. His humor has a habit of going past you like a smorgasbord on a fast moving assembly belt unless you listen closely.

And for a young man of 28, he can surely cover some ground. In one sentence Wednesday night, in a bit referring to the red light houses of his childhood district, he worked in, credibly, football star and movie idol of the '30s, Johnny Mack Brown, and '40s bop singer King Pleasure.

Pryor's mobile face, expressive hands and liquid torso movements are important tools and his occasional use of falsetto fits just right.

Things started out innocently enough, with blonde singer Joan Brant and her medley of tunes, which reminded me that World Series time is nearly here. The curvy Miss Brant, from San Francisco, touched all bases with old and new pop, blues, operatic and Broadway show biz songs.

Then along came Pryor with his knockdown pitch for us WASPs. If I had a sister, I wouldn't have wanted her to hear his first show Wednesday night.

Richard Pryor's comedy show at Isy's was the subject of controversy in 1969. He was cancelled after just a couple of nights, and left town with his name on an arrest warrant. *Credit:* Vancouver Sun *Archives*

Vancouver city bylaw officer and notorious killjoy Milton Harrell, who labelled Bruce's act an indecent performance, one that, in his estimation, was "not for Vancouver."

"That was stupid," Richard says. "We had a lot of comics that were dirtier than him—like Redd Foxx. Lenny was clever, and was never that dirty. But he said something about Catholics, and two cops that were in the audience happened to be Catholics, and they threatened to pull our liquor licence if we let the shows continue."

In the 1960s, stand-up comedy was undergoing a considerable change to incorporate more jokes about politics and social issues in the acts, and in 1969, Isy's Supper Club faced unexpected problems with another comedian.

In 1965, Isy saw Richard Pryor perform at the Marco Polo and then booked him for his own club in 1967. The entire Walters family got along well with Pryor on that occasion, and on an afternoon off, Pryor even took Richard's children for a fun visit to the Stanley Park Zoo. But by 1969, Pryor had changed his act from the relatively mild stand-up comedy of his early career to the much more biting social commentary for which he later became so well known. During that second run at Isy's, on top of the controversial material, the audience also wasn't ready for the string of four-, seven-, and twelve-letter words that Pryor now used in his act, and the only laughter in the room came from a sole bartender wiping a glass at the back. *Vancouver Sun* columnist Bob Smith described Pryor's act as "a show I wouldn't want my sister to hear."

"Isy didn't like Pryor's show. It would be different now, but he just thought it was too controversial. He asked him to drop some of the show, but he refused," says Richard. Pryor was cancelled after four appearances out of the seven he'd been booked. Richard paid him his guarantee, but when Pryor left town, he skipped out on his $433.97 bill at the Ritz Hotel. The court in Vancouver issued a bench warrant, and for a few weeks, Pryor was a wanted man in Vancouver, but he later settled the tab by cheque in the mail, and the criminal complaint was dropped.

The Ritz Hotel was the accommodation of choice for Isy's acts, but Richard Pryor's stay was perhaps just one more incident that made them question the worth of the nightclub's business. In 1967, during an engagement at Isy's of the Four Tops, the band and their entourage were arrested in their hotel room for possession of marijuana, with additional charges laid on singer Levi Stubbs and the group's tour manager for each possessing a handgun. With a sold-out show booked that night, Richard had to post a $7,500 bond to get them out of jail. "[Motown Records president] Berry Gordy called us and thanked us for doing that, and said he owed us one," Richard says. The show went on that night, but weeks later, after the group had returned to the United States and failed to appear in court, part of the bond was forfeited, leaving Gordy to cut a cheque to the Walterses. The criminal charges were eventually dealt with via court-issued fines.

There were always hiccups when dealing with talent, but for the most part, business at Isy's was good. The club attracted full houses with a variety of performers from Cannonball Adderley, Dizzy Gillespie, and Oscar Peterson to the Everly Brothers to Xavier Cugat to Charo. One advantage Isy's and the Cave under the Walterses' ownership had was that both clubs had gotten their liquor licences long before other nightclubs in the city. How they had achieved this while so many other clubs were being raided by the Vancouver police mystified club owners for years. Richard confesses today that it was thanks to friends in high places: provincial politician and member of the BC legislature Thomas Bates from the Point Grey

riding had pushed both liquor licences through. "He liked to drink and liked the girls," Richard says with a laugh. "I delivered a case of Scotch to his office as thanks. He liked to drink Scotch and milk—a strange drink—but, hey, he pushed our licence through, so we didn't care what he drank."

The constant nighttime flow of booze and women at Isy's attracted more than just thirsty politicians. Although Isy Walters was a teetotaller despite all his years in the club business, Richard took a different tack. "There were a lot of girls. I had a lot of girlfriends," Walters confesses. "We got treated like rock stars, in a way." In the 1940s and '50s, club owners rarely attached their own names to their establishments, but at the height of the lounge era in the 1960s, owners were beginning to garner a bit of local celebrity status for themselves—especially if their clubs were popular.

But after a while, Richard's lifestyle began to catch up with him. One night, after the bar had closed, Richard was relaxing with the staff with a drink when the phone rang. "It was Isy. He'd left a little bit earlier and, walking to his car, noticed that there were a couple of cops he recognized across the street watching the club. Once he got home, he called to tell me not to drink too much and drive home. About an hour later, I locked up and walked to my car and started to drive home when the police turned on their lights and pulled me over. Well, they get out and I wind down my window and they ask me if anybody else had driven my car that day. I told them no. So they ask me to pop the truck, and there they find a bag of marijuana. Now, I had never even smoked marijuana before, but they took me down to the police station. When I got down there I said, 'Do you want to search me or something? Do I have to take my clothes off?' but they told me not to worry about it, they just had to go through procedure with me. It turns out they'd got a phone tip on me. Somebody had set me up. I figured it was the bar porter at Isy's, because I'd made a pass at his girlfriend who worked at the club."

Jealous boyfriends or husbands were a recurring problem at Isy's. One night, during a set by Jack Jones, a woman was seated in the bar with her pimp when her husband came in, sat down, and fired a gun under the table at him—but he missed. Richard later pulled the bullet out of the wall and threw it over the side of the Lions Gate Bridge. "I didn't want to protect any of the pimps or rounders. I just didn't want the bad publicity," Richard explains.

"It was definitely a place where the rounders went. They'd be at Isy's all the time," recalls Tringham, who kept a cautious distance from them. "I knew a singer who'd mentioned his suit measurements to one of them, and a couple of nights later, the guy showed up to give him a stolen suit tailored to his size."

After the failed shooting, Richard says, "I started banning them, and the prostitutes who hung around. If those people and the rounders are around, they're always trouble. Isy got along with the rounders, but they didn't like me, and it only got worse from there." Richard's ban did not go without repercussions. "I left my convertible parked out by the club once and they cut it up, completely ripped the canvas top to shreds. I knew it was them. Witnesses who'd seen them later picked out George Bier, one of the rounders who had been one of the regulars," Richard recounts.

The name George Abraham Bier was well known to Vancouver police for decades. Born in 1933, Bier had a thirty-year criminal career in the city and was involved in everything from robbery, fraud, prostitution, running an illegal gambling house, forgery, and drug trafficking. Bier wasn't typically violent, but he was certainly friendly with those who were.

"I got along well with the police. I'd always have a double Scotch ready for them if they dropped in," Richard says. "A Vancouver police detective I knew well told me word was out they were going to shoot me when I was dropping the night deposits up the street at the bank." The police enacted a plan to see

George Bier's mug shot photo, circa mid-1970s.
Credit: Vancouver Police Museum

if they could catch the assailant in a sting. "I was about thirty-one at the time and about six foot tall. So they brought in this cop who was going to pose as me and walk the night deposit bag to the bank," Richard explains. "But this guy was in his mid-fifties and about five-foot-five. I'm looking at this guy and I tell the police, 'Nobody is going to believe his guy is me, even in the middle of the night.' He looked nothing like me. I started noticing he was really shaking, too. He thought for certain he was going to get gunned down. The plan was stupid. Nothing happened in the end."

But Richard reasoned that if he stayed at Isy's, sooner or later, he'd be killed—by either one of the rounders he'd crossed or an angry husband looking for revenge. By the late 1960s, he was also having more disputes with his father. The two not only worked closely together, but they also shared a penthouse apartment, and father and son began to have diametrically opposing views on the business.

"Isy was always bringing back successful acts too soon, where they often wouldn't do as well because people had just seen them. We fought over that. The business was changing, too. We were facing some of the same problems the Cave and other clubs were dealing with by the later sixties. The successful acts were getting more and more expensive and moving into big theatres or even arenas. I didn't want to

Left: Isy Walters. *Credit: Ross Kenward/Vancouver Sun Archives* Right: In the early 1970s, the club's name changed to Isy's Strip City. *Credit: Brian Kent/Vancouver Sun Archives*

give up my playboy lifestyle, but I knew it was time move on."

Richard parted ways amicably with his father professionally and took a job in California, where he lived for the next four decades, first getting involved in the book publishing business and later producing consumer boat shows. In turn, Isy sold the club to Danny Baceda in 1971, but a year later, he took the business back when Baceda got into financial trouble. He turned the club into a strip bar and changed the name to Isy's Strip City.

Bump-and-grind music replaced the Motown hits as Isy passed over the expensive nightclub acts for more affordable stripper entertainment provided by agents and choreographer Jack Card. As Isy got older, and the girls around him got younger, the club played out its next act as comb-over businessmen in check-

ered blazers used their expense accounts to entertain visiting sales reps. Without Richard overseeing the room, the rounders ran free once again—and with them came younger, edgier players who were out to prove themselves. Isy's was still known as a good time, but it was a shabbier version of its former self.

In 1976, Isy died of a heart attack while working in the club. He was sixty-seven. The club was sold and its name was changed to things like the New Isy's and then the Skunk Club in 1980. The Body Shop even temporarily relocated there after it closed on Hornby Street. Eventually, the club emerged in 1980 as a rock and country bar called Outlaws, but its final incarnation in 1986 as a heavy rock and metal bar called the Metro really stood out.

The rat pack cool of Isy's was now well in the rear-view mirror as the Metro packed in the hard rock

Isy Walters with staff of Isy's Strip City. Isy's career as a nightclub manager in the Vancouver entertainment industry spanned decades.
Credit: Vancouver Sun Archives

acts. Bryan Adams, Loverboy, the Killer Dwarfs, and Bob Seger played the club, as well as a host of local acts who could fill the room on their own popularity, including Pretty Boy Floyd, Young Guns, Simon Kaos, Wild Child, and Roxxlyde.

"The Metro and Club Soda were really the two best-known clubs for rock bands in those years in Vancouver," says Chuck Prudham, a lighting technician who has toured with many bands and worked in countless venues in the city. "They were different times. Big hair and big production! Like Club Soda—it was the place where a lot of Canadian bands showed up later to jam after their bigger shows elsewhere. And that was everyone from Syre to Lee Aaron."

The Metro established itself as the epicentre of sex, drugs, and rock 'n' roll. "The Metro used to have these ladies' nights," recalls Steve Lang, a regular at the club in the 1980s. "They started busing up girls from Bellingham who were under twenty-one and couldn't get into bars in Washington State but were over nineteen so they could get into Vancouver clubs.

Outlaws free pass, circa early 1980s.
Credit: Neptoon Records Archives

They had these male strippers onstage who would wrap at ten p.m., and then the long-hair metal guys would come and swoop in. It was a zoo. I remember there was a notice in the news in those years that Vancouver had become the herpes capital of Canada. I'm sure the Metro played its part in that."

The hedonism of the Metro continued unabated through the 1980s until 1989, when the club's owner Hilmar Seussmaier died after Hells Angel Lloyd Robinson fractured his skull in an altercation when Seussmaier asked him to leave the club.

Scene outside the Metro, during the fire of February 8, 1990. *Credit: Paul Dixon*

The incident and the police attention it brought to the club cast a shadow, but the final tragic night for the Metro was February 8, 1990, when a three-alarm fire destroyed the building. Far worse, once firefighters put out the blaze, they found twenty-four-year-old Metro patron Beverly Ann Simpson dead from smoke inhalation. A coroner's inquest revealed that she had somehow remained behind in the women's restroom after the club had been locked up for the night. Simpson might have passed out somewhere in the club, woken to find the bar closed and the lights turned off, and tried to light her way with matches, starting the fire herself. There was no suspicion of foul play. The old Isy's building, which was built before sprinklers were a requirement, was simply vulnerable to a fire.

What was left of the building was demolished, and the nightclub that had seen everything from Martha and the Vandellas to Marshall stacks was gone. Today, a fountain wall between the Shangri-La tower and a Keg Steakhouse stands roughly in the nightclub's place on Georgia Street.

Richard Walters has fond memories of those nights at Isy's, and he has begun to include many of his photos and memoirs of the period of his family's involvement with the Cave and Isy's on his personal website *(richiewalters.com)*. It is not lost on him that he's lived much longer than his father did in the club business, and that he's had more of a chance to look back and reflect than his father ever did.

"It was an interesting life, but I'm not sorry I left. I loved what we did, and what we put together with the productions. They were great days—I adored it," Richard says with a smile.

In 2017, both Isy and Richard Walters were inducted into the BC Entertainment Hall of Fame at a ceremony in North Vancouver. If there were any old arguments left between the father and son who had worked together so closely in the club business fifty years earlier, they were forgotten that day. Richard held his framed certificate and gave a short speech that ended with him looking up and saying, "And I just want to add one thing … Dad, I love you."

THE MARCO POLO

WE TAKE PLEASURE IN INVITING YOU
AND A GUEST TO ATTEND

GEORGE MINAMI TRIO
"The Original Cast of Flower Drum Song"
MARCO POLO CHINA DOLLS
CARSE SNEDDON & his Orchestra

GOOD FOR MONDAY TO THURSDAY
ADMIT TWO   9:30 p.m.

PHONE: 682-2875

MARCO POLO
THEATRE RESTAURANT   No. 983

Welcome to the Marco Polo! Victor Louie with the China Doll dancers.
Credit: Tom Carter Archives

Left: Officially opening in 1964, the Marco Polo billed itself as "Canada's only Oriental Nightclub," which also often showcased Chinese Canadian performers. *Credit: Tom Carter Archives* Right: The Marco Polo Theatre Restaurant at 90 East Pender in Chinatown. *Credit: Tom Carter Archives*

On the night of November 18, 1964, the Marco Polo nightclub at 90 East Pender Street hosted its gala grand opening. Harvey Lowe, looking sharp in a suit and tie, took to the stage to emcee. Once the owner of the Smilin' Buddha Cabaret, Lowe was more widely known to the public as both a radio host and a world champion of the yo-yo during his childhood in the early 1930s. Tonight, as he emceed, Lowe whirled his yo-yos back and forth, up high and down low. One expected to see him pick off the drinking glasses along the tables in the front row. These were well-worn tricks he had once displayed at talent shows as a kid

and now continued to perform during his nightclub appearances. The shtick might have worn a bit thin by the mid-1960s, but on this night, Lowe earned a healthy round of applause from the full house.

Waiting in the wings was Ayako Hosokawa, a singer who'd come direct from Japan. Vocalists were backed by the house band, the Marco Polo Orchestra, featuring local bandleader Carse Sneddon. The Marco Polo promoted this night's entertainment as "Canada's only Oriental Revue," showcasing a floor show that featured "a glamorous line of Chinese Beauties" called the China Dolls.[13] If all that wasn't

[13] John Mackie, "This Day in History: 1964," *Vancouver Sun*, November 16, 2012, 2.

Bill Haley & His Comets at the Marco Polo in 1966.
Credit: Tom Carter Archives

enough to satisfy, a 300-pound barbecued whole pig was the centrepiece of the restaurant's massive Chinese smorgasbord. Chinatown had never seen anything quite like it.

Among all the clubs that have existed in Chinatown over the years—including its many nameless illegal gambling and opium dens from the very early days—the Marco Polo is perhaps the most legendary nightspot in the neighbourhood's history. The club became one of the city's significant live entertainment venues of the 1960s and '70s. Although local popular opinion might deem the Cave, the Palomar, and Isy's to be the city's pre-eminent supper clubs, the Marco Polo, a late arrival on the scene, quickly acquired an audience and atmosphere all its own.

Between 1904 and 1917, 90 East Pender Street housed the terminal station for the Great Northern Railway. When the train line was decommissioned, the track was removed, and by the 1950s, the station's walls and foundation were repurposed to build the Forbidden City, a Chinese restaurant owned by Jimmy Lee, who also owned the May-Ling Club at 442 Main Street.

In 1959, Lee consulted a Chinatown fortune teller, who advised him it would be a bad year for business. Although he hadn't experienced any problems with the business, this ominous warning made him fearful, and he sold the Forbidden City. By 1964, the space was given new life as the Marco Polo theatre restaurant by owners Victor Louie and his brothers.

The brothers were from one of the most successful Chinese Canadian families in the city. Their grandfather H.Y. Louie had emigrated from China, around the time the Marco Polo was still a railway station, and become a produce wholesaler. Their uncle Tong Louie was owner of the London Drugs and IGA supermarket chains. Another uncle, Tim Louie, had become a judge and police commissioner.

However, the Marco Polo didn't cater exclusively to Chinese Canadians. The name alone seemed to convey that non-Asian Canadian diners were more than welcome to come and explore Chinese cuisine.

The Platters onstage at the Marco Polo, 1966. *Credit: Tom Carter Archives*

With its fourteen-page menu, the club offered a seemingly endless variety of dishes—at a time when dining choices in Vancouver were nowhere near as varied as they are today.

"You could usually rely on Chinatown being a good option for restaurants," recalls legendary local radio DJ Red Robinson, who had ample opportunity to sample restaurants while broadcasting from practically everywhere across the Lower Mainland over the years. Back then, Robinson recalls, "there was nothing. The White Lunch? It was just diner food! Just boiled stuff, and maybe some tapioca pudding to finish, with the little eyes staring back at you! Trader Vic's was a big deal when it opened, because before that, the benchmark places in Vancouver were the Devonshire Hotel restaurant or the Georgia. So Chinatown was always an option and welcome relief, with places like the Mandarin Gardens, the Ho Ho, and the On On. What was different was the Marco Polo was a cross between those places with Chinese food, but it also had the shows."

Former *Vancouver Sun* editor and columnist Alex MacGillivray, April 1964. The background was cropped out to spotlight him for his column, which often focused on nightclub happenings and new restaurants in the city. *Credit: Deni Eagland/ Vancouver Sun Archives*

14 Denny Boyd's column, *Vancouver Sun*, March 8, 1968, 23.

The Cave and Isy's featured more of the A-list performers in town, but the Marco Polo hosted many varied and notable acts. Hip American comedians Richard Pryor and Redd Foxx performed at the Marco Polo, as did musical comedy nightclub mainstays like Pete Barbutti. The club also hosted groups such as the 5th Dimension and Sly and the Family Stone, as well as retro acts like the Platters and Bill Haley & His Comets.

But it was a March 1968 engagement at the club by Nina Simone that was perhaps the most notable of all the shows at the Marco Polo. It even caught the attention of *Vancouver Sun* columnist Denny Boyd. Boyd wasn't a regular music reviewer and tended to enjoy the more mainstream style of entertainers, like Dean Martin and Frank Sinatra, and he wasn't normally inclined to offer effusive praise about any musical performer—but even he was bowled over.

"In this day of kiss-blowing entertainers, who beg their audiences for love, Nina is an iconoclast," Boyd wrote. "A glorious singer and sensitive pianist, she thrilled a Marco Polo audience into respectful silence last night. She doesn't smile because she is totally absorbed in her music, none of which is frivolous. When she finishes a song there simply isn't another word to be said about the subject."[14]

During Simone's set at the Marco Polo, an audience member unexpectedly spoke up and questioned her right to sing songs that criticized racial injustice while she was in Canada, where, the patron apparently insisted, there wasn't the same kind of discrimination. Simone's reaction was immediate: "Literally shaking with emotion," Boyd wrote, "she reduced him to ashes with a fiery outburst in which she attempted to bring him up to date. Go see her, and hear her message."

If there was one newspaper columnist who was completely at home at the Marco Polo it was *Vancouver Sun* entertainment editor Alex MacGillivray. If the Cave was Jack Wasserman's beat, then the

Marco Polo was surely MacGillivray's. He wrote regular dispatches about the wide variety of entertainment on display at the club. But his writing did not always please everyone.

"In one review in the newspaper, he gave the China Dolls a bad review," recalls his daughter, Caroline MacGillivray. "The next time he came into the Marco Polo, Pamela Hong from the China Dolls walked up and needled him about it, and really told him off." MacGillivray must have made amends somehow—they eventually married and Pamela gave birth to Caroline. And for Caroline, it was always a treat for her as a child to visit the place where her parents first met. "It was my favourite restaurant. I loved the smorgasbord and the almond cookies," she recalls.

By the mid-1970s, the Marco Polo greatly reduced the number of shows they offered. As the Cave also experienced around that time, the era of the supper club acts was coming to an end, and with it, so did the clubs themselves.

The Marco Polo continued to function as a popular restaurant for a few more years but moved to North Vancouver in spring 1982. When the Marco Polo closed in Chinatown, it seemed to mark the end of a unique time in the history of Vancouver's nightlife, especially for those who had been moved by the performances they'd seen in the club—people like Denny Boyd, who would never forgot that Nina Simone show, and believed that the Marco Polo closing, after the closure of the Cave a year before, marked the end of an era.

Boyd delivered a passionate eulogy for the Marco Polo in the *Vancouver Sun*, lamenting how quickly the city had changed, and expressing cautious optimism about where he thought the city was heading. "It wasn't too long ago that this was nightclub city," he wrote. "You could go downtown with a $20 bill in your pocket and see a class act. Uptown we got the major acts at the Cave and Isy's. Downtown, we got the new acts, plus gold coin beef and steamed broccoli, at the Marco Polo."[15]

"Talent broke at the Marco," he continued. "The bad ones are forgotten, but some went onto stardom. They were new, they were hungry, and they worked hard at the Marco Polo, and they respected your entertainment dollar. It was a fun place, and there aren't any fun places left. Maybe I'm missing something. Maybe Vancouver doesn't want to chuckle any more. Maybe the climate's too wet and the economy's too dry for laughing. All I know is I never saw a bank tower I liked."

In 1983, the Marco Polo building was demolished. A new structure was erected on the site that currently houses one of the campuses of Vancouver Film School.

---

[15] Denny Boyd, "The Curtain Drops on Marco Polo," *Vancouver Sun*, January 27, 1982, 3.

CHAPTER FOUR

THE EAST END

The Hi-Fives at the New Delhi Cabaret.
Credit: Neptoon Records Archives

Cabin Inn advertisement, 1940.
Credit: Author's personal collection

Whereas Vancouver's downtown clubs and ball-rooms generally attracted the city's middle-class and wealthy patrons, the cabarets and nightspots in the East End, particularly those in Chinatown and along the north end of Main Street, catered to a more culturally and economically diverse clientele and maintained a reputation for being a little more offbeat. The clubs downtown may have drawn the big-name acts and marquee performers, but Vancou-verites could always count on the East End clubs to provide something different. Featuring everything from tight R&B combos to burlesque troupes—and, years later, from punk rock bands to exotic striptease acts—these clubs flourished in the 1930s, with some remaining active well into the 1980s.

In the 1930s, 544 Main Street was home to the Venice Cafe, owned by Louis Pozzebon, a well-known businessman who ran a variety of nightclubs and cafés around the city. He got into trouble with the law in 1934 for having liquor in the café—not for *selling* liquor but for some of his patrons bringing it into the café with them. In those years, police charged both customers and businesses for the consumption of alcohol in a public place. The Venice lost its business licence after too many such infractions, but Pozzebon won it back after an appeal to city hall. The Venice reopened in 1936, marking the return of the café's house band—the Venetian Orchestra, led by Sandy DeSantis.

The exact date of the final closure of the Venice Cafe is uncertain, but Pozzebon sold the business and moved to Port Alberni on Vancouver Island, where he lived until his death in 1965. The Log Cabin Inn opened in its place around 1940.

Almost twenty years before the days of the Har-lem Nocturne, the Log Cabin Inn was one of the earliest black clubs in Vancouver. (The Lincoln Club, which was operated by Missouri-born Reg Dotson at 102 East Georgia Street in the late 1910s and '20s, was possibly the first significant black club in town, presenting performances by black vaudevillians.) The Log Cabin Inn advertised itself as a place that provided Southern hospitality to the people of the Pacific Northwest. Patrons got a chicken dinner with hot biscuits and a night of music provided by the six-piece house band—all for an admission fee of $1.05.

It wasn't the most serene establishment, however. On October 31, 1942, a packed house of 200 peo-ple had gathered at the Log Cabin Inn to celebrate Halloween. At one point in the evening, Chester Snowden, a black Canadian Pacific Railway porter seated with a number of friends, set off a small pack of firecrackers on the floor behind another table.

Those not from Vancouver often find the local Halloween custom of lighting firecrackers peculiar. Some city historians suggest that British celebrations like Guy Fawkes Night combined with the readily available fireworks sold in Chinatown made for a uniquely Vancouver tradition. But setting them off inside a nightclub was another matter. Chester Snowden's seemingly harmless detonation resulted in damage to a woman's coat and set off a grim chain of events.

A white man named Sidney Stewart seated at the other table took it upon himself to speak to Snowden's party. It was later reported in court testimony that before Snowden could apologize, Stewart called him "dirty names." The particular epithets were not quot-ed in the newspapers at the time, but before Snowden could respond, a friend at his table, twenty-four-year-old Leander Kenneth "Suki" Jones, bolted up and snarled, "I wouldn't take those words." [16]

Stewart turned and slapped Jones in the mouth. Jones lunged across the table and a fight began. Others in the club yelled for them to stop, and then thirty-five-year-old John Wahlenberg stepped in to break up the fight. A large dockworker who had once been a boxer, Wahlenberg perhaps thought

[16] "Witnesses Testify of Inn Brawl," *Vancouver Sun*, November 6, 1942, 17.

THE VANCOUVER DAILY PROVINCE, FRIDAY, NOVEMBER 6, 1942

EYEWITNESSES DESCRIBE FIGHT

Only One Witness Saw Knife During Fatal Night Club Brawl

In the argument and the ensuing melee which so suddenly flared to a white heat, and as suddenly died, only one man, John Hocko, actually saw a knife in the hand of Leander Kenneth "Suki" Jones on the morning of November 1 when John William Wahlenberg died of a stabbing wound a few minutes later in the crowded room of the Log Cabin Inn, 544 Main street.

Hocko of 349 East Hastings, one of the members of the gay Halloween party which went to the inn the night of October 31, told his story of the night's tragic events, as he saw them, to the jury, which later brought in the verdict that "Wahlenberg came to his death at approximately 12:55 a.m.—and that his death resulted from a wound inflicted by a sharp instrument in the chest in the region of the heart by some person or perons unknown."

down. I felt his vest and felt blood. So I and Hansen helped him out down the stairs."

Eyewitnesses of the fight, and those who participated in it, who followed Hocko on the stand, all gave varying versions of what actually happened.

E. Perry Ward, 339½ West Eighth, said he saw Jones "pivot round and strike Wahlenberg right on the solar plexus." Ward told how the fire crackers had been thrown and of Sidney G. Stewart, 6229 Chester, one of the members of the party at the table toward which the crackers had been thrown, getting up to remonstrate.

"It happened the second time, and Stewart called the colored man some pretty tough names, and I looked at Whalenberg and raised my eyebrows as much as to say I thought the black man was taking an awful lot of dirt and doing nothing about it."

MILLING ROUND.

The next thing Ward saw was several men milling round Stew-

The Log Cabin Inn was the scene of a murder that shocked Vancouverites in 1942. *Credit:* Vancouver Sun *Archives*

it was his responsibility to disperse the melee. But Jones then pulled out a concealed knife and, while lunging at Stewart, stabbed Wahlenberg in the solar plexus. The *Vancouver Sun* reported that the packed house "watched in horror as Wahlenberg slumped to the floor." [17]

An ambulance was summoned as a friend helped Wahlenberg down the stairs. Constables George Pinchin and Ian McGregor were in their patrol car on prowler duty in the East End when a radio call advised them of the stabbing. They arrived at the scene moments later to discover Wahlenberg lying on the sidewalk. Police stormed the club, guarding the door to prevent anyone from leaving. Suki Jones was arrested, and after a search, the police found the knife that he had dumped into the toilet tank. Wahlenberg, meanwhile, was rushed to the hospital but was pronounced dead on arrival.

The news of the nightclub murder shocked Vancouver. Salacious stories of the stabbing and subsequent trial made headlines in the daily newspapers in the weeks and months afterward. Suki Jones was

[17] "Shipyard Worker Stabbed to Death in Night Club Brawl Saturday," *Vancouver Sun*, November 2, 1942, 7.

The New Delhi Cabaret in 1967. *Credit: B.J. Cook*

eventually found guilty of manslaughter and sentenced to ten years in prison. The incident seriously affected business for the Log Cabin Inn, which closed by the late 1940s.

In the early 1950s, a new Indo-Canadian restaurant called the Hindustan Cafe opened in the Log Cabin's place. During this period, the city business licences and bylaws that managed the distinctions between cafés and restaurants, ballrooms and cabarets, controlled more than just the presence of liquor. They also had a direct influence on the kind of clubs that managers could run. Could club owners allow dancing? Could they host entertainers—and if so, what kind? Could they serve drinks? Some club owners chose to ignore such particularities and hoped they wouldn't get caught. Some club goers got a little thrill from defying the rules and getting away with it. The club owners, however, were sometimes forced to swallow a bitter pill. On a warm evening in June 1954, police walked into the Hindustan Cafe on a routine inspection to find

people dancing—something for which the club was not licensed. Hindustan Cafe owner Baskshi Singh was handed a two-week suspension.

The following month, though, a far worse incident spelled the end of the Hindustan. Richard Leon Miller, an American navy seaman visiting Vancouver from Whidbey Island naval base, was stabbed in the back and cut in the face during a brawl at the café. That unfortunate event, along with further liquor infractions, resulted in city hall revoking the Hindustan's business licences, and it closed in 1955.

In its place, Jogi Ram "J.R." Shori opened the New Delhi Cabaret that same year. He had been a part owner of the Hindustan and wanted to reopen more as a supper club that featured entertainment.

"My dad was a heavy gambler, playing high-stakes mah-jong in Chinatown," says Shori's daughter Sylvia Mahal, who was too young to be admitted into the New Delhi went it first opened. Even when she was old enough, her very traditional parents admonished her not to visit. It was not the kind of place for a respectable young woman—even if it was the family business.

If J.R. Shori was an East End rounder who hobnobbed with gamblers and gangsters, he managed to keep a low profile, and his police record was relatively clean but not spotless. In 1932, Shori had acquired forty tons of peas from growers in Yarrow, BC, near Chilliwack. It was arranged that he would pay fifty dollars a ton for the peas, which he received but never paid for. When he was taken to court, it was found that Shori had then sold the peas himself for thirty-five dollars a ton. Shori spent a week in jail for defrauding the growers.

Shori had better success running the New Delhi Cabaret. A music fan and ukulele player, he loved big band music and Frank Sinatra. He also had a studio at home where he encouraged his children to take an interest in music. If his daughter Sylvia was not allowed into the club, her brother, Tab Shori, was a different story.

Born in 1936, Tab won talent shows as a musician in his teens. By his early twenties, he was a skilled guitarist and eventually went on to form the Hi-Fives, a multi-racial band—unusual for that era—that featured a black vocalist named Harry Walker, saxophonist Freddy Carotenuto, bassist Bill Papuc, drummer Larry Krashin, and Tab on guitar. By the early 1960s, the Hi-Fives were the New Delhi house band, a post they held for ten years, playing covers as well as a few spirited originals.

"The New Delhi was dark and intimate. It was a cool space," recalls nightclub manager Gary Taylor, who played drums there. "The house band Harry Walker and the Hi-Fives were great. Tab Shori was a great player."

The New Delhi, like other East End clubs such as the Smilin' Buddha and the Kublai Khan just a block away, provided a full evening's entertainment that often featured dancers as well as a band. As Becki Ross notes in her book *Burlesque West*, in 1964 the New Delhi advertised its "All Star Imported Show Direct from America's Leading Nightclubs and Burlesque Shows," including "Leah Dawson, songstress from Hollywood, Ca, Miss KK Exotic Dancer from Portland, Oregon, Virginia Dare, Exotic Stripper from LA,"—with Harry Walker and the Hi-Fives "for your dancing pleasure."[18]

The New Delhi was also one of the clubs in Vancouver that featured an early performance by a young Jimi Hendrix. Hendrix grew up in Seattle, but he briefly attended elementary school in Vancouver during one of his extended stays with his grandmother in the Strathcona. The Hendrix family had roots in the Hogan's Alley, the first and last identifiably black Vancouver neighbourhood.

"Jimi sat in on a few songs over a few shows there," says eighty-year-old Ronnie Crump, half of the musical duo the Crump Twins, who had begun their showbiz career as child entertainers in the late 1940s and later became popular local club and festival musicians in the '50s and '60s. "We knew him when he was younger, and he happened to be in town when we were playing at the New Delhi. He only sat in with us on a few songs—but I guess I can say Jimi was our sideman back then," he says with a smile.

But it wasn't all good times at the New Delhi. As with other clubs in the area, the New Delhi was a regular stop for the Vancouver police dry squads. Some nights the club got away clean; other nights J.R. Shori got stuck with a fine. Also, the long precarious stairway leading up to the cabaret was the site of more than a few injuries suffered by stumbling, tipsy customers over the years. Tragically, one of these accidents proved to be fatal. On August 19, 1965, Lawrence Salter, a twenty-nine-year-old

[18] Becki Ross, *Burlesque West: Showgirls, Sex, and Sin in Postwar Vancouver* (Toronto: University of Toronto Press, 2009), 65.

railway dining car waiter from Winnipeg, was in town on a night off and accidentally tumbled down the New Delhi stairs, just minutes after he'd been involved in an argument inside. He fractured his skull and died.

The New Delhi remained in business until the mid-1970s, when it changed ownership and became the Falcon Cabaret. The Falcon ran, uniquely, as a country music bar with a Chinese food menu. Perhaps the format was too unusual because the bar later became a jazz venue. It closed in the early 1980s and became the Park Lock Dim Sum and Seafood Restaurant, which closed around 1999. The upstairs floor has mostly remained vacant since then, waiting for its next chapter to be written.

In recent years, Vancouver's Chinatown has been beset by gentrification on all sides. Residential condominiums have cut into the neighbourhood's borders, and many of the local Chinese business owners are aging members of the community who do not expect the younger members of their families to be interested in taking over. New businesses have moved in—particularly hip, contemporary restaurants. But the late-night activity in the area is minimal, save for the booming bass sounds coming from the Fortune Sound Club on East Pender Street most nights of the week. Perhaps the upstairs floor of 544 Main Street could be reinvented and become a nightclub again, to help Chinatown once again become a nighttime hot spot. If it does, just be careful on those stairs.

THE HARLEM NOCTURNE

In the late 1940s, Ernie King was just one of Vancouver's regular working performers. He kept busy with a variety of gigs as both an actor and a musician, appearing everywhere from the stately Orpheum Theatre to small Chinatown nightclubs. But King would eventually emerge as one of the most respected entertainers in Vancouver, not only as a musician and actor but also as an entrepreneur, whose tireless work on and off the stage made for a lifetime commitment to the black arts scene in the city.

King came to Vancouver from Alberta in 1929 as a six-year-old with his mother. After serving in World War II, he returned to Vancouver to work as a stage performer. One day in 1958, while he was scrounging for gigs as a trombonist in the East End cabarets, King made a deal that altered his career path and ultimately enriched the East End club scene. According to *Vancouver Sun* entertainment columnist Jack Wasserman, King visited a place that day where management told him they simply couldn't afford to hire him. By the end of the conversation, King had agreed to buy the nightspot from the beleaguered club owner and, there at 343 East Hastings, the Harlem Nocturne was born.

King, in 2002, recalled the formation of the rudimentary space: "We painted it, cleaned it, put a hardwood dance floor in. I built all the tables—little ones, twenty-eight inches square, to seat four people. I bought a hundred chairs. Had booths coming along the east side, with a couple on the west side.

The kitchen was in the back. The dance floor was about ten by twenty feet. I raised the bandstand [and] I had a small band, and the guys could cook it up—R&B Louis Jordan style, and some Latin music."[19]

It would have only made sense if King had initially been reluctant to take over the business, because the building came with a history. It had previously been a laundry owned by an elderly Chinese immigrant, Dang Yee Gee, who had arrived in Canada thirty years earlier. Gee had made headlines in 1948 when he successfully claimed in court that two Vancouver police officers had shaken him down on the street, stealing twenty-five dollars from him. The two officers were dismissed, and the whole incident contributed to rumours at the time that the VPD was corrupt under Chief Constable Walter Mulligan.

King might have also remembered a newsmaking occurrence in 1951 when Dang Yee Gee found himself on the opposite side of the law, along with two other men and a woman named Toni Silvey, a heroin addict who was well known to police in the 1950s. The foursome was charged with contributing to the delinquency of minors when two fifteen-year-old girls who had escaped from juvenile detention were found at the East Hastings laundry.[20]

The building's sketchy past certainly did not deter crowds from coming to King's new nightclub, which was an immediate success. The Ernie King Orchestra often presented a floor show featuring his wife, dancer Marcy "Choo Choo" Williams. Other performers included Thelma Gibson and the Brownskin Models and a long list of local jazz musicians. In the late 1960s, the club featured local R&B groups like Little Daddie & the Bachelors as well as the occasional burlesque show. The club was popular not only among those from nearby Hogan's Alley—home of Vancouver's working-class black community—but also among a student crowd who favoured it on weekends.

"The Harlem Nocturne was the coolest place," recalls drummer Gary Taylor. "It was an R&B soul club. Just a great little room with great music. To me, the Harlem Nocturne was a big influence on a lot of us guys, and [it was] a real honour when I got to sit in and play with Ernie myself."

"[Ernie] was a very competent trombonist," says saxophonist Gavin Walker, who played with King on and off for years. "One thing that struck me through the years was that despite having to face all the usual obstacles and racism that blacks live with and face every day, whether it's subtle or overt, Ernie never complained or blamed anybody if he faced this kind of stuff. He just simply did what he had to do. Ernie would simply say, 'Well, shit, we'll have to approach this in a different way, but man, we'll get it done.' There was never any jive bullshit with Ernie—he was straight up and what you saw, you got."

Walker fondly recalls seeing some considerable jazz talent perform at the Harlem Nocturne, like be-bop clarinetist Buddy DeFranco and pianist Phineas Newborn Jr., an alumnus of bands led by the likes of Lionel Hampton and Charles Mingus.

"The Nocturne was something [Ernie had] always wanted," says Walker. "And that was a club that was basically for the black community, but everyone was welcome. In its time the club did well, with Americans coming up and with the personnel from the railroads. He ran the club and the house band, and often employed strippers and occasionally singers to go with the bands, too."

Despite the Harlem Nocturne's popularity, it wasn't the easiest business to run in the restrictive climate of liquor regulations that sent police on dry squad raids. Just a year after it opened, the Harlem Nocturne—along with the nearby New Delhi

[19] Becki Ross, *Burlesque West: Showgirls, Sex, and Sin in Postwar Vancouver* (Toronto: University of Toronto Press, 2009), 70.
[20] "Morals Counts Face Quartette," *Vancouver Sun*, March 2, 1951, 25.

SHUT 3 MORE CABARETS, PROSECUTOR TELLS CITY

★★★★★ **The Sun**
FINAL EDITION
VOL. LXXIV—No. 13 — VANCOUVER, FRIDAY, OCT. 16, 1959   10 CENTS

U.S. GOV'T SEIZES STEEL FOR DEFENCE

WASHINGTON (UPI) — The government ordered today that available steel supplies, dwindling because of the strike, be channelled to the nation's missile and atomic defence programs.

The order applies to the non-struck steel mills which are producing about 15 per cent of the nation's capacity, but the same priority system will apply to the mills now closed by strike when they resume operation.

Records Called Bad

City Prosecutor Stewart McMorran has asked the city licence inspector to consider suspending or cancelling the licences of three more Vancouver cabarets.

They are the New Delhi, 544 Main, the Club Utopia,

Not long after it first opened, the Harlem Nocturne, along with the New Delhi and the Utopia Club, became a target for Chief Prosecutor Stewart McMorran.
Credit: Vancouver Sun *Archives*

Cabaret and Club Utopia—was in danger of having its business licence suspended by Vancouver city prosecutor Stewart McMorran with police citing "poor management."

Some local historians suggest that police targeted the Harlem Nocturne in particular simply because of race. At the time, King was the only black nightclub owner in town. The New Delhi was owned by an Indo-Canadian, which might have influenced the city's attitude toward the cabaret. Indeed, the motivation for the crackdowns might have come in large part from notorious alderman Halford Wilson, one of the most racist civic authorities in Vancouver's history. Wilson was one of the most prominent local voices to applaud the internment of Japanese Canadians during World War II and went to his grave believing it had been the right thing to do. As well, two decades after the war, Wilson initiated a motion at city hall that would force the owner of any cabaret whose patrons had been charged with illegal possession of liquor to appear before city

council to show why their business licences should not be revoked.

King, who had no one on his side at city hall, harboured bitter memories of the police raids and insisted he was the target of racism. "No one was harassed more than me," he said. "No one. It got to the point [where] they would harass me two or three times a night."

Whether or not the Harlem Nocturne was singled out, or, as a busy, popular establishment, simply had bad luck with the number of liquor infractions is a more complex question. Joe and Ross Filippone, who ran the Penthouse Nightclub during this same period felt their club, too, was targeted several times a night. In fact, many club owners during these years made similar frustrated statements that they were singled out more than other clubs. The dry squad raids were frequent enough to make life difficult for the owners of a variety of nightspots in the city.

As for the Vancouver police, they were arguably just following the regulations of the period. Retired detective Grant MacDonald joined the VPD in the mid-1960s and experienced the final years of the dry squad raids. He claims to have seen no specific targeting or strategy with the raids; they were just carried out randomly—and, yes, frequently.

"We'd get pulled off other beats to do these liquor raids," recalls MacDonald. "We'd hit a few of the East End clubs, like the Smilin' Buddha or the Shanghai Junk. I don't know if the Filippone brothers had upset somebody higher up, but we always had to hit the Penthouse, too. You'd come in and shine your flashlight around looking for a bottle. None of us really liked to do it. But it was a great policing tool in the East End clubs that were known as 'rats' nests,' or always had problems with fights or thefts in them, so we could keep them in check."

MacDonald denies that the Harlem Nocturne was ever racially profiled and insists that the dry squads only visited clubs once an evening. If police happened to be in more than once a night, he insists, it was more likely to be a beat cop randomly stopping in, or officers simply addressing problems reported *outside* the Harlem Nocturne—a symptom of the neighbourhood's crime problem.

In 1961, a street brawl outside the club involving thirty-five people had to be broken up by Vancouver police. In 1963, police arrested a twenty-year-old man inside the Harlem Nocturne who had a concealed submachine gun. That same year, twenty-one-year-old Wallace Luthje was charged with the murder of twenty-two-year-old John Wilson, who died after Luthje assaulted him behind the cabaret. Luthje was acquitted but was then given a five-year prison term for a separate near-fatal stabbing incident just a year later. Luthje's stay in provincial correctional services failed to correct him. In 1987, he shot and killed two men at a pub in Port Hardy, BC, before turning the gun on himself.

Like many nightclub operators, King applied for a liquor licence multiple times and was denied. Against the backdrop of constant dry squad crackdowns, he joined Joe Philliponi's BC Cabaret Owners Association.[21] After years of being fined, raided, and repeatedly turned down in their liquor licence applications, a group of establishments banded together to demand that the city address their desire to operate above board. Meanwhile, the dry squad continued their surprise visits. The Harlem Nocturne was one of thirteen clubs raided 107 times in January and February of 1967 alone.

"I trained my customers," King said. "I had them put their booze in an empty Coke bottle, or 7 Up bottle, and they'd pour rum in there, or vodka or gin. And the cops never bothered them. It took the cops a year to wise up!"

The City of Vancouver eventually began to grant liquor licences in 1968, but many businesses waited three or four years for their turn. Had King persisted a couple of more years, he might have finally got his licence. But by 1969, his patience had worn thin.

"I couldn't get a liquor licence," he said. "I could only sell food and soft drinks. After ten years of owning that place and fighting with the cops and letting them get away with all kinds of stuff, I finally said, 'To hell with it, I'm closing up.' I sold the place and got out of there."

King probably saw the writing on the wall when the city decided to build the $10 million Georgia Viaduct, a freeway project that would plough through Hogan's Alley and disrupt the surrounding businesses beyond repair. For him, the hassle of running a nightclub in this tenuous location wasn't worth it. King closed the Harlem Nocturne in 1969 and got into the trucking business but remained active in the local music scene. He appeared onstage and on local television, playing music in a variety of bands. He also founded the Sepia Players theatre company, giving many black actors their first local opportunities. Ernie King passed away in 2004, at the age of eighty-five.

---

[21] The family name is Filippone. Joe's name was misspelled by an immigration office when the family immigrated to Canada from Italy.

CHAPTER FIVE

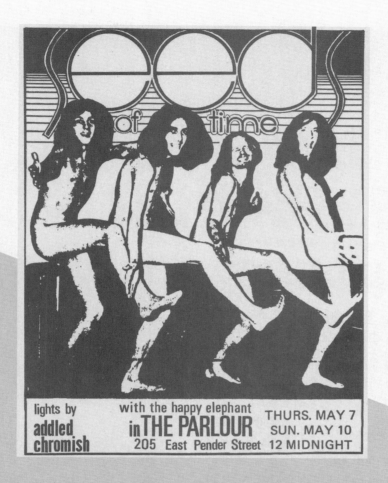

NEVER A DULL MOMENT

Seeds of Time at the Parlour.
Credit: Neptoon Records Archives

Jean Redpath at the Inquisition, 1962. *Credit: Neptoon Records Archives*

In 1961, twenty-three-year-old Howie Bateman felt frustrated that the only options available for young people who sought an interesting nightlife in Vancouver were dreary bars and movies. Determined to create better possibilities himself, he gave up his job selling men's clothing to search for entrepreneurial opportunities of his own. He soon took over a retail space at 726 Seymour Street that had once sold Hammond organs and, after installing furniture and decor from a defunct beer parlour, opened a coffee house that he named the Inquisition.

Howie Bateman opened the Inquisition Coffee House in 1961. *Credit: Vancouver Sun Archives*

Bateman chose the name for no other reason than he liked that it had a questioning tone and was memorable. Without a liquor licence—and despite not even liking coffee himself—he curated a coffee house that became popular with university students and folk music enthusiasts, a demographic that he referred to as the "older young."

A dark and intimate space that held about 150 people, the Inquisition had, according to *Vancouver Sun* columnist Jack Richards, a "macabre stained-glass front window, and murky atmosphere barely broken by the little pool of candlelight by the tables."[22] The chairs were the former property of the First Baptist Church and even had hymnal holders underneath, which could double as hiding places for contraband bottles. The seats were so uncomfortable, patrons wondered whether they had indeed come from an Inquisition torture chamber.

The entertainment at the Inquisition featured everything from acoustic folk acts to local actors reading the poetry of Dylan Thomas, and on evenings when nothing was booked, Bateman himself got onstage to monologue and joke caustically about current events and local news—especially the subject of police going around nightclubs on the hunt for liquor offences.

In November 1962, a dry squad raid interrupted a performance by San Francisco folk duo Bud & Travis. As Jack Wasserman noted in his weekly column, police took to "shining flashlights in patrons' faces, and in the case of the sergeant at one point, actually walked across the stage while the show was in progress." Bateman stopped the show, took to the stage, and in a rare inversion of heckling, barked at the police wandering through the audience, telling them he wished they had come in two nights earlier, when provincial Attorney General Robert Bonner, a folk music fan, had been in attendance.[23]

Despite the police raids, the long hours required to run the club, and offers of more lucrative employment, Bateman liked owning the Inquisition.

"Well, I like Vancouver," he told the *Vancouver Sun* in a 1963 interview. And then, voicing a sentiment that those who lived in Vancouver in the 1960s might miss today, he said, "You can walk down the street and meet people you know. And the Inquisition—I guess it's a small form of expressing myself and very gratifying."

But Bateman perhaps bit off more than he could chew when he booked jazz trumpeter Miles Davis to perform two shows a night at the Inquisition on April 1–3, 1963. Davis was well on his way to becoming one of the most highly regarded jazz musicians of the time, and he didn't exactly come cheap. Davis had recorded the landmark album *Kind of Blue* just four years earlier, but the record's international success, Davis's own notoriety, and even the brand of jazz that

22 Jack Richards, "Howie—How He Grew," *Vancouver Sun*, January 18, 1963, 6.
23 Jack Wasserman, "The Beat Walkers," *Vancouver Sun*, November 15, 1962.

Left: Advertisement for Miles Davis at the Inquisition, April 1963.
Above: The Inquisition Marquee in August 1963.
Credit: Neptoon Records Archives

Davis played, did not make for overnight worldwide success. Despite Davis's high profile, jazz shows in Vancouver at the time attracted a much more niche audience. The Penthouse Nightclub featured more traditional styles of jazz and was popular with older patrons, but younger musicians and younger jazz audiences were left to seek out the smaller modern jazz clubs, like the Cellar (222 East Broadway) and the Flat Five (3623 West Broadway), which later became the Blue Horn. A very busy night at either of those clubs wouldn't attract much more than sixty or seventy people.

That spring of 1963, Davis drove himself to Vancouver from San Francisco in his new Maserati. Bateman met him at the border to escort him into town, where he promptly parked the car at his hotel, the Sands at 1755 Davie Street. For the rest of his stay, Davis travelled around town by taxi—at the Inquisition's expense.

Vancouverite Gary Lee-Nova, then just seventeen, was in attendance with friends at one of Davis's early-evening performances that week and recalls the contemporary local jazz scene in those years. "Audiences for jazz concerts in those days were small. But the audience size seemed to make for a full club during that show." Lee-Nova remembers that although rock 'n' roll had become the dominant form of popular music in the 1960s, there was a dedicated jazz audience in Vancouver back then—though they may not have even recognized each other in the shadows at the Inquisition. "It was very dark inside. The stage was lit, but everything else was more than dim. Miles was very stylishly dressed—Italian-cut suit with cuffless trousers, shirt, and tie. Highly polished black leather shoes. I think the event caused me to feel star-struck, a state beyond being amazed that I was able to see a live performance by Miles Davis and his band in such a small setting."

Reviews in the press were excellent. Even the most irascible critics overlooked the Inquisition's dim interior and uncomfortable chairs to congratulate Bateman for booking a performer of Davis's stature into such a small club. Davis himself seemed to enjoy his Vancouver stay, reportedly drinking a steady stream of Mumm champagne out of sixteen-ounce snifters while out on the town.

But the concerts were a financial disaster for Bateman. He couldn't get rich by merely selling coffee, pizza, and snacks, and he certainly couldn't meet Davis's generous performance guarantee with ticket sales alone in the 150-seat club—unless each customer bought several urns of coffee and six or seven whole pizzas.

In serious debt, Bateman made a considerable gamble. That year, Theatre Under the Stars, or TUTS, which staged productions at the Malkin Bowl in Stanley Park, were in a contract dispute with the venue's management and left. After negotiating a cheap rental fee from the Vancouver Park Board, Bateman announced that he would put on HUTS— Hootenanny Under the Stars—on the evening of July 30, 1963. On the showcase bill were the Milestones, Karen James, Ed McCurdy, Bill Roberts, the Jubilation Singers, and ten other folk acts. Bateman, again defying logic and conventional business sense, charged just one dollar for admission.

It was cloudy on the day of the concert and looked like it might rain. If the show had to be cancelled—or was even poorly attended—because of bad weather, Bateman faced certain disaster. So he devised a backup plan: if the rain came, he would move the concert indoors to the Queen Elizabeth Theatre. Theatre manager Ian Dobbin gave Bateman a considerable break: he didn't have to put up any money or make a final decision until three o'clock that day.

At two o'clock, the sun came out. Relieved, Bateman phoned Dobbin to tell him he wouldn't need the theatre. But practically just as soon as he put the phone down, the skies darkened again at three o'clock, followed by a deluge of rain. "Bateman went and hid in his apartment and was physically ill," Jack Wasserman noted in his column.[24]

With no alternative, Bateman and a group of friends went to the Malkin Bowl, sloshed water out of the chairs, and kept their fingers crossed, waiting for the site to gradually dry out. He must have thought it divine intervention when the sun again parted the skies. An hour or two later, nearly 5,000 people showed up, attracted by the can't-lose price of admission, leaving another 2,500 people without tickets stranded at the entrance to Stanley Park, with traffic backed up for blocks along Georgia Street.

With the debt from the Miles Davis show now partly repaid, Bateman attempted to further dig the club out of its financial hole by booking American singer-songwriter, actor, and civil rights activist Josh White to perform at the Queen Elizabeth Theatre. But Bateman's plans were again disrupted—this time by an event far worse than a rainstorm. The Josh White show was scheduled for November 22, 1963—the day US president John F. Kennedy was assassinated. Local movie houses and restaurants closed upon learning the news. Children were sent home early from school. And the entertainment at the Queen Elizabeth Theatre was cancelled, too, that afternoon, as were Bateman's hopes of a breadwinning concert.

The last nail in the Inquisition's coffin came a week later, immediately following the conclusion of the Canadian Football League's championship Grey Cup game between the Hamilton Tiger-Cats and the hometown BC Lions. The Lions were defeated, and

[24] Jack Wasserman, "Hoot Toots," *Vancouver Sun*, July 2, 1963, 8.

then hordes of rowdy disappointed fans ran amok and clashed with police in the streets of downtown Vancouver. In the wake of the incident, many people avoided the city's core, and local businesses took a considerable hit, leaving a broken Howie Bateman to close the Inquisition in December 1963. He never did fully make back the money from the Miles Davis booking, but as with any veteran gambler, his luck changed. Bateman would depart Vancouver for Toronto, where he found success in magazine publishing and staging theatrical productions.

There is no hint of where the Inquisition once stood. The towering glass skyscraper of the Telus Garden telecommunications building takes up most of the entire block at Seymour and Georgia Streets where the little coffee house once stood. But the venue was the talk of the town for a time and is even remembered by the musician who is often blamed for killing it. As *Vancouver Sun* jazz columnist Bob Smith once noted, whenever Miles Davis happened to meet people from Vancouver, he would somewhat sheepishly ask: "Have you ever heard of the Inquisition Coffee House? Well, I closed it down in one week."[25]

FOUR CLUBS AND A CHONG

T's Cabaret, the Elegant Parlour, the Shanghai Junk, and the Blues Palace are four defunct Vancouver nightspots that are now mostly forgotten, except by Vancouverites of a certain vintage. For the most part, local performers who played those stages weren't especially noteworthy, but there was one figure who passed through all five of them, and eventually onto worldwide fame.

Tommy Chong became best known to millions as the bearded hippie-stoner comprising one half of the legendary comedy duo Cheech & Chong. Before they produced hugely successful records and films in the 1970s, their act had its humble beginnings in a few of Vancouver's Chinatown nightclubs in the 1960s.

"It was night and day in Vancouver from what I was used to," says Chong in 2019, remembering how different Vancouver was compared to Alberta, where he grew up. "Back then Calgary felt like a completely white, racist town from the [American] deep South.

The place was straight, man. They closed down dances there at eleven thirty p.m. Vancouver was much more cosmopolitan, and it was great."

Chong came to Vancouver in 1958 as a twenty-year-old aspiring musician, along with the rest of the Calgary Shades—his racially diverse R&B band. At home, city authorities and police had grown tired of dealing with the rowdy aftermath of the band's performances. Chong says that he and his band were summoned to a meeting with the mayor and the chief of police. "We got told to leave, not asked to leave," Chong says with a laugh. "We got deported from Calgary!"

"I wanted to go to the big city—Vancouver—as soon as the opportunity struck," Chong admits. "My father was born in Vancouver, and every once in a while, he would talk about the fruit trees, the ocean, what it was like growing up there. I had an image of the place in my mind and I was ready to move there."[26]

---

[25] Bob Smith, "Creative Combo Keeps It Quiet," *Vancouver Sun*, October 31, 198, E3.
[26] Tommy Chong, *Cheech and Chong: The Unauthorized Autobiography* (New York: Gallery Books, 2008), 24.

The Moon Glow Cabaret in 1966. *Credit: City of Vancouver Achives CVA 780 335*

It was a hardscrabble existence at first, but the Calgary Shades eventually found a regular gig at the New Delhi Cabaret. They also continued to take other gigs wherever they could around town but were occasionally met with the same response from police in Vancouver that they'd had in Calgary.

The band broke up after a year and the other members returned to Calgary while Chong remained in Vancouver. "Eventually my parents and my girl-friend grabbed me one night—it was kind of an intervention—and they took me back to Calgary. I was having too much fun in Vancouver," Chong says, laughing. But he would not stay in Calgary long. An opportunity to return to Vancouver came in 1960, when Shades singer Tommie Milton called Chong to get the band back together. The resurrected group played its reunion gig in a new club at 331 East Georgia called the Moon Glow Cabaret.

"The Moon Glow was owned by Daddy Clark, a railway porter who loved the Shades and wanted to see us back together," Chong remembers. "The railway porters played a big part in our development because they were the ones who had brought records up from the States. They brought the latest records from Bo Diddley, Muddy Waters, and a host of other blues artists who were really otherwise unobtainable. We would learn these great tunes and then play them for a grateful audience, who would be hearing them for the first time, since they were never played on the radio."

Like so many nightclubs, the Moon Glow had a past. The building had been the Georgia Funeral Chapel in the 1940s, and then became a night-club called Club New Orleans in the '50s, run by a man named John Harris who was arrested in 1960 for smuggling a small amount of heroin over

The Alma Theatre in 1927. Tommy Chong and his bandmates in Little Daddie & the Bachelors took over the venue in 1963 and renamed it the Blues Palace. *Credit: W.J. Moore / City of Vancouver Achives CVA 780 335*

the Washington State border. With those criminal charges pending, Harris abandoned the club, paving the way for Clark to step in and pick up the bar for next to nothing.

"It was a small place," Chong recalls. "At that time, there was such a heroin epidemic going on. That's still happening now, of course, but it was pretty bad then. It was tough to make any club in Chinatown work then because of that. You couldn't charge very much at the door, two or three bucks. And you couldn't sell booze because there was no liquor licences then, so only the bootleggers made money. Daddy Clark was great, but getting the Moon Glow going was a dream that just didn't go. We left after awhile and that was that."

The Calgary Shades were reborn as Little Daddie & the Bachelors (no connection to Daddy Clark). The group took to touring around British Columbia and down the coast to Los Angeles and back on "little homemade tours," as Chong calls them, that the band booked on their own. After the tours, the band would return to Vancouver and play the clubs along Main Street. Chong's next opportunity, though, came in 1963, at the opposite end of the city from Chinatown.

Driving through the west side of town one day, Tommie Milton spotted the Alma Theatre at 3707 West 9th Avenue (near Broadway and Alma). A large venue that had originally opened in the late 1920s, the Alma was now in a state of decay and neglect, but the space could easily hold 400 to 500 people. "It was a big place, and it was for rent," Chong says. "We knew how to rent halls from our days back in Calgary, so we went ahead and took it over, getting a deal when we told the landlord we'd fix up the place."

Chong and Milton renovated the space themselves, and shortly after, the Blues Palace was up and running. The pair next ventured to Seattle in search of a touring R&B act to play at their new venue. They soon returned to Vancouver with their first Blues

Poster designers and newspapers sometimes billed the name of the Blues Palace incorrectly (see opposite page). It was shut down after Point Grey residents rallied to revoke the club's licence. *Credit: Neptoon Records Archives*

Palace booking: the Ike & Tina Turner Revue, for the princely sum of $750.

"The show was packed," Chong remembers. "Little Daddie & the Bachelors opened. We went all out—we added a horn section that night. Everybody played great. I even remember Ike Turner was in the audience at one point, watching our opening set, and he gave me a smile and a nod while I was playing, which felt great as a guitar player."

"Tommy Chong and his crowd really became the centre of that R&B scene in Vancouver then," recalls musician and nightclub operator Gary Taylor. But although the shows inside the Blues Palace were a roaring success, outside, in the surrounding neighbourhood of Point Grey, the reaction was not as

NO ROWDIES AT BLUES PALACE

What Do Jazz Cats Drink? Just Milk, Alderman Finds

Alderman Phillip Lipp found out what the "cats" drink to keep cool at jazz dances.

To his surprise the answer was milk.

He slipped into the Blue Palace, Broadway and Alma, to find out whether complaints of drinking and rowdyism at the dance hall were true.

The city council has received a petition from 56 nearby residents asking for the hall's closure.

NO LIQUOR

"I found no evidence of anyone drinking inside or outside," Ald. Lipp said today. "In fact I was impressed by the young people. They were the type I would be quite happy to invite into my home," he added.

Lipp parked outside the dance hall from 9 until 10 and watched the young men and women arrive.

"There was hardly any noise," the alderman said. "when no traffic was passing I could barely hear the music."

It was a different story when he entered the hall.

"The music was far too loud for my liking, and that's the way the youngsters like it."

Ald. Lipp was careful to conceal his identity. When he was asked if he was a parent, he nodded and slipped unobtrusively into a corner seat to watch the 150 youths twist, rock and jive.

"It was a well-behaved crowd. I did not see anything wrong."

MILK THE DRINK

He looked behind the stage and all around the hall without finding a trace of liquor bottles.

ALD. PHILLIP LIPP
. . . milk his eye-opener

"A few bought soft drinks but milk was most popular. I never expected to see the dancers drinking half bottles of milk. It was a big surprise."

What pleased the alderman most was the lack of racial prejudice.

Here were Chinese and Negro boys dancing with white girls without any embarrassment or resentment, he said.

He watched the dancing for an hour before introducing himself to hall operator Tommie Melton who had invited city council members to the hall after a council debate on the petition.

TYPICAL NIGHT

Ald. Lipp is convinced he saw a typical dance and that it was not a put-up job to fool the council.

"I was told that the worst noises outside the hall are caused by young men hoping to pick up girls leaving on their own. The operator hopes to beat this problem for he has hired bouncers to escort the girls to a bus and wait until they are safely aboard."

Ald. Lipp said he sympathized with the residents who had complained to the council.

"But we have to live with the younger generation," he stressed. "My visit to the Blues Palace did me good. We should encourage more places like this for young people, not try to ban them."

Proud Sub-Chaser Officially Joins the

NORTH VANCOUVER (Staff) — Proud and pretty, HMCS Yukon got her fighting ticket Saturday.

The 366-foot vessel was officially commissioned at Bur-

third of her type to enter service with the navy. Three others are being constructed.

Yukon sails for Halifax next

Alderman Philip Lipp on the Blues Palace in 1963. *Credit: Vancouver Sun Archives*

positive. "All these nice old ladies who lived around the area had their gardens strewn with beer bottles," says Chong. "We actually went around to collect them for extra money, but we couldn't get them all." In reality, the neighbourhood was dealing with more than just a few empties. Complaints from residents about the noise, litter, and disruptive post-concert behaviour soon began to pour into city hall.

Facing pressure to shut down as result of the complaints, Tommie Milton invited members of Vancouver City Council to come see the Blues Palace for themselves in May 1963. Alderman Phillip Lipp of the conservative Non-Partisan Association party showed up unannounced one evening to investigate the source of the complaints for himself. When he arrived, Lipp first lingered outside the club to observe the patrons going in and out of the Blues Palace. After about an hour, without noting any incidents, he decided to go in. The doorman was surprised to see this older, balding man, who looked nothing like the typical Blues Palace patron and more like a parent of one of the young people inside.

"The music's a little too loud for my liking," Lipp later said in an interview with the *Province*. "But these youngsters seem to like it. They say it's got rhythm ... That's a real nice little band they have. It was a nice, well-behaved crowd. I didn't find anything wrong."[27] He reported seeing no alcohol being consumed inside or outside the venue, and even recalled seeing some young people drinking only milk.

It's not known whether the Blues Palace management was tipped off about Lipp's attendance that night, or recognized him, but the venue certainly put its best foot forward and showed him a good time. He later stated that as he was walking out of the club, a young girl even stopped him and asked if he would like to dance.

However, Lipp's positive review as an alderman, if not as a music critic, wasn't enough to save the

Blues Palace. The establishment ran for a few more months, keeping Little Daddie & the Bachelors as the house band and providing a performance space for local rock and R&B groups like the Blues Unman Combo and the Mischiefs, but the older, more conservative residents of the neighbourhood eventually got their way.

In October 1963, a group of fifty-six citizens who lived near the Blues Palace took a petition to city hall requesting that the club's permit be revoked. Despite finding no infractions at the Blues Palace itself, Chief Constable Ralph Booth recommended closure on account of the more than twenty-five reported incidents of drunk and rowdy behaviour outside the venue. In the end, city council voted 5–2, with Lipp and Alderman Ernie Broome opposed.

Chong and Milton moved their enterprise to a smaller space at 119 East Pender Street that they dubbed T's Cabaret. "We named it that because Tommie and I were both nicknamed T," Chong jokes. "The weekends were good, but we couldn't make the rent. T's was small—if there were eighty people in there, it would be crowded."

T's Cabaret didn't last long, but Chong soon stumbled into another business opportunity thanks to Danceland's Jim Wisbey. Wisbey had bought the old Embassy Ballroom as an investment opportunity but was too busy operating the Torch on Howe Street to run it himself. So Wisbey offered the club to Tommy Chong.

By that point, Little Daddie & the Bachelors had morphed once again, with Vancouver soul singer Bobby Taylor replacing Tommie Milton. The new combo took on more of a Motown feel and played regularly at Chong's new space at the Embassy Ballroom that he had renamed the Elegant Parlour. The room was hardly elegant, but it did provide a good place for the band to develop as a unit.

[27] "What's Rock 'n' Roll Drink? ... Milk," *Province*, May 27, 1963, 3.

Tommy Chong in 1969, when he ran the Shanghai Junk.
Credit: Ken Oakes/Vancouver Sun Archives

In an effort to get the group noticed, Chong, in line with his irreverent sense of humour, suggested a new name: Four Niggers and a Chink. Neighbours and passersby were outraged when they saw the moniker on the marquee. The name even came to the attention of Frank Collins, a local representative of the National Association for the Advancement of Colored People, who paid a visit to the club to address Chong himself. Chong said he was simply challenging the mores of the day. The firestorm of controversy was too much, though, and the group became Four Coloured Guys and a Chinese Lad, and then Four Ns and a C. Eventually, they eventually settled on Bobby Taylor & the Vancouvers.

The Elegant Parlour quickly became the place to go. "Lots of people went to the Penthouse, and it was a bit of an older crowd who went there late," Chong recalls. "But younger people came to the Elegant Parlour to dance, and we had some great music there."

"One night, James Brown was in town, and his band had heard about the Elegant Parlour and they all came down. The club was way too full, but we got them in," Ching recounts. "At one point, though, I looked up the stairs and there was Keith Richards, who was also here for a Rolling Stones show, and they were trying to get in, but we had no room. My brother, Stan, who was at the door, didn't recognize any of them, so he shooed them away."

The club was finally garnering Chong the financial success he'd lacked earlier in his career. Also, Bobby Taylor & the Vancouvers had begun touring and caught the attention of Motown Records, which signed them to a record deal.

While in Chicago on tour in 1967, Chong wandered through the doors of the legendary Second City comedy club and into what became a life-changing experience. Chong didn't realize it at the time, but he had walked into perhaps the most influential theatre in the history of North American improv comedy.

"I was mesmerized to the point of obsession and began going to every improv theatre club I could find and stopped to check out when I was on tour," Chong says.

Despite the success of Bobby Taylor & the Vancouvers, a busy touring schedule, and the release of a Top 30 hit, "Does Your Mama Know about Me," written by Chong, his time with the band came to an end in 1968. He returned to Vancouver with a new idea to form an improvisational theatre. And since Jim Wisbey had decided to sell the Elegant Parlour, Chong would again be on the hunt for a suitable venue. The search concluded with a return to Chinatown, where Jimmy Yuen's club, the Shanghai Junk at 442 Main Street, had been foundering.

"We sort of got given the place," Chong remembers, laughing. "It was down the street from the New Delhi, and my family had known the Yuen family, who had owned it for years. It was a beautiful space—and the

Yuens' had approached my brother to take it over. I wanted to offer them ten thousand dollars, and they looked at me like I was crazy. They were ready to give *us* ten thousand dollars. That's why I never went near the business. I tried to stay near the stage! At any rate, we took over the club, but I thought, the only way we we're going to make money here is if we open a strip bar."

In the 1940s, the building was home to a cabaret called the May-Ling Club, run by Jimmy Lee, who had also owned the Forbidden City restaurant on Pender Street. The May-Ling was a supper club that featured floor shows and presented acts like championship accordionist Karl Karleen, the Art Hurford Orchestra, comedian Harry Thomas, as well as Harlem Nocturne owner Ernie King and his wife, Choo Choo Williams, who was billed as "Queen of the Shimmy." The May-Ling was also the site of a sensational murder in March 1957, when twenty-one-year-old Joseph McKenna, after an argument with someone in the club, opened fire on patrons, killing a man before the club bouncer tackled him.

Jimmy Lee sold the May-Ling in 1959, and it was renamed the Kublai Khan in the early 1960s, before being rechristened the Shanghai Junk in 1966. Chong and his brother took over in 1969.

There seemed to be no end to the appetite for strip bars in Vancouver in the 1960s, and the Shanghai Junk was no exception. Meanwhile, Chong, the veteran guitarist who always seemed to be in a band, had no group to perform with. Instead, he became the club's lighting tech for a time, and his time away from music only strengthened his drive to pursue the comedy project that would develop into the troupe called City Works.

"After seeing the Second City guys in Chicago, I thought to myself, 'There's nothing like that in

Vancouver's first improv comedy group, City Works, featuring Tommy Chong (second from left) and Richard "Cheech" Marin (far right). *Credit: Neptoon Records Archives*

Vancouver!' There were no dedicated comedy clubs at all in the city then," Chong says.

But the Shanghai Junk had to be the least likely incubator to hatch what would become arguably one of the biggest comedy duos of the mid-twentieth century. The rough-and-tumble, blue-collar Main Street crowds at the club were not accustomed to improv theatre. "We did sort of have a rule," Chong says. "If you were too drunk to walk up the stairs, you couldn't get in. If we had to throw somebody out, we'd sort of take them to the top of the stairs and let gravity do the rest."

Around this time, an American from Los Angeles who had been staying in Vancouver came into the Shanghai Junk on a whim after he'd delivered some carpets next door. His name was Richard "Cheech" Marin. "He was fast and funny and tired of laying carpets," Chong recalls. "I offered him five dollars a week more than he was getting laying rugs, and that's how he joined City Works."

Today, live comedy is popular in Vancouver, but fifty years ago, Main Street, much less the rest of

Cheech and Chong perform at the War Memorial Gym, October 20, 1973. *Credit: Vladimir Keremidschieff/Vancouver Sun Archives*

Vancouver, was not ready for the City Works troupe. And *Vancouver Sun* drama critic Christopher Dafoe definitely wasn't ready: "A sign on the front door warned us that powerful words would be used; shocking things might happen," he wrote in a review. "When the lights finally went up on the small stage we were treated to a fairly dreary two hours of sketches and blackouts, some of them featuring naked breasts of fair quality. The material was replete with salty dialogue and boring incident."[28] Dafoe did admit, though, that there were "occasional flashes of talent to be seen."

After disbanding City Works in February 1971, Tommy Chong and Cheech Marin decided to try their luck as a comedy duo and took their act south of the border. That year, producer Lou Adler saw them perform at the Troubadour club in Los Angeles and promptly signed them to a record deal. Their first album, released in 1971, was simply called *Cheech and Chong*, and a year later, their follow-up, *Big Bambu*, became the best-selling comedy album in history at the time. The pair went on to perform sold-out arena shows and film a wildly successful series of movies, making them the most successful comedy duo of the 1970s.

[28] Christopher Dafoe, "Improvising a Rover Boys Smoker," *Vancouver Sun*, November 7, 1969, 30.

"Vancouver has changed so much, it's a new city now," says Tommy Chong. "I still think of it as home." *Credit:* Vancouver Sun *Archives*

Chong looks back fondly on those early years in Vancouver, as do many grateful performers and friends, like singer-songwriter B.J. Cook, who says, "A lot of us owe a debt to Tommy because he ran some of the clubs in those days where we could hone our craft. It was a great time for music in Vancouver. The city was a real music mecca. On one hand, at the Cave and Isy's you had the major acts from Vegas breaking in their shows. But even if you were playing the clubs, you could make a good living in the bars. Tommy was a big part of that."

Chong now spends much of his time in Los Angeles, but he returns to Vancouver often to visit family. It's not the same city he knew so well in the 1960s, of course, but he's pleased to see that some of the old landmarks are still here.

"The Celebrities club where the Elegant Parlour was is still there," he says. "The Shanghai Junk building is still there, even though it's a bank now. I went by the Penthouse was I was in town, and the Commodore is still there. Vancouver has changed so much, and it's a new city now. But it's cool to see those places still around, and there's still great people and lots of cool things going on up there. I still think of it as home."

RETINAL CIRCUS

Most Vancouverites are probably unaware that the unassuming four-storey brick building that stands at 1022 Davie Street is perhaps the oldest continually running venue in Vancouver—older, even, than the Commodore Ballroom, the Orpheum Theatre, and the Hotel Vancouver. The names of the clubs that have operated within its walls have changed more frequently than the music that came with them, but save for the odd period of vacancy or renovation, this building has always been a gathering spot for people in search of entertainment.

First opened in 1914 as the Lester Court Ballroom, the space was named for Maud Lester, who used it as home base for her Lester Dancing Academy. Designed by local architects Thomas Hooper and Robert T. Garrow—who was known for designing

SATURDAY, 12th NOVEMBER, 1932

DANCE

Every Saturday from 9 P.M. to 12 P.M.
—AT—
LESTER COURT, 1022 DAVIE STREET
Snappy Music supplied by "Six Jolly Minstrels"
Come and get acquainted.

ADMISSION 25 CENTS

Costume party at Lester Court Ballroom, circa 1920s. *Credit: City of Vancouver Archives CVA 99-5231*
Inset: Ticket for a dance at the Lester Court Ballroom, 1932. *Credit: Neptoon Records Archives*

the Hotel Georgia—the Lester Court was built less than thirty years after the Great Vancouver Fire in 1886. It was a considerably ornate building for its time, with an entrance of marble and tile that led to the main dance hall and a mezzanine that ran around three-quarters of the room, allowing patrons to watch the dancers below.

The dance academy was the building's main business, but the ballroom was rented for social functions, meetings, and even rummage sales in the 1920s and '30s. With the ballroom situated close to St. Paul's Hospital, it was a convenient location for annual functions like the nurses' ball or special events like the 1927 Empire Ball benefit for tuberculosis patients that local ex-servicemen organized.

New owners took over the ballroom in 1933 and had a contest to name the space. A woman named Mabel Green came up with the winning entry: Embassy Ballroom. Throughout the 1930s, the ten-piece Barney Potts Orchestra was the house entertainment, along with the occasional appearance by Frank and Francis Dowie, a popular local father-and-son

Bobby Bland Revue at the Embassy Ballrooom, 1966.
Credit: Neptoon Records Archives

The Drifters at the Embassy Ballroom with Tommy Chong's band Little Daddie & the Bachelors.
Credit: Neptoon Records Archives

comedy duo that would perform skits between orchestra sets.

Years later, in 1961, Embassy Ballroom manager Murdo MacDonald sank $30,000 into the building's downstairs cloakroom and turned it into a 110-seat nightclub. When construction was underway, MacDonald discovered the pillar and post he had planned to move were solid steel and had to stay put since they supported the building. As a result, the club was called the Pillar and Post. There was a kitchen, the music was Dixieland-style jazz led by bandleader Lance Harrison, and it was open until three a.m.

Vera Marchant worked at the Pillar and Post as a waitress not long after it opened, when she was just twenty-one years old. "I had to wear a playboy bunny costume with fishnet stockings," recalls Marchant, who, decades later, still sounds a little bowled over by the experience. Marchant's only previous nightclub experience had been working at the Jazz Cellar, where she'd been the cashier at the front door. The owners thought she looked "classy" and figured having her at the door wound inspire those patrons who looked too drunk to come in to turn around. Whereas Marchant felt safe behind the cashier's desk at the Jazz Cellar, being a waitress at the Pillar and Post was right in the trenches.

"I was carrying a tray of empties and a bunch of loggers who were in town drunk there that night started chasing me around. The band was on a break, and some of the musicians were seated at a table—one of them got up and stopped the logger and asked him what he wanted, and he drunkenly said he wanted to dance. So the musician grabbed the guy's hand and started dancing with him." Laughter erupted and the situation defused, Marchant remembers. "At the end of the night I went to ask who the musician was. It was [legendary local trumpet player] Arnie Chycoski. A few months after that, we got married and we were together for twenty-five years!"

George Vickers leased the Pillar and Post until 1965, when Jim Wisbey bought the building. He approached Tommy Chong and his brother about the downstairs space, and there the Chongs established the Elegant Parlour (see p. 80).

Vancouver concert promoter Jerry Kruz had booked a variety of local coffee house concerts in the early 1960s under the production name the

Vera Marchant worked at both the Jazz Cellar and the Pillar and Post. *Credit: Vera Marchant*

Advertisement for the Pillar and Post, January 1965.
Credit: Vancouver Sun *Archives*

Dante's Inferno poster. *Credit:*
Neptoon Records Archives

United Empire Loyalists at the
Retinal Circus in 1968. *Credit: Neptoon*
Records Archives

In 1967, the club upstairs at 1022 Davie Street was named Dante's Inferno, where that summer, the booking of rock acts really started to gain momentum. In July, the Doors came north on tour and played there. "The one thing I remember about that one is every woman in the place had her eyes on Jim Morrison," says Jim Allen, one of the owners with Roger Schiffer and Blaine Culling. This ownership group soon changed the name of the club to the Retinal Circus.

Throughout the rest of 1967 and into 1968, the Retinal Circus booked a number of new psychedelic bands, including the Seeds of Time, Painted Ship, Mother Tucker's Yellow Duck, Paisley Rain, Papa Bear's Medicine Show, and My Indole Ring. These were bands that, essentially, had nowhere else to play.

"The bands in the other clubs were selling liquor; we were selling dreams," quips Richard Cruickshank, drummer from the United Empire Loyalists, who fast became regulars at the Retinal Circus. "At the time, as young hippies, there was this attitude that the guys who were out getting drunk—we looked down on [them] a bit. And getting stoned, we thought we were better." He stresses, though, that more than anything, the real focus was the music.

The Retinal Circus proved popular right from the start. It was unlike other clubs in Vancouver at the time. There was less cheering or dancing to the music, as young men and women tended to sit on the floor and listen intently as undulating gel light shows were projected on the wall behind the performers.

"Those were good times to be a musician," remembers Cruickshank. "Besides the Retinal Circus, you could play five or six nights a week around town back then if you wanted, especially if you didn't mind where."

Afterthought. He then managed to secure rental of the Russian Community Centre on 4th Avenue for larger rock shows. The community centre had been having difficulty renting its hall to community groups partially because of local Cold War paranoia over communism and its perceived connection to Russia, so the centre's managers were more than happy to rent Kruz the venue. He successfully hosted American rock acts there, like the Grateful Dead and Country Joe McDonald. Concerts in the Afterthought series became popular meeting spots by for the burgeoning hippie community in Kitsilano. But by 1967, police hit Kruz with his second drug arrest and a jail term, which effectively shut down his promotions.

Psychedelic rock and new folk music only grew in popularity after the Afterthought shut down, but very few of the older club managers were interested in this new, strange music, much less the even stranger hippie audiences that came with it. A team of younger music and entertainment entrepreneurs would have to take the initiative to give these new sounds a venue.

The Doors appeared at Dante's Inferno just before the name of the club was changed to the Retinal Circus, in July 1967.

Credit: Neptoon Records Archives; poster designed by Bob Masse

The Velvet Underground at the Retinal Circus in 1968. *Credit: Neptoon Records Archives*

While musicians found gigs at one club or another, the club business itself, especially for a less mainstream place like the Retinal Circus, was still up and down. Within a year, the club closed. It went out with a bang, though, as the venue's final shows featured a four-night appearance by legendary New York art rock band the Velvet Underground over Halloween 1968.

Soon afterward, the owners of the Elegant Parlour moved and set up shop in Chinatown as the Shanghai Junk. In the following years, the clubs at 1022 Davie Street changed names and formats many times over. In 1976, young club operator Marvin Goldhar ran it as a strip bar called the Crazy Horse, until Goldhar was murdered, stabbed in an apparent cocaine deal gone awry, in 1982.

In the 1980s, the West End became the centre of the gay community in Vancouver, with a number of gay clubs, stores, and community groups opening there. Newer gay clubs arrived on Davie Street after older ones in other parts of town like the Gandy Dancer shut down. In 1987, Celebrities opened at 1022 Davie and became a popular gay dance club.

That bass beat pounded the walls of Celebrities until perhaps it became too much for the building to take. In 1999, after falling bricks led the city to declare the venue unsafe, the club closed for more than four years while significant renovations and upgrades were undertaken. Today, Celebrities is one of Vancouver's busiest nightspots.

The old Lester Ballroom has seen trends come and go, and the building has held more than 100 years' worth of Vancouver nighttime crowds. The Dixieland sounds of Lance Harrison and the psychedelic reverb of the Retinal Circus are long gone. So, too, is some of the unique diversity that once flooded Davie Street and the rest of the West End. As a result of prevailing trends and economic pressures, some of the gay nightclubs are changing. Celebrities is now marketed to a "gay and post-gay" nightclub clientele that isn't much different from those found at the Granville Street dance clubs. There are certainly more changes coming to Davie Street nightspots, but if history is any indication, it won't be last call at 1022 Davie Street anytime soon.

A poster for Celebrities. *Credit: Blueprint/BC Gay and Lesbian Archives-CVA*

THE BEROLINA CABARET

Many stories about post-war Vancouver nightclubs include references to the police's dry squad liquor raids and the city's restrictive licensing bylaws, but they were not the only obstacles that nightclub owners had to contend with. Sometimes they would also have to deal with shadowy and unsavoury characters who had agendas of their own. In the early 1960s, owners of the Berolina Cabaret were faced with two such characters: the notorious Gardner brothers.

The Berolina was located across the street from the Hudson's Bay department store, at 641 Granville Street. The cabaret space had originally been the John Goss Studio theatre and later the Goss Auditorium in the 1940s, before the name was changed to Empire Hall in the '50s. Then on December 8, 1962, an urbane German Canadian couple, Mr and Mrs Heinz Rohloff, officially opened the Berolina Cabaret. Advertisements encouraged Vancouverites to come and "enjoy the continental atmosphere" with "Canadian/German cuisine." By all accounts, the Rohloffs' intent was to run a civilized establishment for sophisticated people with discerning taste. Dress code deemed that gentlemen could only enter if they were wearing a suit and tie. The club even featured its own tasseographer, a fortune teller who read tea leaves.

Advertisement for the Berolina Cabaret, 1964.
Credit: Vancouver Sun Archives

The Berolina was a dine-and-dance establishment, regularly featuring local musical talent such as the Bernie Sneed Combo. Sneed, the keyboardist from Tommy Chong's group the Calgary Shades, had moved to Vancouver with Chong and found good work playing in the local clubs. This combo performed tunes that were jazzier than the R&B the Shades played, and the gig provided steady pay for Sneed and his band.

A favourite feature in the cabaret was a system of booth-to-booth telephones, a popular gimmick for singles at some nightclubs across North America in the early 1960s and one that enabled Berolina patrons to call people at other tables. Vancouverites of a certain age might recall that the Bayside Lounge near Denman and Davie Streets maintained a similar phone system until the mid-1980s.

But who came calling on March 20, 1964, was another matter. That Friday night, shortly after closing time, when most of the staff had finished their shifts, six men burst in and ransacked the club in what police called an "orgy of destruction," causing more than $7,000 in damage.[29]

Two men led the gang: one carried a heavy chain and the other a lead pipe. The thugs pushed Berolina manager Donald Trudeau out of the way, telling him, "We're not after you, stay out of this." They ripped

[29] "Chain-Swinging Hoodlums Wreck Granville Night Club," *Vancouver Sun*, March 20, 1964, 1.

The Berolina was the site of an attack on the club by gangsters in March 1964.
Credit: Vancouver Sun *Archives*

Aftermath of the Gardner brothers' attack on the inside of the Berolina. The owners of the club disappeared not long after. *Credit:* Vancouver Sun *Archives*

out two of the booth phones and started destroying the rest of the cabaret. They took to the bandstand, smashing the Hammond organ, electric guitar, and drums, before going on to break 100 glasses, twenty glass ashtrays, ten tables, fifteen chairs, and other furnishings. To hide from the violent chaos, the Rohloffs locked themselves in a washroom, along with band members Sneed, Harry Van, and Ross Kearney.

It was all over in five minutes. Silence fell over the cabaret, and the trembling Berolina staff and musicians emerged from the washroom to find the club destroyed. The police were summoned, and later that night, the two thugs that had led the attack, Frank "Red" Gardner, twenty-four, and his brother John "Tony" Gardner, twenty-seven, were arrested at the Torch Cabaret just a few blocks away on Howe Street.

The Gardner brothers had been living in Vancouver for about a year. Although their declared occupations were "salesmen," there was a rumour going around the city that they were actually Montreal gangsters who'd come west to set up shop. It was not the first time they'd been named in a criminal incident. Red Gardner had previous convictions for robbery and drug offences, and his younger brother for theft, burglary, and possession of a weapon.

This ransacking of the Berolina was allegedly connected to an incident that occurred the previous night, when the club's bouncer Hector Pegararo had intervened in a fight involving the Gardner brothers. Pegararo himself was a colourful character. A year earlier he'd been signed as an offensive end with the Calgary Stampeders of the Canadian Football League but was cut at the end of the season. He then started working as a nightclub bouncer.

But the fight may not have been the real reason behind the incident. "It was talked about how these gangsters had come in looking for protection money and they trashed the place," recalls Tommy Chong.

What exactly precipitated the incident remains a mystery, but when the case went to trial, it made headlines in the city. Red and Tony Gardner got four years in jail each, with Red getting an additional two years for possession of a dangerous weapon—the heavy chain.

Having the Gardner brothers thrown in prison did not calm the waters for everyone at the Berolina Cabaret, though. Hector Pegararo got into trouble later that year when he avenged an attack by a woman named Wanda McMillan, who'd allegedly thrown a Coca-Cola bottle at Pegararo's girlfriend. Witnesses said he stormed into the Torch Cabaret to find McMillan and slugged her to the floor. When club employees at the Torch tried to break up the fight, Pegararo pulled a loaded handgun from his pocket and threatened them. He got six months in jail and was never welcome at the Torch again.

The drama must have been too much for the Rohloffs to handle. Before the end of 1964, they simply stopped coming to the cabaret—and then they disappeared. Not even the insurance adjustors could find them to deliver the cheque to cover the ransacking damages.

The Berolina Cabaret closed in December of that year, and Pegararo kept a low profile after he got out of jail. The Gardners less so. Over the following years, Tony Gardner became a familiar rounder at clubs around town, such as the Penthouse and the Living Room.

In the late 1960s, the Berolina became an Arthur Murray Dance Studio. In the same space where the Gardner brothers and their goons had once destroyed the nightclub in a five-minute ballet of vandalism and violence, men and women now came to learn the rhumba and cha-cha. Eventually, the whole block that once housed the Berolina was developed into the Pacific Centre shopping mall that opened in 1971.

When the Berolina was shuttered and its contents auctioned off, Jim Wisbey tried to find a new home for Danceland there, renaming it the Birdland Cabaret. The Birdland lasted less than two months, but Wisbey wasn't out of the nightclub game yet. He already had a fire going with the Torch.

CHAPTER SIX

NIGHT PEOPLE

Poster for Oil Can Harry's nightclub.
Credit: Neptoon Records Archives

THE TORCH / DIAMOND JIM'S / CLUB ZANZIBAR

Selwyn Pullan, *Ritz Hotel, Lounge*, 1956.
Credit: West Vancouver Art Museum

The Ritz Hotel at 1040 West Georgia Street was one of the more popular hotels in downtown Vancouver and was the frequent accommodation of choice for performers at the nearby Cave nightclub or Isy's Supper Club. Originally designed in 1912 to be a YMCA facility, the seven-storey building was sold during construction and, for a time, served as an apartment building. In 1929, it became the Ritz, offering both hotel rooms and fully serviced apartments. In 1956, the owners transformed the Ritz's rudimentary old beer parlour into an upscale—indeed, ritzy—cocktail lounge. However, by the 1960s, the bar had become a favourite nightspot for local rounders and mid-level gangsters—quite the contrast from the elderly widows and widowers who ostentatiously lived their final years as permanent guests of the hotel.

One of these long-term residents was Gretchen Day Ross. In 1973, she died in the hotel—but not of natural causes.

Ross had been married to wealthy local investment banker John Campbell Ross. The couple had no children of their own, but when he died in 1961, he made local news by leaving hundreds of thousands of dollars to local children's charities, in addition to bequeathing considerable sums to various brothers, sisters, nieces, and nephews. Gretchen, too, was taken care of by her husband's estate, and eventually Mrs Ross sold their West Vancouver home and moved into the top floor of the Ritz, where she lived peacefully for some time.

"Hotel Fire Kills Woman," read the headline of a short piece tucked inside the June 22, 1973, edition of the *Vancouver Sun*. The article simply noted that police had found Mrs Gretchen Day Ross, eighty-five, a permanent guest of the hotel, deceased in the fire. Damage was restricted to her suite on the top floor of the building, but there was no suspicion of foul play. A fire department spokesperson said the blaze had apparently started in a bed. Most likely it was ignited by Mrs Ross's lit cigarette that had smouldered as she carelessly dozed off. This brief news report on the incident would connect with the story of another fire that ended one of the more controversial and notorious nightclubs in Vancouver history.

The building that once stood at 1129 Howe Street in Vancouver's West End hadn't always been a nightclub. In 1917, it was International Motors Ltd., a car dealership. By the late 1940s, the space became a meeting hall for the fraternal organization the Loyal Order of Moose. Though a few Vancouverites of the era recalled it being rented out for some memorable stag parties, it was better known for hosting wholesome events such as bingo nights, square dancing, and waltz parties—certainly nothing like the activities that would occur there just a few years later.

The changes came when "Diamond" Jim Wisbey arrived on the scene. Wisbey was one of the prominent figures in the Vancouver entertainment industry in the 1960s. In the early part of the decade, he was a manager at Danceland, and then diversified as a concert promoter, bringing Ray Charles to perform at the Pacific National Exhibition Forum in 1962. In fall 1963, Wisbey, then just twenty-nine years old, converted the old Moose Hall into a new nightclub he called the Torch Cabaret, featuring live music, two floor shows, exotic dancers, and "San Francisco Style A Go Go." The roster of performers included R&B bands like the Madcaps, the Noteables, the Fabulous Viscounts, and Mike Campbell and the In Crowd. On weekends, silent movies were shown on a big screen during intermissions between bands.

Soon, the Torch was also hosting comedy performances. Tuesday nights were billed as "Telephone Night," when "World Famous Celebrities such as Sinatra, Castro, Elvis," and other famous figures of the day were supposedly called on the phone live onstage. The bit was perhaps inspired by the popularity of Bob Newhart's very successful nightclub act in which he had one-sided telephone conversation routines. This two-sided version featured an emcee and an offstage impressionist—"Everyone will hear these exciting calls through our SPECIAL PA SYSTEM," an ad declared.

DUSK TILL DAWN . . . 10 p.m. to 6 a.m.

DINING & DANCING, TUES. THRU SAT.

Now! Back by Popular Demand!

THE NOTEABLES Sensational Singers, Comedians, Instrumentalists

plus Miss B. J. COOK, Popular Songstress

EXTRA! Next Wednesday Night

AMATEUR BURLESQUE NIGHT

Cash Prizes & Night Club Engagements
YOUNG LADIES WISHING AN AUDITION
Phone MU 2-9630, 10 p.m. to 2 a.m.

TUESDAY NITE IS TELEPHONE NITE

In Addition To Our Regular Floorshow

We will phone WORLD FAMOUS PERSONALITIES
such as SINATRA, CASTRO, ELVIS, etc.
IN NEW YORK, HOLLYWOOD, LAS VEGAS, ETC., ETC.
Everyone will hear these exciting calls through our
SPECIAL PA SYSTEM.

TORCH CABARET

1129 HOWE ST.
Opp. Ramada Inn
RESERVATIONS
MU 2-9630 - AL 3-3222

Newspaper advertisement for the Torch Cabaret in 1964. *Credit:* Vancouver Sun *Archives*

Wisbey himself would sometimes emcee the Telephone Nights. He also took the microphone on the club's weekly "amateur" burlesque nights, when lingerie-clad dancers would bump and grind to a five-piece band. More often than not, the performers were actually professional dancers, but the shows were popular regardless. Occasionally, Wisbey would feature a dancer known as Zsa Zsa, whose campy act was straight out of the traditional cabaret shows of 1930s Berlin and concluded with her dramatically removing her top to reveal that *she* was in fact a *he*. Wisbey would then take to the stage with a big show

of shock and surprise, saying that nothing had been rehearsed, and he didn't have a chance to turn off the spotlight. There were typically a few puritans in the audience who wouldn't clap as loudly, but the novelty went over well, and the Torch Cabaret started to pack the house regularly. It soon developed a reputation as a swinging nightspot, thanks, in part, to the hundreds of younger Vancouverites that were moving into the new apartment buildings being built nearby in the West End.

Like most nightclubs in Vancouver of the period, the Torch operated without a liquor licence, leaving it with the unofficial status of bottle club. Although the nearby Penthouse Nightclub was the downtown establishment most often targeted by the VPD's dry squad, there's no question the Torch Cabaret was a frequent runner-up, and the club earned attention from the press because of it.

"The police swoop on The Torch Cabaret minutes after 2:00am today was one of the most coldly, efficient booze raids I've seen in 20 years on the beat," wrote Jack Wasserman in his December 5, 1964, column in the *Vancouver Sun*. "Fifteen policemen, led by an inspector and including five dry-squad detectives, sealed off every entrance and exit before moving inside. The officers then turned on the lights and proceeded to go through all 300 patrons for illicit booze. Slight protest resulted in a fast trip to the paddy wagon. 40 bottles of liquor were carried away as well as 15 patrons."[30] Wasserman went on to note that a senior officer explained they were "merely checking on a situation which we feel has been deteriorating." Wisbey was later fined more than $1,000 for permitting patrons to drink alcohol in his cabaret.

[30] Jack Wasserman, "The Town around Us," *Vancouver Sun*, December 5, 1964, 31.

The situation came to a head on September 30, 1967. That evening, two plainclothes Vancouver police officers, one male and one female, dropped in at the Torch and produced a bottle of rye that they kept openly on the table. Staff at the club, who thought these two were simply a couple out for a fun Saturday night, never informed them the bottle was not permitted, or even suggested they hide it—they just let them enjoy their night. Three nights later, the dry squad staged a raid, found more illegal alcohol in the building, and cited Wisbey and the Torch for doing nothing about those two plainclothes officers.

Wisbey now considered himself a target of police harassment. He was also frustrated that his applications for a liquor licence had been turned down repeatedly. He sought to politicize this by being a vocal attendee at city council meetings. This wasn't his first foray into activism; Wisbey had unsuccessfully run as a candidate in the 1966 provincial election, and he'd become the treasurer of the BC Cabaret Owners Association.

At a city council meeting in March 1968, Ernie Broome—one of the aldermen who had voted against the closure of Tommy Chong's Blues Palace five years earlier—asked for details on charges against the Torch. Wisbey stated the two undercover officers went beyond the requirements of their job description and "partied all night. They had a good time."[31] When Wisbey said the dry squad police raids he'd witnessed had often included as many as ten police officers, Broome interrupted and asked, incredulously, "How can we afford to spend hundreds of thousands of dollars a year on such stupidity as this?" He recommended that city council ask the police to stop the raids until the various issues surrounding liquor licence applications were resolved.

The tide was finally turning. At the same time that Vancouver police chief constable Ralph Booth stated to the press that month that the bottle clubs had become havens for organized crime and would continue to be unless the law cracked down on them, Alderman Broome again raised eyebrows in the council meeting, stating that the VPD's recent request to hire another fifty men shouldn't be granted if they were going to "send men sneaking into cabarets to drink and eat New York steaks" at the taxpayers' expense.

City council decided to send a letter to the liquor control board in Victoria declaring that the Torch met city regulations and recommending the issuance of a liquor licence.

Wisbey lost the battle—he was fined fifty dollars for the liquor infraction—but he won the war. Perhaps a point was reached where too many Vancouverites, for too many years, had their sociable evenings interrupted by being caught with a harmless bottle of gin. Perhaps they had paid fines too many times. Perhaps the chorus of complaint from all of the beleaguered restaurants and cabarets in Vancouver had finally been heard, and enough was enough. There had to be a change.

There were even members within the VPD, including officers who had participated in the dry squad raids, who thought that police manpower was simply better used elsewhere and the time had come to do away with the raids and properly license otherwise law-abiding establishments.

The hearing over the Torch Cabaret wasn't the only event to turn the tide, but it was remarkable that city council had finally agreed with a venue owner, and so publicly, as well. It was a significant shift in the municipal attitude toward nightclubs. So after being turned down four times, the Torch Cabaret finally got its liquor licence in September 1968, as did a number of other establishments over the following two years.

Perhaps to usher in a new era, or to symbolically cast off some of the burdens of the past, Wisbey

---

[31] Bud Elsie, "Police 'Party' Was Followed by Charges against Cabaret," *Vancouver Sun*, March 27, 1969, 25.

Poster for the Rodger Collins
Show appearing at Diamond
Jim's in 1969. *Credit: Neptoon
Records Archives*

rechristened the newly licensed establishment Diamond Jim's. But some challenges remained. There was competition from other nightclubs to contend with. The Cave and Isy's were still perhaps the most popular spots in town, and other new clubs, like Oil Can Harry's, were breaking onto the scene.

In November 1970, Wisbey received an offer for Diamond Jim's and decided to sell. Whether this was because of the years of frustration running a nightclub or simply a desire to step away from the late-night lifestyle, he chose to turn his attention to a more lucrative trade: real estate.

Less than a month after the sale of Diamond Jim's, a new venue opened under the name Club Zanzibar. While the Torch had been a controversial nightspot thanks to its bawdy burlesque shows and seemingly endless stream of liquor infractions, the Zanzibar would take the establishment's reputation to whole new levels of notoriety.

From the start, Club Zanzibar was a different kind of nightclub. It scrapped the comedy and floor shows. It also scrapped the R&B bands and replaced them with a simple live combo, but this house band would not provide music for patrons to dance to.

This music would accompany a whole other kind of entertainment that went with the club's new business direction.

Readers of the January 18, 1971, edition of the *Province* would certainly have noticed that day's headline about two armed gunmen who held up the front desk clerk at the Ritz Hotel—but it was the small advertisement on the corner of page 2 that raised more eyebrows.

The Zanzibar announced "Topless Wraslin' [sic]... see it to believe it," and promised "topless dancers trained to kick, maul, pinch, eye-gouge, and hair-pull." Assuring customers that the evening would be "zany—wackey—hilarious—violent," the ad was accompanied by a small black-and-white photo of two women wrestling. A discreet black bar was superimposed over the ample chest of one of the combatants. Baron of beef would be served at the event, promised the ad.

The reaction was immediate. Exotic dancing certainly wasn't new to Vancouver, but this was a different kind of exhibitionism altogether. Columnist Allan Fotheringham tackled the subject in his column in the *Vancouver Sun* the following day: "There are those parochial critics among us who contend that Vancouver is lacking in the avant-garde, and is sadly deficient of the cultural breakthroughs that mark more progressive centres. They, carping complainers, obviously did not catch the ad on page 2 of the *Province* yesterday."[32]

Fotheringham said he called Club Zanzibar to find out more and chatted with an anonymous spokesperson who noted that the management had previously "tested the act for audience appreciation" at the Gulf Club on Hastings Street, which was under the same management.

"There were a few things that had to be worked out before being put before a more critical audience,"

In 1970, Vancouverites were shocked by advertisements and help wanted notices for the new Club Zanzibar operated by Martin Roitman. *Credit: Vancouver Sun Archives*

the spokesperson told Fotheringham, leaving the columnist to remark that the man sounded like a theatre director about to move a new act from New Haven to Broadway. "One never knew the typewriter salesmen and stock hustlers of Howe Street rated so high in the pantheon of noon hour buffets," Fotheringham wrote. "Students of foreign culture will recall the girls 'wraslin'' in mud on the Reeperbahn in Hamburg. Can Howe Street compare? Wednesday's opening, with the violent baron of beef snapping at the customers, will tell."

It was probably the Zanzibar's young owner, Martin Roitman, who spoke to Fotheringham that day. A graduate of Vancouver's Sir Winston Churchill Secondary School and a former sailor in the Canadian navy, Roitman seemed to enjoy creating an

[32] Allan Fotheringham's column, *Vancouver Sun*, January 19, 1971, 25.

aura of controversy around himself. His nightclub-operating company, which he dubbed "the Syndicate" (it included the Zanzibar, the Gulf Club, and the O.K. Corral in New Westminster), had a distinctly seedy reputation that some observers saw as a playful put-on, with Roitman playing up his role as a sleazy nightclub owner. Others took him more seriously, however, and thought he might have legitimate connections to organized crime.

Either way, the Zanzibar ad caused such a furor, the club was suddenly the talk of the town. The controversy forced Roitman himself to step forward with a letter to the editor in the *Vancouver Sun* the following week. "With regard to the 'Topless Wraslin,' that I have put on for the Club Zanzibar," he wrote, "I would like to inform your readers, in order to call a halt to the barrage of telephone calls we have received from 'irate' women, that it is definitely not an obscene performance."[33]

Roitman probably viewed the letter as another opportunity for free publicity. Subtly dropping the name of one of his other nightclubs into the letter, he continued, "I have carefully trained five ex-stripteasers at afternoon rehearsals at the Gulf Club, to put on a very entertaining and humorous act. Nothing more. The girls and the midget, billed as 'one mad dog vs. five chicks,' have been selected very carefully with regards to the law of the land. Interestingly enough, it is the women in the audience who yell and cheer the loudest."

A month later, Roitman doubled down. The Syndicate ran a new advertisement for Club Zanzibar that welcomed "nurses, stewardesses, waitresses, maids, secretaries, and beauty parlour attendants" to join the cast of entertainers at the club, assuring patrons that "a whole new crew of girls to replace the topless wraslers currently undergoing treatment at hospital for body injuries" had been brought aboard.[34]

And he didn't stop there. Roitman also showcased a 300-pound stripper by the name of "U.C. More" at the Zanzibar. Even some male performers got up onstage, first at a luncheon featuring a demonstration by local weightlifter Joe Hing, and then for a karate demonstration during another topless wrestling night. Listings in the local classified sections that called for "young girls" and "midgets" only added to the wild reputation.

Classified ad in the *Vancouver Sun*. *Credit:* Vancouver *Sun Archives*

By the summer of 1971, the Zanzibar's standing as one of the city's more ribald pleasure domes was firmly established. And Roitman ignored all complaints from the public. In one of the events that summer he advertised a "Slave Auction" in which "3 beauties from the east will be auctioned off by Abdullah, our horrid little slave trader from Marrakesh." The event promised that three successful bidders would gain the company of some of the Zanzibar's featured exotic dancers, the "beautiful LOVELY GALORE ... MISS JUDY ... and the fantastic MARSHA for ONE night ... painting the town red ... paid for by Club Zanzibar." Entrants in the auction were assured that no public profiles would be jeopardized—all bids would be processed under aliases, leaving husbands free to use the excuse that they were quite discreetly "entertaining out of town clients for the night."

In a candid interview with the *Vancouver Sun*, Roitman said of the nightclub business, "I find there's more honesty in this than there is in mining promotion. At least when we fool people we tell them

---

[33] Martin S. Roitman, "Not Obscene," *Vancouver Sun*, January 28, 1971, 5.
[34] Advertisement for Club Zanzibar, *Vancouver Sun*, February 19, 1971, 8.

we're fooling them. I thought that when I left the Canadian Navy eight years ago that I would achieve the self-satisfaction all of us desire." He added that he had become a nightclub owner for the freedom and lifestyle it gave him: "No one does this for money, really. Anyone who does it for money is crazy."[35]

Roitman also offered some insight into how he envisioned his life unfolding: "Knowing your own future is not a blessing ... [Life] is a difficult and complicated jigsaw puzzle. It's been getting to me the last three, four months. I wonder what it's all for. Jack Ruby had two nightclubs and he became famous for shooting [Lee Harvey] Oswald. Where does that leave me? I'm waiting for the mafia to move in and buy me out," he said, laughing. "I'll get a yacht and a cook. Be my chance to relax. Off to Jamaica."

The party continued at Zanzibar for the rest of the summer, but come autumn, an incident occurred at the club that was so lurid, not even Martin Roitman could have anticipated it.

It had been an otherwise unremarkable evening at Club Zanzibar on November 9, 1971. The topless wrestlers were off for the night, so the quiet Monday crowd had to be satisfied instead with "bottomless dancers." "Miss Shelly"—billed as "Queen of the Strippers"—was onstage performing her final dance for the club's thirty or forty patrons before closing time.

Witnesses later said they'd seen one of the customers, a short, stocky man in his late thirties, sitting alone at his table and nursing a drink for about half an hour. The man stood out—he wore a blond wig. Others who got a closer look said he also wore a fake moustache.

Miss Shelly gyrated onstage in an exciting conclusion to her act as the house drummer, who had accentuated her bumps and grinds with snare rolls and cymbal hits, now reached a tumultuous crescendo

An advertisement for Club Zanzibar. *Credit:* Vancouver Sun *Archives*

on his kit. Patrons hardly noticed the man in the wig walk calmly across the floor, kneel beside a cigarette machine, and fire four shots at the head of a man seated in front of him, as the cymbals and drums crashed onstage.

It was as if the man had timed the shooting perfectly—the pop of the .38-calibre pistol was mostly drowned out by the cacophony. But those sitting closer to the table where the man was shot screamed in horror. Heads turned. People at the bar who'd been staring into their drinks suddenly bolted upright. There was shouting, and confusion erupted. No one got a good enough look at the man in the blond wig, who by that point had calmly walked out the front door, gotten into a pickup truck, and driven away.

[35] Allan Fotheringham's column, *Vancouver Sun*, November 10, 1971, 2.

The notorious Club Zanzibar made altogether different headlines in November 1971.

Credit: Vancouver Sun *Archives*

Few clues to nightclub shooting

Drum-roll murder suspect still eludes police

By JOHN GRIFFITHS

Police today were still seeking a man who shot and killed a nightclub customer early Tuesday as drums rolled during the finale of a Vancouver striptease show.

However, police apparently had no adequate description of the suspect, who was wearing a blond wig when he shot James Thomas Brennan, 40, formerly of Whitehorse.

Nor, they said, have they been able to establish a motive for the killing, which resembled the plot of a film on television at Halloween.

In the film, The Man Who Knew Too Much, a man tried unsuccessfully to shoot his victim as cymbals crashed during a symphony concert.

In Tuesday's killing the murderer waited as a "bottomless" dancer finished her act and left the stage at the Club Zanzibar, 1129 Howe Street.

Then, as the drums rolled, he calmly walked to another table, fired four shots into the head of the victim and fled amid the confusion.

Two men at nearby tables were injured by shots.

They were cab driver John Micka, 25, of Coquitlam, who was reportedly in good condition in hospital, and Elwood Watson, 28, of Vancouver, whose condition was said to be fairly good. Watson re-

WILLIAM HARRIGAN

quired surgery later in the day.

A friend of Brennan, snake dancer William Harrigan, said the murderer knelt beside a cigarette machine as he fired the shots.

Harrigan, who has occasionally performed at the club with a nine-foot boa constrictor, said Brennan was to have been his manager.

"He was going to promote my act. He was a happy-go-lucky sort of guy. He was a good talker. He was always joking."

Harrigan dismissed reports that the slaying was connected with a love triangle.

He said he met Brennan about 10 years ago in Montre-

al. Brennan moved to Vancouver about eight months ago from Whitehorse, where his parents live.

Brennan and Harrigan had since shared an apartment on Bute Street.

Harrigan said Brennan was a steward in a Vancouver steam bath.

Both visited the Zanzibar regularly. Brennan was well known at the club.

"When we went last night, I told him I didn't like it." Harrigan said. "I'm psychic. It seemed sort of strange, but he wanted to stay for a couple of drinks."

Harrigan said he was looking at the bandstand when the

shots, barely audible above the sound of the drums, were fired. He said he did not get a look at the gunman because of the confusion.

Others in the club told him the suspect was wearing a false moustache in addition to an unkempt, blond wig.

Police said the gunman, who used a .38-calibre revolver, apparently had been sitting quietly drinking for about half an hour before the shooting. About 40 to 50 customers were in the club.

The gunman is believed to have driven from the club in a pickup truck. He was described as being 35 to 40, short and stocky.

Vancouver Sun article on the shooting at the Zanzibar. *Credit:* Vancouver Sun *Archives*

James Thomas Brennan, a forty-year-old man from Whitehorse, Yukon, lay dead with two bullets in his head, and two other men seated at nearby tables were injured by a stray bullet each.

The incident hit the front page of the following day's newspapers. Reporters noted the shooting mimicked the plot in the Alfred Hitchcock film *The Man Who Knew Too Much*, in which a man tries, unsuccessfully, to shoot his victim as cymbals crash during a symphony concert.

A man named William Harrigan, who had performed as a snake dancer at the club with a nine-foot boa constrictor, said that Brennan had planned to become his manager. They had met each other ten years earlier in Montreal, and Harrigan said they'd shared an apartment on Bute Street in Vancouver, near where Brennan worked as a steward in a local steam bath.

"When we went [to the Zanzibar] last night, I told him I didn't like it," Harrigan said. "I'm psychic. It seemed sort of strange, but he wanted to stay for a couple of drinks."[36]

Premonitions aside, Harrigan could not help the police with any suspects or motive in Brennan's murder. The subsequent investigation did not indicate that Brennan was killed for being part of any sort of love triangle. The crime left many unanswered questions. Had the killer seen Miss Shelly's act before? Did he rehearse the crime or know Miss Shelly's act well enough for the drummer's finale to mask the

[36] "Drum-Roll Murder Suspect Still Eludes Police," *Vancouver Sun,* November 10, 1971, 1.

Reward offered for nightclub killer

VANCOUVER (CP) — A $1,000 reward was posted by the police commission Wednesday for information leading to the arrest of the nightclub killer of James Thomas Brennan.

Brennan, 40, of Whitehorse, was watching a floor show in the Club Zanzibar Nov. 9 when another patron blasted four shots at him, hitting him twice.

The bullets struck Brennan in the face and head. Two other patrons in the premises were injured in the shooting, but neither seriously.

Police announce a reward to find James Thomas Brennan's murderer.
Credit: Vancouver Sun *Archives*

Credit: Vancouver Sun *Archives*

shooting, or was it a coincidence? Even the drummer was questioned. The following week, stumped police offered a $1,000 reward for information leading to the arrest of the "nightclub killer of James Thomas Brennan."[37]

The investigation into the murder of James Thomas Brennan remains a cold case for Vancouver homicide detectives. Strangely, it's not the only unsolved murder in Club Zanzibar's legacy. In December 1974, a waitress and go-go dancer at the club, Barbara Ann LaRocque, twenty-two, went missing shortly after finishing her shift. Three days later, her strangled body was found dumped in an area north of Langley.

Business immediately soured after Brennan's murder, and for a time, Roitman considered selling off all three Syndicate nightclubs and getting into another line of work. It was one thing to put up with the late nights and the licensing headaches. Dealing with what seemed to be a professional hit was quite another. As the rain fell deeper into the winter of 1971, perhaps the idea of living in semi-retirement on a boat in Jamaica looked more appealing than ever.

A month after the shooting, the Zanzibar placed a notice in papers that was altogether new—far more stern and conservative than the promotions of the past. The austere "Notice to Patrons" read that the "Zanzibar will permit NO FIREARMS on the premises."

About a year later, Roitman changed the name of Club Zanzibar to Syndicate City, perhaps in an effort to shake free of the stigma of the shooting

[37] "Reward Offered for Nightclub Killer," *Vancouver Sun*, November 18, 1971, 31.

CLUB MANAGER TO FACE ARSON TRIAL

The former manager of the Club Zanzibar at 1135 Howe, which was gutted by fire Feb. 21, is free on $10,000 bail pending trial June 23 on a charge of arson.

Martin Roitman, 35, who gave his address as 1135 Howe, appeared in provincial court Monday.

A ban on publication of evidence during the bail hearing was imposed by the provincial court.

After Club Zanzibar burned down, in the subsequent fire investigation, manager Martin Roitman became the main suspect and was charged with arson. *Credit:* Vancouver Sun *Archives*

that had shadowed the club ever since. Regardless, the nightclub continued to face resistance from city bureaucrats, who pressured Roitman to ensure his dancers were clothed and repeatedly threatened to revoke his licence or close the business altogether.

Within a couple of years, the club went back to being named the Zanzibar—perhaps to recapture whatever compelling notoriety it had when it first opened. By 1976, with the Penthouse Nightclub now closed, the Zanzibar's main competition was, at least temporarily, out of business, and the club became successful again.

Before it closed its doors for the final time, the Zanzibar would be the site of one last spectacle. On February 21, 1977, after a late night working in the club, Roitman decided to sleep in his second-storey office. A city health inspector would be reporting to the club early the next day for an appointment, so Roitman wanted to supervise the morning cleaning by staff and ensure that all went smoothly. He was joined that night by the club janitor, who later claimed he was too intoxicated to drive home and had decided to sleep on an office couch.

Roitman would testify he was awakened by the smell of smoke. He tried to lead the janitor to a main floor exit but was forced back by heavy smoke. He then smashed a window with a chair, yelled for help, and awaited rescue. When the fire department arrived, they found Roitman yelling from the upper floor window and the front doors to the club not only locked but also chained and barred from the inside, so they had to use axes and chain cutters to get in. Roitman and the janitor were rescued.

Firemen later found a large quantity of barbecuing fire-starter briquettes strewn around the cabaret and discovered that the office safe had been tampered with. It didn't take long for Roitman himself to come under investigation. Police learned that the business had been insured for $359,000 and surmised that Roitman had deliberately set fire to the building to collect on the policy. Charges were laid, and although there was a publication ban during the trial, details leaked out.

At considerable expense, Roitman hired prominent Vancouver lawyer Allan McEachern (later appointed chief justice of the Supreme Court of British Columbia) to fight his case. McEachern asserted that there were others who could have set the fire, including a hot-tempered exotic dancer who stormed out of the club one night after getting into a pay dispute with management. According to witnesses, she had ripped a phone from the wall, kicked in a door, and threatened to "burn down the place."[38]

When Roitman took to the stand, he claimed his innocence, stating that his cabaret was earning $250,000 a year and he'd be an idiot to get rid of what

38 "Zanzibar Boss Wins Acquittal," *Vancouver Sun*, February, 2, 1978, 4.

he considered a "gold mine." "How dumb would I have to be to try to burn down my place while I was in it?" he said in his defence.

The court said the fire was arson, but the Crown could not prove that Roitman was the culprit, so he was acquitted in 1978.

It was during the trial that the name of Ritz Hotel resident Gretchen Day Ross surfaced. It was discovered that the wealthy widow had been the owner of the Zanzibar building when Roitman took it over from Jim Wisbey. We don't know what the distinguished widow Ross thought of the Zanzibar and all the lurid activity that occurred on a property she owned. Perhaps she never knew. Perhaps she paid no attention to what was simply another item in her late husband's collection of assets. Perhaps she didn't want to think about it, preferring to keep the memory of the Ross family name associated with the philanthropy carried out by her husband's will, rather than having their good name attached to some filthy late-night circus. All we know is that she quietly deposited the rent cheques, until she died in that accidental fire in her room at the Ritz.

As for Martin Roitman, he never did make his getaway to Jamaica. He died in a plane accident on July 10, 1980, when the Cessna he was piloting crashed on Bowen Island in Howe Sound near Vancouver.

The place where the Torch Cabaret and Club Zanzibar once stood is now home to the Cinematheque art house movie theatre. Film noir festivals and Fellini retrospectives have replaced the topless wrestlers and strippers on roller skates. The transition inevitably leaves one to reflect: the goings-on at the old Zanzibar would have made one hell of a movie.

OIL CAN HARRY'S

There is no single figure in the history of Vancouver nightclubs quite like the legendary Danny Baceda. There is certainly no one else from the halcyon days of the city's nightlife scene in the 1960s and '70s who achieved success so quickly—and with such panache. But despite all his larger-than-life talent, skill, and personality, he disappeared from the city just as quickly as he rose to prominence, never to be heard from again.

As a young man, Baceda was a clothing salesman at the Vancouver Eaton's department store in the early 1960s, but he was eager to get into the nightclub business. In 1965, with some financial assistance from his mother, he became a minority owner in the Pink Pussycat at 352 Water Street with Harvey Izen, Roger Gibson, and Basil Pantages. Baceda didn't stay for long, though, selling his shares back to the others before the club was ensnared in a morality charge in 1967. Two off-duty Vancouver policemen who were moonlighting as doormen at the Pink Pussycat took part in a drunken stag night performance with two of the club's dancers when the morality squad raided midway through the show and charged the two men and the dancers with committing an indecent act in a public place. The details of the misadventure were splashed all over the *Vancouver Sun* and *Province* newspapers, and the subsequent trial resulted in fines and dismissals of the two constables from the police force.

Baceda was on to his next business venture by then, though. With $7,000 of his own money, and a few $4,000 minority-partner shares from other investors, he opened Oil Can Harry's at 752 Thurlow Street in 1966. The venue had previously been

Hostesses at Oil Can Harry's, circa 1970. *Credit: Peter Hulbert/ Vancouver Sun Archives*

Inside Oil Can Harry's. *Photo: Dan Scott/Vancouver Sun Archives*

Danny Baceda (age twenty-four) and Frank Hook (age twenty-three), proprietors of Oil Can Harry's. *Photo: Dave Buchan/*Vancouver Sun *Archives*

Mike's 752 Club, which was known as a gay-friendly club, and prior to that it had been the Bavarian-themed restaurant and cabaret the Rathskeller.

There was nothing quite like Oil Can Harry's in Vancouver at the time. The club featured two separate rooms—Harry's Go-Go Room upstairs and Dirty Sal's Cellar downstairs—so the club could essentially host two acts and two different crowds at the same time. (In 1969, the club expanded with a third room.)

"Danny was a visionary," says Vancouver reggae concert promoter Mel Warner, who, in 1973, his final year of high school, became a busboy at Oil Can Harry's. He later became a doorman there. "Danny had an idea that the whole area around Oil Can Harry's could be a new Las Vegas. He wanted to have valet parking, and guys in suits at the front door that would hand you a glass of champagne when you walked in. He was even thinking about the potential of slot machines that early, when nobody was even considering it at that time—he always had great ideas!"

VANCOUVERS' SWINGINGEST, LIVELIEST ADULT . . . . .

A·GO·GO

Featuring . . .
**HARRY'S GO-GO GIRLS and the tops
in NORTHWEST ENTERTAINMENT.**
21 and over, Jacket and Tie.
Wed., Thurs., Fri., Sat., nine till . . . ?
752 THURLOW, VANCOUVER   683-7923

Poster for Oil Can Harry's nightclub, 1966.
Credit: Neptoon Records Archives

TONIGHT ONLY AT OIL CAN HARRY'S
The Great Rhythm 'n' Blues Sound of
JASON . HOOVER
AND THE EPICS
Plus TONIGHT ONLY in
DIRTY SAL'S CELLAR
VANCOUVER'S JAMES BROWN
KENTISH STEELE & the SHANTELS
JACKET & TIE, PLEASE
752 Thurlow St.
Phone 683-7923

Jayson Hoover and the Epics and
Kentish Steele were just two of the great
acts to come out of the Vancouver nightclub
scene in the 1960s. *Credit: Vancouver Sun Archives*

Oil Can Harry's quickly became the city's new place to go. The club burst nightly with young singles now living in the new West End apartment buildings nearby.

"Those were the days that everyone used to dress up in suits and ties to go to nightclubs," Warner says with a laugh. "On Fridays, everybody—businessmen, rounders, pimps, you name it—used to go down to Murray Goldman's clothing store to get a brand-new tie or jacket—whatever the latest style was—and then come down looking sharp to Oil Can Harry's. By eight p.m., the place was packed!"

Oil Can Harry's became a unique training ground for Warner and his early efforts to get into the local music business. He not only watched Baceda run the club, but, as doorman, he also got to meet some of the local band managers and agents who frequented the place.

Baceda brought in performers like American soul singers Edwin Starr and Wayne Cochran, but it was the local Night Train Revue, the club's house band, that kept the dance floor full of beehives and skinny ties. Additionally, go-go girls danced in miniskirts and boots on platforms on either side of the stage.

Danny Baceda was just twenty-three years old when he started Oil Can Harry's and became almost overnight the young tycoon of the Vancouver entertainment industry. Flush with money from the successful club and new investors, in 1971, Baceda bought the Cave one week and then Isy's Supper Club the next. In the space of just a few years, he'd grown from pushing double-breasted suits at Eaton's to owning the three biggest nightclubs in Vancouver. He was the talk of the town, where he could often be seen driving around in a Ferrari, sporting a fresh Acapulco tan.

But it was a case of expanding too quickly. With cash flow issues and investors who'd promised more than they could provide, financing became a problem. Just a year later, Baceda was forced to sell off both the Cave and Isy's. Oil Can Harry's was at least partially rescued by Baceda's cousin Frank Hook—one of the club's original minority investors—who, after securing some loans, took over the business in 1972. For a time, the club seemed to be back on its feet again.

By the mid-1970s, Oil Can Harry's programming took a more sophisticated turn toward jazz. Charles Mingus, Bill Evans, Stan Getz, Pharoah Sanders, McCoy Tyner, and Gil Scott-Heron all performed at the club.

In 1974, Baceda was back in business with a new club: Baceda's, at 1609 East Hastings Street. Where Oil Can Harry's had featured two to three rooms, Baceda's had five! There was Danny's Disco, a theatre space called the Purple Pit that could hold 700 people, another 300-person showroom, a piano lounge called the Hunter's Lair, and a restaurant called Rubina's named for Baceda's mother (who operated a Mexican restaurant in Gastown). Outside the club, a thirty-foot-long sign spelling "B-A-C-E-D-A-S" in blood-red letters left no doubt about who was in charge.

"It was a beautiful, amazing club," recalls Mel Warner. "When it first opened, it was really doing well. But Danny was bringing in the biggest artists he could—paying out huge money. I think a year or so later, he got into some stock market stuff at the same time—how shall I put this—some undesirables started showing at the club. The rounders and hookers started taking over. There were a lot of rumours that Danny was involved with the mafia—all of that was ridiculous, though. But the atmosphere changed at the same time the owners of the building jacked up the rent on him."

Both Baceda's and Frank Hook's Oil Can Harry's closed in 1977. Warner believes that if Baceda had chosen to simply stay at the old Oil Can Harry's location and not expand so quickly, he might have stayed in business. But there was another factor affecting the nightclub business in the late 1970s: the arrival of disco. Older rooms were being passed over by younger audiences in search of flashy clubs where they could be the stars of their own dance floors, not mere onlookers facing a stage.

A year later, with Oil Can Harry's in receivership, Baceda tried to reopen the Thurlow Street club as the Raspberry Patch. He had difficulty getting it off the ground, though. Faced with financing problem and licensing issues, the club never opened.

Undeterred, the unsinkable Danny Baceda ran for mayor of Vancouver as an independent candidate in 1978 against the incumbent Jack Volrich. "People don't realize when I left the nightclubs and the rock music I'd go home at night and listen to classical records and follow politics," Baceda told the *Vancouver Sun* during an election campaign interview, trying to assure voters that he had potential as an outside candidate. "The city is full of small civic groups telling them how to vote, but the voters have wisened up and they're saying, 'Let's get someone who's got some smarts upstairs and isn't politically oriented.'"[39]

Baceda promised to cut through red tape at city hall. He said he would facilitate Sunday shopping,

[39] Alan Merridew and Andy Ross, "Who Will Be Sitting in the Mayor's Chair," *Vancouver Sun*, October 24, 1978, 12.

Danny Baceda in the "Hunter's Lair" room of his East Hastings nightclub, Baceda's, June 1974.
*Photo: George Diack/*Vancouver Sun *Archives*

eliminate bus fares for people over sixty, pressure the provincial and federal governments to implement mass transit, prevent construction along the waterfront to preserve city views, and bring in legalized gambling monitored by proper oversight. He came fifth out of seven candidates.

Baceda, it seems, had finally had enough of Vancouver. He left the city in 1979 for California. But no one knows—or no one is talking about—what exactly became of him. Rumours abound: he invested in a sailboat company, he became either a B-movie or an adult film producer, he opened a motorcycle sales shop and got entangled with biker gangs. There is no end the speculation. He is believed to be living in the Los Angeles area, but the author's attempts to reach Baceda proved fruitless, and members of the Baceda family who still reside in Vancouver remain private, adding to the man's enigma.

"I heard that he opened a lounge in Los Angeles," Mel Warner says. "But I never heard much again. He must be doing something interesting. He was that kind of guy."

If he prefers not to return to the city, or to keep his life today separate from those early days in Vancouver, he might at least know that his exploits still stand tall in the history of the entertainment business here. There has never been anyone else quite like Danny Baceda.

THE LIVING ROOM

In the early 1970s, people strolling at night down the west side of Hornby Street, just north of Dunsmuir Street, couldn't miss the eye-catching sign that depicted smoke, coiling and drifting up from a cigarette in an astray. It was a subtle invitation to passersby to venture down into the subterranean retreat of George Vickers's Living Room.

The Living Room may have been one of the smallest nightspots around, but for a time, the intimate club, and Vickers himself, were big in Vancouver nightclub scene.

Born in 1926, George Albert Vickers started out at the Cave in the 1950s as a nightclub photographer, taking pictures of patrons at their tables, a job that soon had him doing the rounds of other downtown clubs. "When I first knew him he had a beat-up camera and he ran from club to club taking those souvenir pictures which then sold for a buck," recalled Jack Wasserman in his newspaper column in 1966.[40] Vickers took photos not only of patrons out for the evening but also many of the club owners who wanted a keepsake shot of themselves posed with headliners who were playing in town.

Vickers took a number of the vintage photos that are still hanging on the walls of the Penthouse Nightclub, and many long-time Vancouver families have a photo of their parents or grandparents seated at a nightclub table that was quite likely to have been

George Vickers's *Vancouver Guide* steered tourists to the local nightclubs, including his own.
Credit: Roger Vickers Archives

taken by him. These snapshots were the pre–social media equivalent of selfies. The key difference being that without the universal convenience of cellphone cameras, *someone* with a camera had to capture the moment. Enter George Vickers. With his camera ready, he became well known and welcomed as he moved from nightspot to nightspot and, more often than not, was invited to sit down with the VIPs he'd photograph. Often, he would stay after hours to drink with staff and the visiting performers.

But he was more than just a barfly who was handy with a camera. In the mid-1950s he decided that the city needed a tour guide, and he set up the one-man operation for which he took photos, sold advertising, wrote copy, and handled circulation for his *Vancouver Guide* long before any similar publication existed in town—which he continued to publish successfully well into the 1970s.

But the lure of getting off the sidelines to run a club of his own was too much to resist. So with profits from the *Vancouver Guide* and a timely bank loan, in 1961, he opened the Living Room in the basement of 617 Seymour Street, which had previously been the location of the Dugout, a Hawaiian-themed supper club.

---

[40] Jack Wasserman's column, *Vancouver Sun*, March 10, 1966, 37.

A busy night at the Living Room. *Credit: Roger Vickers Archives*

Above: "I have the most intimate nightclub in Canada," claimed George Vickers. "In fact, it's a real living room." Right: Outside the Living Room on Hornby Street. *Credit: Roger Vickers Archives*

The setting of the Living Room was just that: a low-key array of white chesterfields and some tables and chairs spread around the room. "You try for the right atmosphere and here, at least, I feel I've succeeded. I have the most intimate club in Canada. It is, in fact, a real living room," Vickers once told the *Vancouver Sun*.[41]

The business became somewhat of a family affair, with Vickers's wife, Candy, working at the Living Room, as well as his young son, Roger, whose time at the club made for an early education in show business —though perhaps not with the most glamorous beginning. Today, age sixty-eight, Roger resides in Lethbridge, Alberta, but vividly recalls his teenage years at the Living Room, where he started out cleaning toilets but quickly graduated to dishwasher. The club might have been able to hold only 200 people at the most, but it became popular very quickly, and the Vickers family squeezed in as many eager patrons as they could. "In those days we were packed," Roger says. "Jammed! Over-jammed on some nights, really. My dad wouldn't care. If we had to jam in another couple and put the two couples together, he'd do it. That's just the way it was. But it became a good way

[41] Robbi West, "George Vickers: Cabaret Owner," *Vancouver Sun*, September 9, 1966, 20A.

George Vickers: Cabaret Owner

Or, How Being in Show Biz Can Send You Up the Wall

By ROBBI WEST

Have you ever thought you'd like to own a big, fancy night club and walk around elegant as all get-out and chat with the celebrities and lug away a sack of $10 bills each night?

Okay, meet George Vickers.

He owns a night club.

Local boy makes good, or . . . frustrated at 40.

He's a tall, thin chap whose face looks like it's been through some kind of a war, and he's too busy being cook, hat check boy, bookkeeper, electrician, sweeper-upper to be as elegant a host as he'd like to be, although he tries hard.

George hasn't seen that sack of $10 bills, except in his dreams, which come only between the nightmares.

Five months ago, he became the proud owner of a nice and shiny liquor licence for his Living Room Cabaret. He wanted that licence for a long time. He wanted to be legit. So he got it - - - but good! Right between the pocketbook and his sanity.

But let him tell it. He does it well:

"There's a saying among cabaret owners that you'll always make the wrong decision once you have a liquor licence.

"After six months of holding a licence, I can vouch for the truth of that saying.

"When you have a 'bottle club' (a cabaret without a liquor licence) all you do is sell seats. The people don't care what type of entertainment you have, if any. And they don't care what the music is — record player, juke box, or live combo. All they want is a place to sit and drink from their bottle. Their own bottle. They don't care about the rest.

"However, if you have a liquor licence, this means, by virtue of the B.C. Liquor Act, that you must have a cover charge (of at least a dollar) and then price the drinks accordingly.

"And because the people are now paying for more than the price of their bottle and some ice, they expect more. If they come out.

"So, to get the people out, we have to add incentive. And this is where all the wrong decisions arise. Especially if you're just a baby in this business as I am.

"You get the wrong type of entertainment or pay too much for it because you don't know how to bargain. You install a kitchen and find people won't eat at your place

GEORGE VICKERS
. . . he has his problems

because they are accustomed to eating in restaurants and drinking in nightclubs.

"Then you try for the right atmosphere and here, at least, I feel I've succeeded. I have the most intimate club in Canada. It is, in fact, a real living room.

"But atmosphere, I'm afraid, won't draw the people. On Friday and Saturday nights it's all right because people go out just to go out. But from Monday to Thursday you have to have an act to draw the crowds. And acts cost money which increases the overhead which necessitates drawing larger crowds and you only do that by having better and bigger acts.

"It's just a great big vicious circle. You're no longer selling just seats — you're selling a show.

"This vicious circle will, I hope, come to an end on

January first when the city by-law changes become effective, making it impossible for a cabaret to have a city licence without a provincial liquor licence.

"No licence, no cabaret.

"At least the licensed clubs will have a fighting chance.

"As it stands now, a club that gets its liquor licence is almost dead before it starts.

"I know the truth of this too.

"I've invested about $30,000 into this club since it opened in 1961. I did okay. It was furnished with comfortable lounge chairs, two-seat sofas and small coffee tables. I sold food and, of course, soft drinks.

"I had a small combo for soft background and dance music.

"It was considered one of the better little clubs around.

"Then, in 1965, I applied for a liquor licence. And the struggle was on. For almost a year, I and other small club operators tried to get licences from the LCB. Some of us won. Some of us lost.

"In March, 1965, the Johann Strauss got a full cabaret licence — the first non-floor show club around to get one.

"The Duke's got one. Then the Kublai Khan. I got one. That made seven licensed clubs among the 40 or so clubs around.

"By July 30, this year, the city had 34 cabarets licensed by the city. Nineteen had provincial liquor licences. And some of these were going broke.

"I wasn't going broke, but I sure was struggling hard.

"Fourteen hours a day. Sometimes a lot more.

"A club owner doesn't mind working a 14-hour day if he can see the results and knows he's doing the best possible job.

"But what really annoys the liquor-licensed operators is the fact that while we have invested thousands of dollars into a nicely-decorated, well-run club with good food and entertainment, we're still struggling to keep our heads above the water and all the while the bottle clubs, which provide not much more than a loud band, a table and some chairs, are packing the people in.

"It's not fair to any of us, but there doesn't seem to be much we can do about it for a few months.

"Just hang in there."

That's why George Vickers has a great big red circle around January first on the calendar.

New year — new deal.

A central figure in the Vancouver nightclub scene for over twenty years, George Vickers was frequently spotlighted in the media and was named "Clubman of the Year" in 1972. *Credit:* Vancouver Sun *Archives*

for strangers to get to meet one another—you made friends. Clubs just wouldn't do that today."

The entertainment tended to be small local combos or acoustic duos—as well as the occasional comedy act. American comedian Pat Paulsen performed there several times before he moved on to bigger clubs like the Cave and Isy's Supper Club.

At first, the Living Room—like almost all nightclubs of the period—had no liquor licence. "We'd sell pop and a bucket of ice, and you brought your own bottle down," Roger remembers. "When we got raided, the girl upstairs at the cashier window who took the two- or three-dollar admission would reach down as the police were coming down the stairs and turn the lights in the club off and on. My dad would jump up onstage and shout to everybody to hide their bottles—we had these coffee tables that had drawers in them. Police couldn't confiscate anything unless it was in open view. We were raided many times."

George Vickers was a vocal proponent of the government finally granting proper liquor licences to nightclub operators and a member of BC Cabaret Owners Association. Vickers applied for a liquor licence in 1965 and, after multiple appeals, was finally granted one. His lease for the Seymour Street space was ending, though, and he was forced to look for a new location at the end of 1969.

Vickers found an even smaller space at 569 Hornby Street, closer to the action of the Cave, Hy's Steakhouse, and other clubs. Vickers announced his arrival by putting up a sign outside the Living Room that read, "Glad to join you, Ken, Hy and Herb." It was an open letter to Ken Stauffer from the Cave, Hy Aisenstat from the steakhouse, and Herb Capozzi, who ran the successful Men's Athletic

Recreational Centre (MARC) in the penthouse of the Marc Building at 595 Hornby.

It was the beginning of the boom on Hornby Street. Around the time that Vickers opened the new Living Room, another club operator, Pat McCleery, with Capozzi, opened Sneaky Pete's in the Marc Building. Later, a restaurant called Charlie Brown's opened there. By the end of the 1970s, that stretch of Hornby Street would also include 12 Caesars, Misty's, Gary Taylor's Rock Room, and Sugar Daddy's.

Unfortunately, after the new Living Room opened with its official liquor licence, Vickers found that business hadn't gotten any easier. "When you have a bottle club, all you do is sell seats," he said in an interview with the *Vancouver Sun*. "The people don't care what kind of entertainment you have, if any. And they don't care what the music is—record player, juke box, or live combo. All they want is a place to sit and drink from their bottle. Their own bottle. They don't care about the rest. However if you have a liquor license, this means by virtue of the BC Liquor Act, that you must have a cover charge of at least a dollar, and then price the drinks accordingly. And because the people are now paying more than the price of their bottle and some ice, they expect more. If they come out."

He continued, "So to get the people out we have to add incentive. And this is where all the wrong business decisions arrive. Especially if you're just a baby in this business as I am. You get the wrong type of entertainment or pay too much for it because you don't know how to bargain ... It can be a bit of a vicious circle—you're not just selling seats, you're selling a show."

Fortunately for Vickers, singer-guitarist Howie James began to regularly draw crowds at the Living Room. An unlikely nightclub star, James had become a devout Christian in 1964 and didn't smoke or drink but had built up a popular local following at a few

select clubs around town. He would frequently appear at the Living Room performing solo, or in duos or trios, often with Kichi, a Japanese Hammond organ player who was a Living Room mainstay. Frank Sinatra songs were particular favourites: "Crowds used to flock down to the Living Room to hear [Howie] sing 'My Way,'" Roger Vickers recalls.

Another popular musician was Marty Gillan, who later went on to host and perform in a corny weekly local television show in the early 1970s called *Banjo Parlor*, produced by what was then called BCTV at their studios in Burnaby. There was also Norm Canover, a jazz musician, and Rudolph Boyce, the Singing Star from Trinidad, who performed calypso music that capitalized on the mainstream popularity of Harry Belafonte.

With Vickers's relatively low overhead and his policy of sticking with good local entertainers he could afford, he quickly grew out of being the "baby in the business" he'd considered himself to be just a few years earlier. The Living Room soon became a roaring success, so much so that the *Vancouver Sun* leisure section named Vickers "Clubman of the Year" in 1972.

"He doesn't wear mod clothes, he doesn't drive fast motor-cars and he doesn't give champagne parties for a bevy of beauties in his Living Room cabaret," stated the article, "yet he is the most successful operator among Vancouver's night club owners simply because he has found a magic formula which, night after night, the customers respond. He mixes the voice-guitar talent like Howie James with a low-key atmosphere at his Hornby Street club and, as a result, has been laughing all the way to the bank all year."[42]

Vickers rode this success for the rest of the 1970s. For a time, the club became popular with the local rounders, who would rub elbows with the regulars —the stockbrokers and bankers. "There was a guy named Andre who was the biggest bookie in

---

[42] "The Clubman," *Vancouver Sun*, December 22, 1972, 5A.

Top: Rudolph Boyce and band at the Living Room in 1966. Boyce, originally from Trinidad, was one of the first local Caribbean performers who became well known in the city's nightclub scene.
Bottom: George Vickers in the Living Room.
Credit: Roger Vickers Archives

Vancouver then," Roger Vickers remembers. "I should be careful of some of the names I say, but they all came down and mixed with everybody."

By the end of the decade, though, the club business was changing. Even the local media joked that George Vickers, now in his early fifties, was ancient compared to the younger club owners of the day. "My dad was kind of old school," says Roger. "With acts like Howie James singing Sinatra. We really catered to a forty-and-up crowd. Everything was going more disco and rock 'n' roll, and times were changing."

Vickers eventually sold the Living Room to Barry Williams (of Williams Moving and Storage), who later sold it to a Chinese investor. Roger Vickers joined former Cave owner Stan Grozina to run the new club, which was renamed the Crystal Room. But by the early 1980s, the club scene had changed so dramatically—and the regulars had gotten older and moved on from places like the Living Room—that they got out of the business after two months.

George Vickers may have gotten out of the club business, but he continued to work in nightlife—just not always in Vancouver. Vickers went on to work for the MGM Grand, taking groups of people to Vegas, Reno, and, on a few occasions, Monte Carlo, hosting tours of well-heeled gamblers looking for a good time.

Today, although a new bar on ever-changing Granville Street has adopted the name the Living Room, there's little evidence on Hornby Street of Vickers's legacy and what was once one of the more popular Vancouver nightspots of the early 1970s. The building that once housed the original Living Room in its basement was torn down in the 1980s, and an office block now stands in its place. George Vickers passed away in 2007, a few months after his eighty-first birthday.

One aspect of George Vickers's legacy that does remain, however, is the innumerable number of souvenir nightclub photos he took at the Cave, Penthouse, and Palomar to amass a photographic record of Vancouver that by sheer size approaches the archive that legendary street photographer Foncie Pulice, of Foncie's Photos, took of the city in action. It's only because Vickers took so many of his photos after dark, in nightclubs, that he doesn't get as much attention.

The faces in his pictures—tucked into curling photo albums, filed away in shoeboxes—smile back at their children and grandchildren, who might barely recognize these younger versions of their elders. But if they look closely, perhaps they can imagine that, although the music and fashions were different, they had just as much fun on the town as they did at the same age.

CHAPTER SEVEN

FLY BY NIGHT

Jayne County and the Electric Chairs at
Gary Taylor's Rock Room, June 19, 1980.
Photo: Gordon McCaw

THE BOPCATS

GARY TAYLOR'S
661 HORNBY St.
VANCOUVER

OCTOBER
21—25

A special evening with
"MARTHA & THE MUFFINS"
Gary Taylors Rock Room

Doors 8 p.m.
Special Guests:
the "Hostages"
684-3616

Tuesday, November 18, 1980
Tickets $10.00
661 Wassermans Beat (Hornby)

Credit: Neptoon Records Archives

Those who work in nightclubs today tend to quit before too long. Some get sick of the long hours and the unrelenting lifestyle that doesn't begin until after dark. Even the successful ones prefer a change of pace and an existence that provides more daylight after a few years. In Vancouver in the 1970s, few had stuck around as long as Joe Philliponi, who by then was in his sixties and had been in the cabaret business for more than thirty-five years. But by that time, people like him and George Vickers of the Living Room were being replaced by a new generation of up-and-coming club owners with new ideas that were more in tune with contemporary culture. The young lions grow old, of course, and of this new rock 'n' roll generation, nobody has managed to stay in the game longer than musician, club owner, and manager Gary Taylor.

Born in Vancouver in 1941, Taylor moved shortly thereafter with his family to Quadra Island, just off the eastern coast of Vancouver Island. He got his first job on Quadra—as a paperboy delivering the *Province* newspaper. Although he was probably born with his legendary gift of the gab, that job would provide formative training in the art of salesmanship. "You want to learn how to talk to people? Try going door to door as a kid like that—trying to make a newspaper sale," Taylor says with a laugh.

Taylor showed an early interest in music, too, when he played drums in the Duke of Connaught's army cadets marching band. (Despite the literally regimental style of play, the experience would later serve him well during his time as a jazz drummer.) When his family moved to Burnaby, he began to take drum lessons from tutors who taught him how to sight-read sheet music. This allowed him to show up and play a song with much greater ease than drummers who needed more time to rehearse with the band. Soon, by the early 1960s, he was a working musician on the local club scene.

"Those were the good old days," Taylor recalls— but not because he considers the music to have been better then. It was simply exciting because rock 'n' roll was still relatively new, and a fresh kind of live performance was coming along with it.

"Everyone was innocent," Taylor says. "The innocence of the world is kind of vanishing now, but back then, it was just a whole different era."

Taylor stayed busy as a session and pickup player. In February 1964, Taylor opened for English rock band the Dave Clark Five at the Queen Elizabeth Theatre, where he was enlisted to play in Freddy Cannon's backing band. Cannon, an American who had scored a Top 10 hit in 1959 in the USA with "Tallahassee Lassie," had a sore throat that evening, but it didn't stop the show.

"I'll never forget," Taylor recalls. "Freddy said, 'Gary—play as loud as you can.' His voice was shot that night and he couldn't sing, so he just wanted the band to play as loud as they could and he'd do his best to mouth the words and have the audience sing along."

But not everyone was pleased with Taylor's burgeoning success as a local musician. "My father didn't want me to be a drummer, so he got me a job—cleaning out cement trucks. Every morning, I'd have to put this spacesuit on and sandblast the trucks. At night, I'd go back up playing music to strippers at the Smilin' Buddha with the Gary Taylor Trio. On the second day of the cement gig, I was looking at my lunch kit and I saw the miserable people around me that were working there. I thought to myself, *I could clean out cement trucks for a living, or play music for strippers at the Smilin' Buddha.* It was an easy choice. I quit after that second day."

It was his group the Classics that brought Taylor more local prominence as one of the first Vancouver rock 'n' roll bands to be televised. In 1964, the Classics were enlisted as the house band on *Let's Go*, the CBC TV program for youth. Along with Taylor on drums, the group featured Tom Baird on keys, Brian Russell on guitar, Glenn Miller on bass, Claire Lawrence on saxophone, and Howie Vickers on vocals.

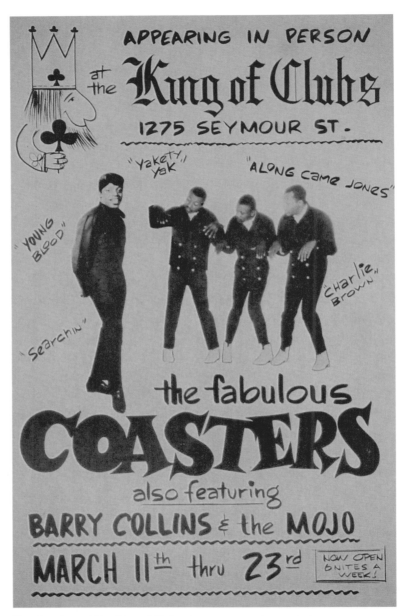

The Coasters at the King of Clubs. *Credit: Neptoon Records Archives*

"We were pretty versatile, and honed on R&B, so we played a lot of Sam & Dave, Marvin Gaye, but we could really play anything," he recalls.

While on tour with the Classics, Taylor became interested in another aspect of the business. The group had done some short tours down the US coast and back when he began to realize that many of the nightclub managers he dealt with didn't recognize what he considered to be good music. Certain he could do better job, Taylor found an old garage, built in 1937, at 1275 Seymour Street that had been part of a Volkswagen dealership. There, with some old friends helping as investors, he opened the King of Clubs in 1966.

"My partners were all sports guys I grew up with," says Taylor. "Neal Beaumont—who was an all-star defensive back for the BC Lions—he had a big name in town, Bill Bradley, a hall of fame lacrosse player —guys that knew teamwork and not to fuck each other around. We didn't really know what the fuck we were doing. All I knew was I could drag people in, and I could play."

Since they were unsure of what the future held, Taylor and his partners continued to sublet a space in the back of the garage to a transmission shop to help with rent. But Taylor excelled at promotion, and the Gary Taylor Trio, with him on the drums, and Tom Baird and Glenn Miller from the Classics, became the King of Clubs house band.

"I was only about seventeen or eighteen when I first came down to sing there," recalls Gillian Russell, sister of Brian Russell from the Classics, who also appeared as a featured vocalist on the *Let's Go* TV show. "I sang some of those same songs from the show down at the King of Clubs, also some Diana Ross songs, Dusty Springfield, and even some Elvis songs. It was a really fun time and always packed. But this was when the clubs didn't have a liquor

Advertisement for the King of Clubs in 1966.
Credit: Vancouver Sun *Archives*

licence—when I saw people had brown bags under the tables, I was so young I didn't even realize what was in the bottles or why they were hiding them!"

The King of Clubs lasted three years before Taylor and his partners sold part of the business to American singer-songwriter Buddy Knox, a Nashville recording star who'd scored a number-one hit in 1957 with "Party Doll." In the late 1960s, Knox settled in Vancouver for a time. In October 1969, with Knox as a co-owner, the King of Clubs became a country music bar—one of the first of its kind in downtown Vancouver—and was renamed the Purple Steer. The club opened to considerable fanfare, with local radio legend Red Robinson acting as emcee, reading aloud telegrams from Knox's famous friends—everyone from Glen Campbell to Robert Mitchum—passing along best wishes for the new venture.

The music featured a mix of local performers, like Irene Butler, a gifted singer who'd performed with the Valentines in the early 1960s, as well as electric honky-tonk touring acts like the Chaparral Brothers. When he wasn't on the road, Buddy Knox himself would perform regularly at the Purple Steer.

Pass for the Purple Steer. *Credit: Neptoon Records Archives*

Les Stork, owner of the Bunkhouse coffee house on Davie Street, launched a new trend: topless waitresses. Following Stork's lead, Taylor began organizing topless luncheons at the Purple Steer, which evolved into burlesque shows in the evening. But at the Bunkhouse, city licensing authorities came down on Stork, insisting that if waitresses were topless, they couldn't dance or move like anyone onstage. So Taylor found a middle ground. "I got a custom Victorian-style chaise longue made, and we had this girl Anne—she wore a see-through blouse. She was seated by the buffet, so all [patrons] really could do was talk to her. We were packed every lunch!" Taylor boasts.

By 1973, the cowboy hats had gradually disappeared from the Purple Steer, and the club was renamed the Garage Cabaret. The crowd at 1275 Seymour was now predominantly made up of bikers. Strip shows had become the main feature of the club, thanks to new investor Martin Roitman.

"Some of the other owners stayed on, but I wasn't a big fan of Marty, so I moved on," Taylor says. It was perhaps for the best that Taylor left the club, because on May 29, 1973, Robert Leigh Wilkins, a twenty-nine-year-old man from North Vancouver, crashed his car into the front doors of the Garage, nearly killing the club's assistant manager, who was forced to leap for his life. He had been ejected from the club earlier than evening. Wilkins was charged with attempted murder that year, but the Crown dropped the charges and instead booked him for dangerous driving and mischief. He paid a fine of $300.[45]

Taylor used his experience managing the strip shows at the Purple Steer and Garage to briefly run

But by the late 1960s and into the '70s, it was getting harder for country bars or jazz clubs to operate, with more and more people staying home and watching the big-name entertainers on TV variety shows, essentially for free. Only twenty-nine percent of households in BC owned televisions in 1955, but by 1975, this figure had increased to ninety-five percent.[43]

However, the Purple Steer didn't turn its back on country music; instead, it made the move that so many other Vancouver nightclubs had done to improve business and gave patrons something they couldn't see on TV.

As Becki Ross notes in *Burlesque West*, "In spite of opposition to toplessness, the trend continued as Vancouver clubs began to advertise topless pool rooms, topless go-go girls, topless lunches, topless shoeshines."[44] Martin Roitman at Club Zanzibar would push the boundaries of his outlandish Howe Street circus to the limit during this period with topless teeter-totter.

[43] *Household Facilities and Equipment*, Table 25: Telephones, Radios, Television Receivers, *Province*, September 1955, 198; *Household Facilities and Equipment*, Table 29: Black and White TV Sets, *Province*, April 1975, 23.
[44] Becki Ross, *Burlesque West: Showgirls, Sex, and Sin in Postwar Vancouver* (Toronto: University of Toronto Press, 2009), 54.
[45] *Vancouver Sun*, August 3, 1973, 9.

the luncheons at the Penthouse Nightclub. Eventually, he found his own space in the Castle Hotel at 750 Granville, naming it the Gary Taylor's Show Lounge. This was an unlikely spot for an exotic dance bar. The four-storey hotel, built in 1908, had a ground-floor beer parlour and had quietly been known since the 1950s as a gay establishment—though not a completely enlightened one. A no-touch rule was in place to prevent any physical displays of affection. Despite that, however, the Castle had become a social hub for the city's gay community in the years before more openly gay bars existed.

"The pub that was on the one side of the lobby was all gay," says Taylor. "The show lounge was up front on the other side. So when I moved in there, that shook things up a bit!"

The show lounge did well, nonetheless, even though Taylor and some dancers were charged in November 1973 for putting on an obscene show—the city had not yet adapted to allow full nudity onstage. "There was some lawyers convention going on in town, and a bunch of conventioneers dropped in one night. They probably had a great time, but I guess this got back to [prosecutor] Stewart McMorran, who had it out for me and they tried to shut us down." Taylor later won the case in court.

It was during these years that Taylor's reputation began to precede him. The quote repeated throughout nightclub circles was that "Gary Taylor could talk a nun into stripping."

"I would say that's basically true," says the unabashedly candid Taylor today. "I realize it's a funny comment—I'm not embarrassed by it. In all my clubs, none of the dancers there had ever danced before. I trained them all to dance for themselves. I didn't allow the audience to yell and scream. We had jazz, and beautiful girls. It's different now. It was sort of a time of discovery then. With live music, and striptease.

The discovery isn't as important anymore—there's not a lot of mystique going on."

In the late 1970s, Taylor became interested in running a club dedicated to music again. In 1979, while Gary Taylor's Show Lounge was still going, he found an upstairs space at 661 Hornby Street, across the street from the Cave. He named it, simply, Gary Taylor's Rock Room.

"Gary Taylor's Rock Room was a lot of fun," recalls Colin Hartridge, a veteran Vancouver drummer whose band Sparkling Apple played there regularly. "On Monday nights they had a live CFOX radio broadcast, which originated at Gary Taylor's, segments of which made their way onto the first *Vancouver Seeds* compilation album." Hartridge says that although there were certainly lots of places to play in Vancouver back in those days, the Rock Room was special for its variety and quality of performers. One night, a mainstream local rock group like the Headpins would play; the next, an out-of-town new wave band like the Battered Wives; and after that, a mainstay band such as the Powder Blues.

"Taylor's was always a great place," wrote Les Wiseman in the *Vancouver Sun*. "The rock crowd could sit in upholstered banquettes and swill with the approximation of nightclub sophistication ... Taylor's had become a mini Manhattan where any given week you could catch Johnny Thunders and the Cosa Nostra, Jayne County and the Electric Chairs, or the Lenny Kaye Connection."[46]

That June 19, 1980, appearance by Jayne County was unlike anything the city had ever seen before. County was rock 'n' roll's first openly trans singer. Taylor was prepared for some controversy, but he was determined not to let things get out of hand.

"When they got up to play, the place was packed," Taylor recalls. "There was a guy in the audience, he had come to target Jayne—that she had been a guy

[46] Les Wiseman, "Rear Window," *Vancouver Sun*, April 2000, C31.

Jayne County and the Electric Chairs at Gary Taylor's Rock Room, June 19, 1980. *Photo: Gordon McCaw*

One of the most colourful figures in the history of Vancouver entertainment has to be Les Stork. *Credit:* Vancouver Sun *Archives*

In 1966, Les Stork was charged with obscenity for featuring topless waitresses at his folk music coffee house. *Photo: Ron Allen/*Vancouver Sun *Archives*

expand if it means giving up the Bunkhouse."[49] It was a bold statement to make, but although Stork might have had that attitude in the beginning, he probably realized there was more money to be made *with* a licence.

That same year, a concert by legendary folk-blues duo Sonny Terry and Brownie McGhee immortalized the venue in a recording that would be released as *At the Bunkhouse.*

In 1964, Stork made headlines when he broke up a robbery at the Bunkhouse. Two men had come into his office one night while he was counting the previous night's earnings. Threatening Stork at knifepoint, they demanded the cash. But Stork, a trained heavyweight boxer who'd spent time in the Canadian army, beat up the two would-be thieves, who managed to flee the club before the police arrived.

In 1966, Stork had another run-in with law enforcement—this time, from the other side. One night, police and city licensing officials came to the Bunkhouse and charged Stork with obscenity because of a new feature at the venue, and a first for the city: topless waitresses.

During the mid-1960s, city officials in Vancouver were just beginning to come to terms with the concept of topless entertainment in cabarets, but restaurants did not fall under the same licensing category and rules. Because cafés weren't initially covered by the bylaws, Stork and the Bunkhouse were at first free from scrutiny. As a folk music club with topless waitresses, the Bunkhouse definitely had a unique atmosphere compared to other places. News that it had originally managed to avoid licence inspectors gained considerable attention—newspapers

[49] Leslie Millin, "Dream Comes True—Live Recording Success Mark," *Ottawa Journal*, April 10, 1965, 67.

Menu for the Bunkhouse after it moved from Davie Street to West Hastings, 1970. *Credit: Kevin Stork*

from as far away as Pennsylvania were writing about this intimate little coffee house on Davie Street, though one Bunkhouse patron, noting the dimly lit atmosphere, said, "Girls? It's so dark in here I can't see my food."[50]

Stork cleverly used the headlines to promote his club, and his trials became the ongoing feature of several Jack Wasserman columns. Stork protested the city licensing but was forced to comply with regulators and have the waitresses wear see-through tops. City bylaw officers probably didn't appreciate his flippant attitude to the whole affair. When the time came to be apply for a liquor licence in 1968—when the city's nightclub regulations began to relax—Stork found himself bumped further down the list.

He may not have been popular with city licence inspectors, but Stork was well liked among his peers.

"He was a colourful guy, and fun," recalls drummer and club owner Gary Taylor. Beneath the fun, though, lurked an increasingly dark lifestyle that ultimately led anyone who got near Stork to disaster.

"My father's is a rags-to-riches, and back to rags, story," says Kevin Stork. Born in 1961, Kevin Stork is not without some fond memories of his father. He can recall his parents taking him to visit the Bunkhouse on a few evenings when he was five years old, sitting on José Feliciano's lap and meeting some of the stars who played there. At some point in the mid-'60s, though, Les Stork developed a serious cocaine addiction, which quickly began to affect not only his personal life but also his business.

"I think my father was attracted by the aura of the nightclub business," Kevin says. "He was successful in the beginning. He had all it took to make it big

---

[50] "Go-Go Girls Must Cover Upper Torsos," *Wilkes-Barre Record*, September 20, 1966, 20.

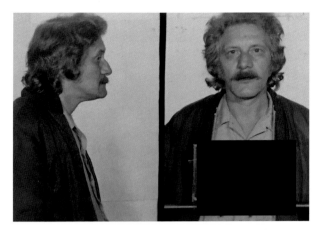

By the early 1970s, Les Stork had become seriously involved with members of Vancouver's underworld. His exploits were not successful. *Credit: Vancouver Police Museum*

and had a real knack for being a showman—he could have promoted anything. But he went another way. His ego and cocaine use led to everything coming crashing down. He went from being a nightclub champion to a drug-dealing gangster."

The Bunkhouse's decline followed Stork's addiction. He had begun to associate with various underworld figures. He hosted them at the club and would pick up their tabs, doing further damage to his bottom line. Stork also cheated on his wife, Terry, and became violent with his family. This resulted in the couple separating in 1968. Terry had handled the accounting at the Bunkhouse, so without her, the Bunkhouse sunk deeper into disarray. The club closed in 1969, reopened briefly in 1970 near Gastown at 303 West Hastings, then closed again, permanently.

With his business in ruins and his family life in tatters, Stork only fell further. He relocated to Toronto for a short time but returned to Vancouver in a characteristically headline-making fashion.

In 1973, the Royal Canadian Mounted Police had become suspicious of a Land Rover, a boat, and a trailer that had arrived in Toronto from Europe.

The RCMP tailed the vehicles all the way to their final destination in Surrey, a suburb just south of Vancouver. Police arrested the two men who were there to meet the vehicles, as well as the man who had driven the Land Rover across the country: Les Stork.

The RCMP had inspected the vehicles in Toronto before Stork picked them up and found 280 pounds of hashish hidden in the boat—which they replaced with sand. The approximately $700,000 worth of hash Stork thought he'd successfully transported to Vancouver was in fact Toronto dirt. Stork was sentenced to eight years in Kingston Penitentiary but only served two years, thanks to a technicality raised during an appeal. But this would not be his last run-in with the law.

When Stork left prison, he bought a moving company that he named Stork Delivery, Moving and Storage. The business did very well, and it looked like he might turn his life around. He bought a house and a boat, and began enjoying a lifestyle that others would have envied, but his regard for his estranged family remained negligible.

"He didn't support my mother at all," recalls Kevin Stork. "We'd get the odd photo or letter of him acting like a big shot, while my mother tried to support me. There were certainly no Christmas presents, or even a birthday phone call. We lived very poor. The money wasn't the thing—he just wasn't interested in us. One day, he came by for a rare visit to pick me up, saying he was going to buy me some clothes for school—I was practically dressed in old rags. He ended up going to a discount store and buying eight dollars' worth of socks and underwear while he went next door and bought himself a pair of alligator shoes."

Despite being out of the nightclub business, Stork returned to his old habits. He started using cocaine again and fell in with the wrong crowd, including infamous 1970s Vancouver underworld figure John Eccles, who, along with criminal associates Eddie Cheese and Al Oda and others, held court at the Penthouse Nightclub. During the notorious 1975 police investigation of the club, a witness identified Stork as a pimp.

Despite his father's continued drug abuse and personal problems, Kevin moved in with him in the early 1980s in an effort to make amends. The results were a disaster. At one point, Kevin was awarded a $2,000 grant to attend a broadcasting school—an amount his father promised he could double. Instead, Stork spent his son's money on cocaine and never paid it back, let alone matched it.

In 1982, Stork told Kevin he had to go away on business for a couple of weeks. Kevin dutifully said he'd stay at the house to keep an eye on things while his father was away. "It turns out that he was trying to do the same drug run he'd done before in 1973, and he got arrested again. The next day, a guy came to the house and put a gun to my head, demanding to know where he was. I managed to calm him down and convince him that he'd truly been arrested, hadn't skipped town, and that I didn't have his money. But that was it for me. I was done with him."

Stork returned to Kingston Penitentiary, this time for a six-year sentence. While incarcerated, Stork learned the art of stained glass, and when he got out of prison, he practised his new hobby while living in Abbotsford. Although he was finally drug free, the ravages of years of serious cocaine abuse had taken their toll, and Les Stork died in 1999.

"It was a tough life being the son of Les Stork," says Kevin, who finds it difficult to forgive and forget.

"The cocaine slowly destroyed everything he had, and he hurt and used a lot of people on the way. There is some good that has come out of it. A few years ago, I discovered I had a half brother. My father had cheated on my mother and they had a son. He tracked me down and I've discovered a whole new family that I've been happy to get to know. If any good can come from it all, it's been that."

As for the Bunkhouse, the old space became a restaurant called the Canvas Company in the 1980s, and then a music and comedy club called Poco Locos in the 1990s. In the early 2000s, it was home to the Atlantic Trap & Gill, an East Coast–themed bar that did a roaring trade for a few years with homesick Maritimers living in Vancouver. It closed in 2007, but Les Stork might have at least been pleased to know that acoustic folk songs—played by the likes of the Town Pants, Pat Chessell, Adrian Duncan, and Roger Buston—were pouring from the open windows at that corner of Davie Street once again. Some of the foot-stomping spirit found at the original Bunkhouse had returned.

Kevin Stork hasn't been back to see the Bunkhouse space in almost fifty years, but he and his half brother want to make a pilgrimage soon. The visit is likely to be bittersweet. One brother never met his father, and the other might have been better off never knowing him at all. They will be going not only to an empty nightclub but also to a place that perhaps holds the ghost that connects them.

THE RIVERQUEEN

Jesse Fuller performing at the Riverqueen, September 1969. *Photo: Vladimir Keremidschieff*

The Riverqueen, at 1043 Davie Street, was a coffee house run by Vancouver musician Ron Small and wife, Shirley, that primarily showed folk and blues acts. Ron, an African American entertainer from Chicago, had first visited Vancouver to perform at Isy's Supper Club with his group the Fabulous Pearls. He decided to stay. In the early 1960s, Small was a regular performer at venues like the New Delhi Cabaret until, eventually, he decided it was time to have a club of his own.

The Riverqueen opened in 1968 in a snug room that left no audience member more than thirty feet from the stage. Gordon Lightfoot was the first notable performer to play the room, but Charlie Musselwhite,

Freddy King, John Hammond, Big Mama Thornton, Reverend Gary Davis, Jesse Fuller, John Lee Hooker, and many others performed there. It also hosted some intimate theatre productions, like those by Ernie King's Sepia Players.

It was a theatre production that unexpectedly played a role in sinking the Riverqueen. In 1969, the Gallimaufry theatre company booked the Riverqueen to stage a production of the Michael McClure play *The Beard*, about an imaginary encounter between American pop culture icons Billy the Kid and Jean Harlow. The play is not only full of sexually explicit language but also concludes with a scene of simulated cunnilingus. On the evening of the November 5 performance, police entered the Riverqueen, stopped the show, and arrested the actors, the stage manager, as well as Ron and Shirley Small, charging them with obscenity. Many in the audience protested, applauding the actors and booing the police, as the five were hauled away.

This same play had previously been staged at both the Arts Club Theatre and the Vancouver Art Gallery without incident. Those connected to the club suggested that because the Riverqueen was a popular venue whose audience regulars included pimps, prostitutes, and drug dealers, Vancouver police kept a close eye on the establishment—certainly more than they did the Arts Club or the Art Gallery—and took advantage of the staging of a controversial play to shut it down. Both the theatre company and the Smalls fought the obscenity case vehemently, eventually gaining their acquittal in 1973.

The Riverqueen closed in 1971 and is still remembered fondly by those of a certain age who caught some of the considerable talent at the West End nightclub. Ron Small remained active in the music industry well into his later years, performing with the Sojourners, as well as other local gospel choirs. He passed away in 2018.

10★★★   THE PROVINCE, Tuesday, October 13, 1970
Obscenity charges

Special 'Beard' show may aid court: Judge

The provincial court hearing obscenity charges in connection with the play The Beard will probably be given a special showing.

Judge Larry Eckardt has agreed that a special performance of the alleged obscene production could help the court in reaching a decision.

Five persons connected with the play and the Riverqueen Coffee House, 1043 Davie, where it was being staged, are named in the charge.

They are Angela Slater, the leading lady; Wayne Robson, the leading man; Ronnie Small, the coffee house proprietor; Shirley Small, his wife and cashier and ticket-seller; and Henry Yeager, technical director and light operator.

Judge Eckardt ruled those permitted to attend the special showing should be limited to court officers, police officers, clerks and counsel.

Prosecutor Al Cliffe said the showing should be open to anyone. No date has been set for the special show.

Big shop centre

In 1969, Ronnie Small, the proprietor of the Riverqueen, along with his wife, Shirley, were arrested on an obscenity charge for the production of the play *The Beard* at the venue. Both actors were also arrested onstage by Vancouver police during the performance. *Credit: Province Archives*

Credit: Neptoon Records Archives

CHAPTER EIGHT

STEPPING OUT INTO THE SEVENTIES

Vancouver at night in the 1970s.
Credit: City of Vancouver Archives
CVA1435-96

THE DAISY

The Daisy nightclub was in the old Hector's restaurant at 5th and Fir, February 1966.
Credit: William E. Graham/City of Vancouver Archives CVA 1135-21

Daisy swizzle stick.

A night at the Daisy in 1969. *Photo: Vladimir Keremidschieff*

Away from the steady buzz of the Hornby strip, and removed from the hustle and bustle of Chinatown, the stylish Daisy nightclub opened its doors at 1601 West 5th Avenue on September 3, 1969. Opening night featured a packed house of more than 300 people assembled to catch the performance by Carl Graves and Soul Unlimited. Errol Fisher, a Vancouver stock market promoter with no prior experience in the nightclub industry, launched the club in the space that once held Hector's Restaurant. It was open every night of the week except Sundays, with a distinct aim to appeal to what the Daisy defined as the "aware generation."

"As nightclubs go, the Daisy's furnishings are without peer in Vancouver, complete with lush carpeting, balconies, dance floor and drawing rooms where it is hoped the quiet click of billiard balls will be heard in the not too distant future," wrote columnist Brian MacLeod, reviewing the grand opening in the *Vancouver Sun*. "The lighting is dark, in keeping with today's taste, and is augmented by two rows of black light; the kind that makes everyone shine like a tooth paste ad."[51]

The Daisy hoped to cater to a more upscale crowd who wanted to dress up a bit to dance on the club's large dance floor, which was augmented by strobe lights and a large screen, "which will furnish a light show as good as any in town."

In the hope of drawing a hip, sophisticated crowd, the Daisy used ad copy that employed the fab, finger-snapping language of the era, inviting patrons to "submerge yourself in the multi-sensory atmosphere of Vancouver's grooviest most exclusive night club for swinging singles and couples."

"Personally," said MacLeod, closing his review, "I found the atmosphere of the Daisy to be reminiscent of the whole new wave of people and clubs now flourishing from London to Los Angeles. They are the forerunners of the multi-media entertainment everyone will experience in the future."

The club was short-lived, closing in 1971. But it launched the career of a young Sam Feldman, who worked as a doorman at the Daisy. After the club closed, he went on to form the Feldman Agency, which over the years has become one of North America's premier booking and management agencies for musicians. The building that once housed the Daisy remains but has been remodelled significantly. It now holds the offices of the Lazy Gourmet catering company, which services more weddings and corporate events than parties for groovy swingers.

---

[51] Brian MacLeod, "Daisies in Full Bloom on Opening Night," *Vancouver Sun*, September 5, 1969, 3.

ROHAN'S ROCKPILE AND THE SOFT ROCK CAFÉ

Visitors to Vancouver today might have difficulty imagining the trendy, upscale west side neighbourhood of Kitsilano as home to the city's 1960s counterculture. Now, residents of Kitsilano are mostly young, well-to-do professionals and entrepreneurs who hit it big in everything from real estate to yoga pants, mixed with older, long-time residents who have hung on to their increasingly valuable homes. Back in the late 1960s, some middle-class families considered it a novelty to drive through the streets of Kitsilano and catch a glimpse of the many hippies who roamed the area.

A popular meeting spot among locals in those days was Rohan's Records, located in a small commercial building at 2865 West 4th Avenue that looked like a house. The music store catered to discerning fans of the folk, blues, and psychedelic rock of the day. The store only ran for a few years before closing in 1973, but the establishment reopened on December 4 that year as a live music club one block away under the name Rohan's Rockpile, owned and operated by Fred Xavier and partners Lynn Lowther and Thora Sigurdson.

"It was like a neighbourhood pub, but a nightclub," says Lindsay Mitchell, guitarist for Seeds of Time and Prism. "Every scene has its clubhouse. That was ours in Kitsilano."

Rohan's clubhouse appeal may have been because it provided a supportive showcase for local acts. The Cement City Cowboys, Brain Damage, Danny Tripper, Doug and the Slugs, Jerry Doucette, Denise McCann, and Pied Pumkin all performed at Rohan's Rockpile. Word spread and soon it was more than just locals drawn to the club.

"Rohan's was kind of a funny, unpretentious place," says musician and nightclub operator Gary Taylor.

Rohan's in Kitsilano shortly before it closed in 1981.
Photo: Charles Campbell

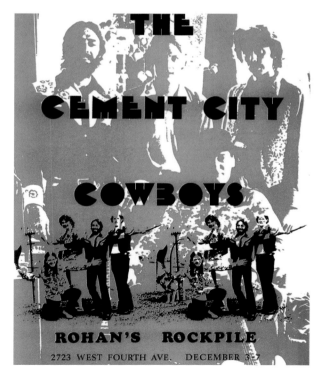

Local band the Cement City Cowboys at Rohan's Rockpile.
Credit: Neptoon Records Archives

"Kitsilano eventually had a club scene of its own, and Rohan's was a big part of that."

Other venues in the neighbourhood also grew in popularity. The Soft Rock Café at 1925 West 4th Avenue opened in May 1976 in a 5,000-square-foot space that had previously been a mattress factory and showroom with huge floor-to-ceiling windows. Owner Sola Fiedler had previously operated a popular coffee house in Toronto during the 1960s, the heyday of Joni Mitchell and Gordon Lightfoot. When she arrived in Vancouver, she discovered the summer of love was long over in the city, and the area around 4th Avenue was experiencing a bit of a downturn.

"Kits was dead in the mid-seventies," eighty-one-year-old Fiedler recalled in a 2017 interview.[52] According to Feidler, the neighbourhood featured "boarded up storefronts and hardly any restaurants. All the hippies were gone." Her new café and music venue, however, instantly became popular.

Despite its tepid name—a play on London's original Hard Rock Cafe—the Soft Rock Café welcomed some decidedly upbeat and energetic acts. "We started out with locals like Jim Byrnes, Powder Blues, and D.O.A.," Fiedler says, "and branched out into international artists like Ravi Shankar, Dexter Gordon, and Dan Hill."

Fiedler sold the business when her lease ended in 1983, and the club, under different management, closed a year later. The building currently houses a bank and a yoga studio.

Rohan's Rockpile didn't last either. In 1981, a property developer bought a number of lots on the 2700 of block of West 4th and constructed the office

The Soft Rock Café's calendar of events, April 1982.
Credit: SFU Poster Archives

complex that is currently home to a dental clinic. The original Rohan's Records building that fought development for so long was finally demolished in 2018. Perhaps it's not surprising, since—according to a 2018 property assessment—that lot alone is worth $4.7 million.

---

52 Grant Lawrence, "Kitsilano's Legendary Soft Rock Café Remembered," *Westender,* July 5, 2017.

LASSETER'S DEN

In the late 1960s into the '70s, a building stood at 1736 East Broadway, just east of Commercial Drive, with a large red door featuring a wood carving of the devil's face. It was not a local chapter of the Church of Satan, or a meeting spot for East Van occultists. It was Lasseter's Den—a bar owned by Bill Lasseter, a fullback and defensive back who'd played 100 games with the CFL's BC Lions during the '60s, most notably as a member of the team that first won the Grey Cup in 1964.

The gloomy subterranean-style interior of Lasseter's Den looked similar to the Cave, at least around the stage area, where local acts like the Silver Chalice Band and Easy Meat presided as the house bands.

Other acts to have played there included Bowser Moon, Hot Rocks, the In Tensions, Ram, Rocket Norton, Kentish Steele, Stonebolt, Hit and Run, and Spindrift.

Bruce Allen, who would later gain fame and fortune as a manager for such artists as Bryan Adams and Michael Bublé, made his first foray into the music business as an agent booking groups like Crosstown Bus and Five Man Cargo at Lasseter's.

After ten years in the business, Bill Lasseter moved to Abbotsford, BC, and the Den closed. The Commercial–Broadway SkyTrain station now stands where the club used to be. Bill Lasseter died in 2017.

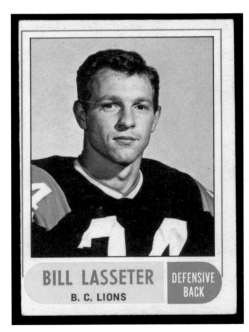

Bill Lasseter's CFL card, 1968. He founded the Lasseter's Den nightclub.
Credit: Author's personal collection

The Silver Chalice Band onstage at Lasseter's Den, 1968.
Credit: Neptoon Records Archives

THE EGRESS

In the early 1970s, the building at 739 Beatty Street was known as home to various short-lived ventures like the Runnymede Supper Club in 1972 and, before that, a topless bar called the Bunny Room. When a live music club called the Egress opened there in 1973, most thought it too would prove to be flop. But, although the Egress lasted for only a year, the club will be remembered for the wide range of folk, blues, and comedy stars that appeared on its stage.

An oddball duo of men in their mid-twenties ran the club. John Bottomley (not to be confused with the Vancouver musician of the same name) was a soft-spoken, denim-clad hippie who knew nothing of the nightclub business. With some money he borrowed from his mother and some small shareholders, he joined forces with Charles "Buzz" Wright, a talkative American who arrived in Vancouver wearing what turned out to be his everyday uniform: a Hawaiian shirt and cowboy boots. Bottomley had met Wright when he was managing the Troubadour and Boarding House clubs in San Francisco, and Wright thought he could use some of his booking agent's contacts from there and bring those acts up to Vancouver—all while dodging getting drafted to fight in the Vietnam War.

The club's name was a reference to an anecdote about legendary showman P.T. Barnum. The story goes, in an effort to get more people to come through the doors of one of his exhibits, Barnum once posted a sign that read, "THIS WAY TO THE EGRESS." He was counting on the curious, easily duped public to not know what the word meant and follow the sign. Those who followed found themselves outside the exhibition with no way to re-enter without paying another admission.

Bottomley and Wright had originally planned to open a club in North Vancouver, but after having trouble dealing with a conservative city council, they

Poster for the Egress. *Credit: Neptoon Records Archives*

pursued a downtown location instead. With a confirmed appearance by blues singer John Hammond just nine days away, they set up shop on Beatty Street and opened on March 13, 1973.

In the early 1970s, long before Rogers Arena or BC Place stadium were there, Beatty Street was lined with warehouses, factories, parking lots, and small restaurants—hardly an area that saw a lot of foot traffic. The duo put a lot of work into turning the place into a suitable venue for the Hammond show.

"A club is three or four guys getting their heads together and working their asses off," Buzz Wright said in an interview. "You work sixteen hours a day, and sometimes you don't get time to sleep."

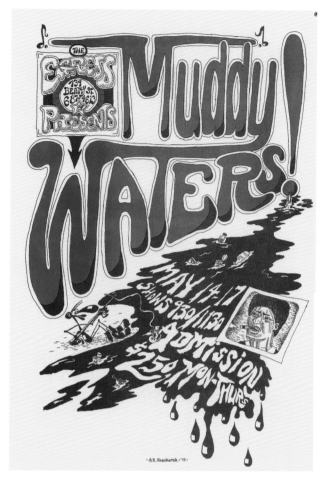

Artist/illustrator Grant Shankaruk designed original posters for each Egress concert while the club was in operation.
Credit: Neptoon Records Archives

"Buzz Wright—what a character," recalls iconic Vancouver bluesman Jim Byrnes. "He had been a circus carny from Oklahoma, and it showed. So not only was Buzz his name, but there was a real buzz when he was in the room. He was a great guy. The whole staff, and the whole vibe of the place, was great." Byrnes remembers seeing performances by Muddy Waters, the Johnny Otis Revue, Taj Mahal, and Tim Buckley at the Egress.

"The cool thing about the Egress was the proximity of the stage," say Byrnes. "It wasn't a big place, so you could get up close." He noted that for Vancouver audiences, it was a stunning experience to see Howlin' Wolf at the Egress.

"Howlin' Wolf was the most intimidating entertainer I ever saw in my life," recalls guitarist Dave Chisholm, who saw that show in his late teens and went on to form the Vancouver band the Fins. "He was a very imposing guy. He would look through the crowd and it would feel he was looking right through you—he had that stare. He was six-foot-three, but he looked taller, and when he held that microphone in his huge hands, it looked like a toy."

Chisholm remembers standout concerts at the Egress such as Mose Allison, Dan Hicks and His Hot Licks, James Cotton, and Albert King. The Egress did well bringing these big acts to town, and the nightclub fast became a going concern. In 1973, the *Vancouver Sun* named Bottomley and Wright the nightclub men of the year.

By September 1973, comedian Steve Martin had appeared on the *Smothers Brothers Comedy Hour* program but had yet to make a name for himself with comedy records and hit movies when he first came to Vancouver to perform at the Egress.

"I remember feeling bad because there wasn't that many people there for my show, and everybody was up the street seeing Gordon Lightfoot at the Queen Elizabeth Theatre," Martin recalled in 2016.

The show may not have been well attended, but it was well reviewed. Martin performed what, years

Steve Martin performed at the Egress as a relatively unknown comedian in 1973. The next day, he went to Gastown and busked with his banjo for extra money.
Credit: Neptoon Records Archives

later, would be considered his classic routines: making nonsensical balloon tricks, juggling oranges, and plucking his banjo. At one point, sanitation trucks in the alley behind the Egress were making a lot of noise, so Martin turned the interruption into a bit by walking out the back doors of the club to continue his show there.

"All in all, the Egress was a great venue," says Chisholm. "The only thing was it was really hard to get a drink. The shows were busy, and I never saw any fights, but the hippie waitresses were kind of slow, and sometimes they didn't want to interrupt the show by having waitresses coming through the tables. Maybe that's why it went under in the end."

Poster for Howlin' Wolf at the Egress, 1973. *Credit: Neptoon Records Archives*

Death of Egress leaves a vacuum

By JEANI READ

The marquee still said John Fahey, weeks after the Egress expired on Beatty Street, a sad little reminder of a year and a half of good music in a city where good music is evidently not enough.

While it survived, The Egress was unique in Vancouver, a small (270 seat) and comfortable folk-blues-jazz room modelled roughly after the fashion of such firmly entrenched Los Angeles and San Francisco clubs as the Troubadour, the Whisky and the Boarding House, and it filled an important entertainment vacuum, bringing in acts like Mose Allison, Freddie King, Albert Collins, Tom Rush, Mimi Farina, Phil Ochs, Tim Buckley, Earl Scruggs, James Cotton, Jesse Winchester, Bruce Cockburn.

Its demise, after operating on a month-to-month financial shoestring since its opening in March of last year, certainly wasn't unprecedented. Clubs of its ilk have closed down with depressing regularity over the years, and The Egress is just the latest domino.

It is easy enough to write the whole thing off as a cut and dried matter of dollars and cents — take profits meagre enough to put the club four or five months' rent in arrears, add an unpaid property tax of $3,500, and you have it.

Except it's never quite as simple as that. Undoubtedly The Egress was insufficiently funded, as John Bottomley, its principal shareholder, is first to admit and reiterate.

Close on the heels of an assortment of ill-fated night spots in the building, Bottomley and his three partners leased the premises, assumed the previous debts, sank $20,000 into it, and were left with no working capital when backers pulled out at the last minute.

"There was no money behind us," says Bottomley. "We were $2,000 in debt when we opened. We could have closed the first week."

But the first two acts, John Hammond followed by Sonny Terry and Brownie McGhee, put the club out of immediate danger and things were off to a precariously optimistic start.

It was, in many ways, a naive enterprise. The only partner who knew anything about the business was club booker Buzz Wright, who had previously managed both the Troubadour and the Boarding House in San Francisco, which is where Bottomley met him in 1972.

"I saw the Boarding House," says Bottomley, who had been working on getting a suitable location and a suitable format for 18 months. "John Hammond was playing there, and then Dan Hicks. And I thought all I had to do was import that up here."

But that wasn't as simple as it looked, either. The original intent was to use the club as a showcase for just-breaking new talent and for local performers, as well as offering a solid line-up of well-established artists, a formula that has proven successful enough in a lot of markets.

But it soon became obvious — as anyone could have told them — that Vancouver was strictly a "name" town. Big acts would draw but local artists had virtually no local support and audiences here were a hair's breadth too slow at picking up on breaking artists to turn out to see them before their prices became prohibitive.

In addition, the clientele, which turned out only for specific acts and never formed a sizeable regular nucleus that would trust the club to bring in quality acts of relatively obscure repute, made a nightmarish guessing game out of the whole business.

"If we had been in a place like Toronto, we could have brought in local acts and broken even," says Bottomley. "As it was, it was better just to close down during slow weeks. In fact, it would have worked even in Calgary, Edmonton or Winnipeg. But Vancouver isn't ready for a music scene, even though it should be. People here have everything going for them. They don't need to get up and do anything."

He blames everything from the climate to the rise in the cost of living for the inconsistent attendance. But whatever the case, at an average of $2,500 a week per act, money got short enough to force cancellations and higher admission costs, and things spiralled downward from there.

So The Egress quietly went up for sale six weeks ago. There weren't any takers. Fahey played there for one last weekend, to cap the — ironically — profitable month of June. Guessing game over, doors closed. But it sure was nice while it lasted.

Vancouver Sun article marking the end of the Egress, 1974. *Credit:* Vancouver Sun *Archives*

The Egress indeed struggled financially. Audiences came out to see the big-name performers, but when locals played, the room was empty. It made for a precarious month-to-month existence, and eventually, five months of unpaid rent, along with unpaid property taxes, crippled the Egress. Dejected, Bottomley closed the club at the end of July 1974, ironically, after they'd had one of their most profitable months.

In the years afterward, the space held a strip bar called the Foxy Lady Cabaret; later, a café called the Something Else; and finally, the Three-Seven restaurant before it and some other buildings on the block were demolished.

When the Egress closed, Bottomley blamed the club's inconsistent attendance on everything from Vancouver's climate to cost of living. Forty years later, managers of failed nightclubs around town continue to make similar complaints. "Vancouver isn't quite ready for a music scene," Bottomley said back then. "Even though it should be."

Perhaps although Buzz Wright had lots of connections to folk and blues acts from the States, Egress management had a poor idea of the best local acts to take the stage on other nights. During those years, there was more of an appetite in the city for cover bands than original acts. Maybe Bottomley was right and Vancouver wasn't ready for a music scene all its own. At least, not yet.

THE WINDMILL

The year 1912 was big one for a few venues and gathering places around Vancouver. On January 5, for instance, the first professional hockey game in Vancouver was played at the new Denman Arena, where the Vancouver Millionaires beat the New Westminster Royals 8–3. A few months later, on April 21, the British & Foreign Sailors' Society held a public memorial service at the Vancouver Opera House in aid of the survivors of the *Titanic* disaster.

What did not make the news that year was the construction and opening of a small building at 1047 Granville Street—although it did not begin its life as a music venue, it would become, almost seventy years later, an unlikely breeding ground for Vancouver punk rock.

Over the years, the space has been home to a wide variety of businesses. It began as the retail store of G.G. Heather Co., furriers and taxidermists. In the 1920s, it was a podiatrist's office, then a bakery, and

eventually, a lingerie shop called Raphael's. Through the '40s and '50s it was the Viking fur hat store. Then, in the mid-'60s, a man named John Iuele opened the Paradise Cabaret, a supper club with music that featured live cocktail jazz performed by a Hammond organist and a drummer.

However, Paradise, in this case, was short-lived. Over the next few years, the space saw a quick succession of fleeting establishments: in 1969, a club called Adam's Rib; in 1974, an exotic dance lounge called the Fox's Den; and in 1975, the Miko Cabaret (a live music spot that served Japanese food).

Finally, in May the following year, it became the venue that it would be best remembered for: the Windmill.

It began primarily as a rock 'n' roll venue, featuring local cover bands of varying quality such as the Blak Smith and the regrettably named Asparagus Band. Sparkling Apple, one of the better acts in Vancouver during the period, played the Windmill in 1978.

The space that was once the Windmill has undergone many name changes. In 1969, it was Adam's Rib.
Credit: Vancouver Sun *Archives*

Before local punk rock found a home at the Smilin' Buddha, the Windmill was one of the few nightclubs that allowed punk bands to perform.
Credit: Province *Archives*

"The club itself was a haven for downtown hookers and drug dealers who mainly would use the Windmill as a place to get out of the rain," recalls Sparkling Apple drummer Colin Hartridge. "One interesting thing—the stage was a good five feet high above what was a steel dance floor. I think the stage was that high because there were so many fights there!"

The club certainly attracted a rough clientele. In September 1976, just months after the Windmill opened, four patrons beat up the club's doorman and fractured his leg.

In the late 1970s, punk rock was growing in popularity in Vancouver and some local nightclubs were beginning to book punk shows. In late 1978, the Windmill was one of them and began to feature punk bands, such as D.O.A., the Subhumans, and Private School, on Monday nights. Paul Wilson-Brown, who had booked some of the early punk rock shows at the Quadra Club on Homer Street, arranged these Monday night shows.

Advertisement for the Windmill, 1976. *Credit:* Province *Archives*

The exterior of the old Windmill in 2019. The space had been empty for many years, and even in derelict condition, the lot was assessed at $6.2 million. *Credit: Aaron Chapman*

It's difficult to ascertain why the steel floor was installed in the first place, but it proved to be a sturdy surface for pogo-dancing punk rock audiences. The unique floor even once provided a memorable night for some unlikely participants.

"I had a housemate who was doing social work with deaf students who were interested in the arts," says Vancouver bassist Bob Petterson, then a student at Simon Fraser University. "He took some of them down to the Windmill that night for what I think I remember was a Subhumans show—they had a great time. They couldn't hear it, but they could feel the volume of the music through their feet, which reverberated through that metal flooring. They really got off on it and had a great time."

On Monday, January 29, 1979, some other particularly memorable patrons came to the Windmill. Two days before the band played their North American debut at the Commodore Ballroom, the Clash's Joe Strummer and Paul Simonon dropped in unexpectedly to check out the local punk scene.

"The punks in Vancouver had the ripped-jean jacket look," recalls Grant McDonagh, owner of Vancouver's Zulu Records, who was in the audience that evening. "But the Clash looked kind of bright. They had brothel creeper shoes; they looked kind of in a different class. But at the same time they were really nice guys; they were very approachable."

The Windmill did not last long, closing in 1980. The building eventually became a pawn shop and then a small grocery store in the early 2000s. In recent years, it has remained vacant, with its doorway and front window covered in posters.

The period of rock and punk shows that happened at the Windmill was very short—barely a blip on the 110-year timeline of the building. And by the early 1980s, the local punk scene had migrated to a Hastings Street dive that granted these new bands more than just one night a week. The Smilin' Buddha would give them a lifetime.

THE SMILIN' BUDDHA

One of the most fondly remembered and mythologized dive bars in the history of Vancouver was the Smilin' Buddha Cabaret at 109 East Hastings Street. The club never made its owners rich, and it didn't launch any bands onto career paths gilded with gold and platinum records, but these facts had no impact whatsoever on the Smilin' Buddha's legacy.

It wasn't always a dive. During the Downtown Eastside's better days, the spot was called the Broadway Café. It occupied one part of a section of three buildings at 105 East Hastings Street. A Greek Canadian restaurateur and bootlegger named Sutro Bancroft ran the café. Born in 1882, Bancroft participated in the Klondike Gold Rush in his late teens and then

settled in Vancouver in the early 1900s. At first, his Broadway Café took up all three lots on the property, but with the arrival of the Great Depression, Bancroft divided it back into three. The new address created at 109 East Hastings became home to Gowdy's Used Clothing, which clothed the area's largely blue-collar workers and their families in the 1930s.

In the 1940s, the space became the Latin Quarter Café, a supper club that served steak and spaghetti, and featured trios or quartets during the week and small musical combos of six or seven on Saturday nights. But the business had problems similar to all other Vancouver nightclubs of the era: without a liquor licence it was targeted regularly by the police dry squad raids.

The Latin Quarter became a vocal member of the BC Cabaret Owners Association, even going so far as to run an ad in the *Province* newspaper in 1948 challenging British Columbia liquor laws, proclaiming, "Over 2/3 of the people are moderate drinkers, yet the 'Government Liquor Act' was written to appease the prohibitionists. Moderate drinking is best encouraged when night clubs are permitted to serve their patrons with cocktails by the glass."[53]

Whether it was because of police harassment or a downturn in business, the Latin Quarter eventually closed, and the space became home to Cardo's Dine and Dance in 1951, but the VPD dry squad certainly didn't back off just because it was a new business. In 1952, a waiter was sentenced to six months in jail for selling liquor, with police later finding a cache of sixteen bottles hidden in the basement. Cardo's was given a thirty-day suspension of its business licence in July 1952, which subsequently led to its closure.

▼▼▼▼▼▼▼▼▼▼▼▼▼▼▼
NOTICE

Over 2/3 of the people are moderate drinkers, yet the "Government Liquor Act" was written to appease the prohibitionists. Moderate drinking is best encouraged when night clubs are permitted to serve their patrons with cocktails by the glass, under Government supervision.

LATIN QUARTER

109 East Hastings St.

MEMBER OF THE B.C. CABARET OWNERS' ASSOCIATION
▲▲▲▲▲▲▲▲▲▲▲▲▲▲▲

In a *Province* newspaper ad, the Latin Quarter defends itself against the Vancouver police's dry squad raids.
Credit: Province Archives

Back when this building was operating as the Broadway Café, Harvey Lowe was a kid developing his yo-yo skills in nearby Chinatown. Young Harvey honed these skills to such a degree that he went on to demonstrate them at theatres, county fairs, and talent shows, winning every contest he entered. Lowe ultimately signed with a promoter who took him to London, England, where he won the 1932 World Yo-Yo Contest and $4,600 in prize money.

By the early 1950s, Lowe was making his first foray into a different kind of money-making realm— Vancouver nightlife. He first became a doorman at the Dye Ning Club, an underground gambling den that was located in the 100 block of East Pender Street. With the odd joke or one-liner, he developed his yo-yo routine into a nightclub act and began performing and emceeing at local clubs like the Cave. By the end of the decade, he was such a well-known personality in the city he even hosted a weekly radio show *Call of China*, the country's first Chinese Canadian radio program.

Lowe and his friend and business associate Albert Kwan were both familiar with the Shanghai nightclubs of the 1940s, which had featured modern cabaret entertainment and served traditional Chinese food. The two thought the same kind of club could work well near Vancouver's Chinatown. Lowe and Kwan, along with other partners, opened the Smilin' Buddha Cabaret on October 16, 1952.

Inside, the club presented music that matched the formal dances of the period: waltzes, foxtrots, and rhumbas played by small combos. Outside, the large Smilin' Buddha neon sign, built locally by Wallace Neon, shone over Hastings Street. By the 1950s, there was more neon in Vancouver than any other city in the world, except for Shanghai—and the Smilin' Buddha sign was just one of many signature neon beacons downtown.

[53] Club listings announcement, *Province*, October 27, 1948, 14.

Harvey Lowe and Albert Kwan opened the Smilin' Buddha Cabaret in 1952. *Credit:* Vancouver Sun *Archives*

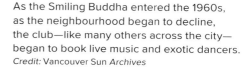

As the Smiling Buddha entered the 1960s, as the neighbourhood began to decline, the club—like many others across the city—began to book live music and exotic dancers. *Credit:* Vancouver Sun *Archives*

The restaurants and cafés along Hastings Street were doing well in the 1950s, and the neighbourhood was still largely considered safe. With an abundance of seasonal workers like loggers and miners coming from the interior of the province to spend some of their wages on a fun furlough in the big city, many hotels and nightclubs in the Downtown Eastside turned a reasonable profit. There was still the occasional liquor raid in the neighbourhood, but Lowe and Kwan ran the Smilin' Buddha without many problems.

But Vancouver was changing, particularly downtown. The city itself increased in population by twelve percent between 1951 and 1961, but the surrounding metropolitan area increased by eighty-seven percent.[54] As a result, by the mid-'50s, Vancouver's downtown was suffering a significant loss of business and retail traffic to suburban areas, and Lowe and Kwan thought, after ten years, it was time to sell the Smilin' Buddha.

Lachman Dass Jir and his wife, Nancy, purchased the Smilin' Buddha in 1962. During this period, it became one of the East End clubs, along with the New Delhi, that catered to the lively local R&B music scene.

"Most of the musicians that worked there were bands that were playing the dance circuit," says Vancouver guitarist Henry Young, whose career goes back decades in the city's club scene. "The format

[54] Bruce Macdonald, *Vancouver: A Visual History* (Vancouver: Talonbooks, 1992), 52.

was the band would play an instrumental set, then they'd do a floor show. The floor show had an emcee; sometimes it would be Teddy Felton or Ronnie Small or even Marty Gillan. And they always closed off with a stripper—that would be Miss Lovie or Lady Scarlett or Lulu Turner, or Lottie the Body, who was always around."

Although rumours persist that the Smilin' Buddha hosted very early Vancouver appearances by Janis Joplin and Jefferson Airplane, there is no evidence of such performances. Touring musicians seldom played the club in the 1960s. Far more common were touring exotic dancers and strippers. The local musical acts were usually small trios or quartets, but the pay wasn't great, and a four-piece act would get a hundred dollars a week in total.

"It was a tough place," recalls Ronnie Crump, who performed with his twin brother, Robert, as the Crump Twins around Hogan's Alley. "When we played there, we made sure our gear was insured in case somebody threw a glass at the guitar or drums."

Either because Lachman Jir didn't run the club as well as Lowe and Kwan, or because the neighbourhood's rising poverty, drug, and crime issues presented serious business challenges, the Smilin' Buddha became less successful during the 1960s. By the end of the decade, it was considered a dump and became a regular trouble spot for city licence inspectors. The Vancouver police blotter from this time is filled with fights, robberies, and even fatal assaults that took place at the Smilin' Buddha.

In 1963, fifty-year-old Walter Kunda was dragged into the washroom and robbed of $175. He claimed five men took part in the attack.

In 1964, while the lights were dimmed during the floor show, someone broke into the club's jukebox. Police didn't need to look far for a suspect—the thief was passed out drunk at a table just a few feet away.

In 1965, twenty-eight-year-old Louis Koszas, a bouncer at the club, was charged with murder for the death of Anthony Van Reenen, a twenty-five-

Twins Ronnie and Robert Crump performed at the Smilin' Buddha in the early 1960s. In 2019, they were inducted into the BC Entertainment Hall of Fame.
Credit: Author's personal collection

year-old South African sailor who was on shore leave from a freighter moored in Burrard Inlet. Van Reenan suffered fatal head injuries when he was thrown out onto the pavement outside the Smilin' Buddha. The charges were dismissed, but a month later, Koszas was arrested for possession of heroin and drug paraphernalia and spent six months in jail.

A year later, a man seated at a table in the club with his wife was stabbed in the head with a fork. The assailant was a man dressed in women's clothing, which resulted in Vancouver police chief constable Ralph Booth calling for a law that prohibited men from wearing women's clothing in public.

Art Bergmann (right) of the K-Tels (later named the Young Canadians) onstage with Ken "Dimwit" Montgomery (left) of the Pointed Sticks/D.O.A. *Photo: Bev Davies*

The Smilin' Buddha is rarely mentioned in any histories of the LGBTQ community in Vancouver, but the club was known in the 1960s as a welcoming place for some of the local cross-dressing community. Musicians who played the club in those years often recall seeing people in drag either onstage or in the audience, but they were not always law-abiding.

"In the couple of years prior to the Montreal Expo, the Montreal police did a very aggressive job of clearing out a number of professional pickpockets who were also cross-dressers that they had persistent criminal issues with. They felt they didn't want them preying on the tourists visiting the fair—so a lot of them driven out of Montreal seemed to end up here in Vancouver," recalls retired VPD detective Grant MacDonald, who joined the police department in 1964 and spent a number of years working on the Downtown Eastside. "I remember coming in to the Buddha one night and looking at the men's washroom stall, and seeing two pairs of feet: one a pair in work boots, and the other one in high heels. I opened the door and this guy in women's clothing was all over this drunk old logger but picking the logger's pocket while they were going at it. I broke things up and cleared them out of there."

Dead Kennedys onstage at the Smilin' Buddha, 1980. *Photo: Bev Davies*

By the late 1970s, the Downtown Eastside had become a markedly different neighbourhood than twenty years earlier. Long gone were those days in the 1940s and '50s when the area was a bustling community of working-class shops and businesses. The nights of orchestras and floor shows at the Smilin' Buddha were a distant memory, and the club had essentially become an East End strip bar, with some occasional country music courtesy of musicians like B.J. Howard and George Poburn, who would also emcee the acts coming on and off stage between shows.

And then punk music arrived. Vancouver's punk rock scene was well underway by the time it came to the Smilin' Buddha; local punk shows had been going on in rented halls since 1977. Managers of those halls, though, were growing less sympathetic to punk rock and had become wary of the violence and vandalism associated with the scene. So the punk bands were starting to look for new venues that would take them. And as more members of the scene were reaching the legal drinking age, bands and audiences alike recognized the need for a licensed club.

In that same year of 1977, Smilin' Buddha owner Lachman Jir was called to defend himself at a hearing before city council. Although the club had a liquor licence, inspectors cited a number of incidents in which patrons were served alcohol despite already being sufficiently inebriated. Jir's lawyers fought successfully against the city's push to have his licence revoked, stating that these incidents were overblown.

The Smilin' Buddha's precarious standing with city council combined with the socio-economic decline affecting the Downtown Eastside, oddly, provided the perfect storm in which a generation of chaotic Vancouver punk rock could flourish. The cabaret found itself at the epicentre of a new musical and cultural scene.

It was Jim Bescott, bassist of local punk band the K-Tels, who first suggested the Smilin' Buddha as a place to play. "He was a denizen of all the old bars, and actually played in them," recalls K-Tels singer-guitarist Art Bergmann. "He knew Lachman and asked if we could play there. We played for a week!"—though Jir initially pulled the plug on the band the first night upon hearing the group's volume. The K-Tels were in good company, though. Jir had kicked a then-unknown Jimi Hendrix off the stage of the Smilin' Buddha one night for playing too loud. The incident had apparently occurred when Hendrix sat in with the band one evening on one of his visits to see family in Vancouver in the early 1960s. By the 1970s, the story had taken on a mythical status in the cabaret's history, one that Jir told reluctantly upon request at the bar.

Bergmann notes that Vancouver was nothing but "cover-band city" in the late '70s, and it was hard to find venues interested in original music—if you wanted to play live music in Vancouver clubs, it had to be Top 40. This was a period when club circuit bands needed first to be signed to select local booking agencies to get a foot in the door, and those agencies would submit playlists for the musicians to learn certain songs or drop others. It was a dictatorial system that a new generation of Vancouver musicians had no interest in.

"The Smilin' Buddha was one of the few places that original bands could play," Bergmann recalls, noting

how quickly the scene moved there. "The Subhumans played the next week, D.O.A. the week after that."

Although Jir thought punk rock music was much too loud, the cabaret's sudden popularity changed his outlook. And the younger punk rock crowd bought more drinks than the previous down-and-out clientele, who soon abandoned the place, driven away by the volume of these new bands. This demographic shift created an unmistakable air of conquest at the Smilin' Buddha.

"One thing that was interesting about those days in the beginning of the punk rock scene was that nobody was from Vancouver," recalls Dennis Mills, frontman of the art punk band AKA. "The D.O.A. people were from Burnaby, Nick Jones and Pointed Sticks people from North Vancouver, the Modernettes and Art Bergmann from White Rock—it seemed like everybody was people from the suburbs—we were the original bridge-and-tunnel people!"

"When I see photos of those nights at the Buddha, I can't help but think how young we all look," recalls John "Buck Cherry" Armstrong of the Modernettes. "We look like we ought to have parents picking us up and driving us home."

For Armstrong, the move from playing the rental halls to the clubs brought relief. Performing in halls required the bands to rent and haul around their own sound and lighting systems. "Sometimes in those rented halls, we'd make a bunch of money but had to give a lot of it back to pay for damages. With the Buddha, now we were in an honest-to-God nightclub. And if somebody kicked the toilet to pieces, that was thankfully Lachman's problem and not ours."

Despite the nightclub being a licensed bar, which meant it was technically off limits for those under nineteen, younger teenagers desperate to see punk bands were often able to watch the shows from an open doorway. Even some of the musicians who performed at the Smilin' Buddha were underage.

"I used to take the bus to school from Marpole up by Granville and 70th, and the bus would go down

Any given night at the Smilin' Buddha. *Photo: Bev Davies*

Hastings and past the Smilin' Buddha," recalls Ziggy Sigmund, who found an early home at the club to nurture his teenage rock 'n' roll aspirations, before going on to play guitar in Vancouver bands Slow, the Scramblers, and Econoline Crush. Sigmund first played there in 1979, at the age of fourteen, with East Van Halen, a punk group composed of very young players, including brothers Nick and Lev Delany and Eric Marxen (who would later perform in Copyright).

"It always seemed an easy place to play, or to get a gig," says Sigmund. "Or to show up opening for somebody, or open for an opening act. It was always kind of disorganized in a way. You'd show up, and people would say, 'Oh, are you playing tonight?'"

Sigmund notes that underage patrons had to gain approval from Igor, the club's notorious six-foot-seven

bouncer. Some youngsters were allowed entrance as long as they promised not to drink. Those who did drink, did so discreetly and would suffer Igor's wrath if caught.

"I was backstage in the kitchen, which was unused and got used as a band room back then," says Sigmund. "Wimpy Roy [Brian Goble] from the Subhumans was there, and he handed me this drink—it was some weird green mixed drink he had. I had just started sipping it when Igor walked in and yelled at me and grabbed me and threw me out the back door. I landed on a garbage bag in the back alley. Then, seconds later, I saw my guitar case flying out the back door over my head after me. He caught me one other time and threw me out the same way. I think I landed on the same garbage bag."

Smilin' Buddha poster
by Ronald Nelson
promoting a show
headlined by Dead
Kennedys. *Credit:
Ronald Nelson*

Photographer Gordon McCaw took pictures of bands at the club and recognized from the beginning that he was witnessing something special at the Smilin' Buddha. "Having lived in Alberta for seven and half years, I found Vancouver's culture refreshingly different and more to my liking," he says. "The fire and passion of these bands and the almost religious fervour of the fans. One of the best examples of that was one of the performances I saw of the Bludgeoned Pigs. I remember at one point the lead singer, Alastair, was still singing with about eight punks pig-piled on top of him. I just thought you'd never see a per-

formance like that at the Queen Elizabeth Theatre."

By 1980, the club was established as *the* punk rock venue in Vancouver. Touring American acts like the Dils, Black Flag, and Dead Kennedys performed there. Many of the performances were captured by Bev Davies, the local photographer most closely associated with the Smilin' Buddha. But for Davies, the club was so much more than a location to get great shots.

"I felt lucky to be there," says Davies. "It was a real community of people getting up on the stage every night. You see moments of that today from time to time but not like it was then. I went there alone, but

"I felt lucky to be there," says photographer Bev Davies, who took hundreds of photos of bands and audiences at the Smilin' Buddha. "In particular, the women I knew there always saved me a seat and looked after me." *Photo: Bev Davies*

all your friends were there. In particular, the women that I knew there always saved me a seat and looked after me. I just felt very welcome there."

Some Vancouverites didn't share Davies's warm feelings toward the new denizens of the Smilin' Buddha. In fact, some members of the city council perceived the punk rock audiences as a legitimate threat to social order. In May 1979, some police on their beat visited the club, prompting nightclub patrons to shout, "Kill pigs!" The incident nearly started a riot, and city council called Jir to appear at a hearing regarding a licence suspension.

At the hearing, alderwoman Bernice Gerard, a notorious conservative and Pentecostal Christian evangelist, denounced punk rock as being "on the fringe of civilization."[55] Meanwhile, angry alderman Don Bellamy, a former police officer, said, "None of our policemen are going to take this kind of garbage."

Lawyers and club management, in turn, insisted that police were prone to "strut" around the cabaret "insulting the patrons." Many people who attended the Smilin' Buddha in those years recall instances of the police storming in to look for underage drinkers and intimidate patrons.

In the end, the Smilin' Buddha avoided licence suspension but did not escape penalties. "The one photo I wish I had was of the official occupancy sign given by city hall," Bev Davies says. "Every time the Buddha got penalized for one infraction or another,

[55] Andrea Maitland, "Near-Riot by Punk Rockers Wipes the Smile off Buddha," *Vancouver Sun*, November 2, 1979, A3.

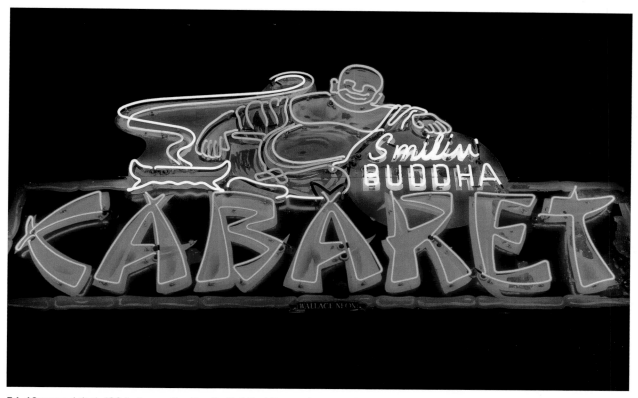

54-40 named their 1994 album after the Smilin' Buddha, and restored the sign from the scrapyard. It is now on permanent display at the Museum of Vancouver. *Credit:* Vancouver Sun *Archives*

that number went down. The number would get crossed out and the next one would be lower, and lower as time went on!"

Playing at the Smilin' Buddha Cabaret in the early 1980s was a rite of passage for Vancouver punk and new wave bands. The flood of independent music that crashed out of Vancouver in those years was so influential that bands like D.O.A., the Subhumans, the Modernettes, and Pointed Sticks were heard well beyond the city limits. The era represents a tremendous burst of energy that was happening in Vancouver's music and art scene. But some of those involved in that scene prefer not to look back at the Smilin' Buddha through rose-coloured glasses.

"There was nothing good about the Buddha," Art Bergmann says sardonically. "It was the only place

to play. It stunk to high heaven from fifty-year-old grease in the kitchen!"

The club was repaired and renovated after a serious fire in 1983, but by 1987, it was all over at the Smilin' Buddha. Other exciting venues had opened in town, like the Quadra Club, Gary Taylor's Rock Room, and eventually, the Town Pump—all of which began to book punk rock bands. The club reopened in the early 1990s as the Smilin' Sports Café, run by Lachman Jir's son, Robert, but it closed in 1996, after which the space languished empty for more than fifteen years.

In 2013, brothers Andrew and Justin Turner, with Malcolm Hassin, signed a lease and led a successful effort to reopen the venue as SBC Restaurant. It was no easy feat. Hassin and the Turners had to haul out more than a ton of garbage and junk from the

SBC Restaurant now occupies the Smilin' Buddha space, where it runs both an indoor skateboard park and music venue.
Credit: SBC Restaurant

basement that had been mysteriously piled up there the while time the building had been neglected. Moreover, the power had been disconnected from the building. But today, SBC is a unique indoor skateboard park and restaurant, featuring a stage that can be placed in and out of a forty-five-foot-long skateboard ramp. On weekends, SBC regularly hosts bands, including some from the Smilin' Buddha Cabaret's legendary past, such as D.O.A. and Pointed Sticks.

Now, young skateboarders who weren't even alive in its heyday of the late 1970s and early 1980s are giving the venue its future. And more than a few of them might be listening to D.O.A. while they're skateboarding on the SBC half pipe. The venue has even been included on the Vancouver Heritage Foundation's list of celebrated cultural and historical "Places That Matter," but despite the encouraging success of SBC, its future is by no means certain. Like any venue not owned by its operators, the owners could raise the rent to prohibitive levels or simply choose to sell or develop the property. Almost all nightclubs in Vancouver today face those same risks. It appears the last chapter of the Smilin' Buddha's history has yet to be written.

CHAPTER NINE

GASTOWN AND BEYOND

Gastown's Blood Alley at night, 1976.
Credit: City of Vancouver Archives CVA 293-083

THE TOWN PUMP

Eddie Vedder of Pearl Jam at a legendary
Town Pump appearance in January 1991.
Photo: Kevin Statham

Vancouver is a young city with a short history, even compared to many of the other still-developing cities along the West Coast of North America. In a way, it's what makes Vancouver unique—lots of the major, fundamental changes to its urban centre have occurred within the lifetime of many Vancouverites.

Even the city's neighbourhood that seems the most historic is not as old as it appears. Today, cruise ship passengers who stop in the Port of Vancouver and stroll the short distance from the modern terminal at Canada Place to visit the shops and restaurants of nearby Gastown might be led to believe that the district—with its old-fashioned bollards, red-brick lanes, and whistling steam clock—is a preserved remnant of what was once a quaint Victorian-era colonial town. But much of that aura is manufactured. Even Blood Alley, the vividly named passageway that cuts through Gastown, is a myth. It gets its name not from once being home to abattoirs, nor from some rough-and-tumble, two-fisted past. This was simply a colourful title pitched by marketing types who sought to conjure a compelling image as part of a major overhaul of Gastown during the early 1970s. Just a few years earlier, the area had been considered a slum that should be cleared to make room for a highway.

Despite Gastown being a deceptive modern creation, it has still been home to some authentically mythical places over the years, places that stamped a real mark in the city's entertainment history. Perhaps the most significant of them all was the Town Pump.

Ruben Kopp and Edward Keate opened the Town Pump in March 1971 at 66 Water Street. A veteran of the club scene, Kopp had worked as a waiter at the Cavalier Room, the cocktail lounge in the Hotel Georgia. With a sizeable bank loan, Kopp had opened his own place called the Sir Walter Raleigh at Granville and Hastings Streets. Keate ran a brokerage company but was also an amateur chef who was keen to get

The Town Pump opened in 1971.
Credit: Vancouver Sun *Archives*

into the restaurant business. The main ingredient he brought to the new Town Pump was financing.

The partners had found the space in Gastown for their new venture in 1970, but they were not entirely enthusiastic about its location. "We were making an expensive move into the worst part of town," Keate recalled in a 1971 interview with the *Vancouver Sun*, noting that the financial outlook at the time was anything but rosy, and many businesses were failing.[56]

The building had once been two separate units, built in 1909 and 1912, respectively. Kopp and Keate put a considerable amount of money into sprucing up the place. The decor featured a Wild West, frontier style, complete with a long oak bar, old brass, red drapes, and vintage photographs of old Vancouver and newspaper clippings. But the look of the space did not please everyone. A group calling themselves the Frank Buck Society partnered with the Keep Gastown Historic Committee and sent an angry letter to the owners of the Town Pump upon their opening. Kopp and Keate were excoriated for "perpetuating an obscenity" because "the Town Pump portrays the

[56] Bill Fletcher, "Town Pump Pair Find Right Market," *Vancouver Sun*, April 1, 1971, 34.

The Replacements at the Town Pump, July 1987.
Photo: Charles Campbell

'movie-lot' American Old West. There is no counterpart in Canadian history, Canadians can do without importing the gunslinger, Indian princess caricatures from south of the border. CANADIAN PRIDE OVER YANKEE COERSION!"[57] However, these dissenters proved to be in the minority, as the Town Pump was an instant success.

While the Town Pump, backed by businessmen with deep pockets, was getting underway in Gastown, Bob Burrows was doing his best on a shoestring at the Pink Parlour—the after-hours space in the back of the Shanghai Junk where Tommy Chong's City Works comedy group got its start. Chong's improv troupe had failed to impress the heavy drinkers in the audience, who were more interested in the strippers that had been incorporated into the act. The club was failing. One day, when Chong was lamenting the club's future, Burrows—who had booked a few bands at the Pink Parlour—and a friend named J.P. suggested on a lark they could take over. Before they

had a chance to reconsider, Chong tossed them the keys and told them rent was $200 a month.

"I knew some of the bands, like Jayson Hoover and the Epics, and the Night Train Revue," Burrows recalls. "And J.P. knew the hippie bands, like the Seeds of Time and Mock Duck. It went well for a while. Then J.P. left for Toronto and I took it over altogether. I must have been the only white businessman in Chinatown. I was down there all the time. I didn't eat anything but Chinese food!" He laughs, recalling dining daily across the street from the Parlour at the King Hong restaurant. "The cooks in there were these young Chinese guys. They really kept an eye out for me. They'd pick up my packages or mail there, and they'd tell me when they overheard the cops eating in the restaurant talking about when they were going to raid me."

Eventually, not even the cooks at the King Hong could save Burrows. One night, Vancouver police nailed Burrows for running a bar illegally and shut him down. By then, though, he was working at a small local booking agency called Whitefoot Entertainments. "It had to be the world's worst agency, and I was their worst agent," he recalls. "I sent a guy to do a gig up in the Interior once, and when he got there it was just a pile of lumber and [the venue] hadn't been built yet!"

Burrows was having better success in Vancouver. He had struck up a business relationship with a stockbroker named Allen Achilles who had bought the Town Pump from Kopp and Keate in the late 1970s. "Allen was the kind of guy who'd sell shares of a gold mine when there was nothing there, just a hole in the ground," says Burrows. Achilles hired him to make weekend bookings for the club. "Back then, the Town Pump did good business in the day as a restaurant but nothing at night. In the daytime, there were a lot of drunks there. The execs over at the Woodward's Building would come over and sit

[57] Lorne Parton's column, *Province*, March 19, 1971, 23.

all day near the bar phone from lunch until the end of the day and drink and occasionally check their calls. No wonder Woodward's went out of business!"

By the early 1980s, Burrows was booking local acts like David Raven, the Beverly Sisters, and the Villains in the club on the weekends, but now the weeknights needed to be filled, too. The house band, Marty Gillan and the Town Pumpers, were a declining draw. The evenings continued to feature hit-and-miss bookings of singer-songwriters, and aside from a deaf piano player named James who, intriguingly, played audience requests he learned by ear, the club needed to change gears.

But then Burrows made a pivotal booking in 1984. He had been following the career of local musician Art Bergmann, so he approached him to play during the week. Bergmann was less than enthusiastic at first. "He didn't think it would be cool to play in there on a weekday," says Burrows, "so I told him, 'Would it be cool if I gave you four grand?'—and he went for it! The show was packed, I made my money back, and from 1984, things really took off. I remember I booked Donovan, the folk singer, which I thought might be a risk, but it sold out in twenty minutes. By the end of the 1980s, it was crazy—so many bands."

As soon as the club started booking bands during weeknights, it scared away the lunchtime crowd, who were forced to sit through the "one, two, one, two" calls over a microphone during sound check. But pretty soon, the nighttime crowds at the Town Pump became so good it didn't matter that the lunch patrons had disappeared. Much of the room's Old West decor of was swapped out for a more rock 'n' roll atmosphere.

During the 1980s, the Town Pump benefitted from not only an incredible wave of good, original live bands but also the public's strong appetite for the music. Promoter Peter McCulloch's company Timbre Concerts represented artists like the Blasters and David Lindley. Booker and manager Frank Weipert brought in bands like the Cadillac Tramps

"The Pump and the Rail and the Commodore all going full steam at once. What a town filled with friends and music," says Craig Northey of the Odds, recalling the vibrant period of live music in the city in the late 1980s into the '90s." *Credit: SFU Special Collections*

and the Beat Farmers. "*Melody Maker* in England was suddenly talking about the Town Pump as a place to play," says Burrows.

And a fleet of homegrown talent from across Canada—including Toronto-based acts like the Shuffle Demons, Bourbon Tabernacle Choir, and the Rheostatics—played the Town Pump, putting the Gastown club on the national music map "I think the first gig that the Tragically Hip did in Vancouver was at the Town Pump," recalls the band's manager Jake Gold. "One big night for the band happened at the 1991 Junos in Vancouver. We played a show at the Town Pump that was sold out way in advance— it was the most talked-about show that weekend.

Gordon Downie of the Tragically Hip onstage at the Town Pump. *Photo: Dee Lippingwell*

It was an 'underplay' for us, because the band could have played a much bigger place. But it had sold out so early, and all these music industry people wanted to get into that one, that was such a big event."

There was a lot of buzz about the club among other Canadian musicians. "We'd already heard of the Town Pump long before we came out here," recalls Headstones singer Hugh Dillon. "But there was no way to get there because it seemed so far away. We'd never been to BC, but I loved bands from Vancouver like D.O.A. and Slow, so coming here was like coming to Mecca! The first time we were at the Town Pump there wasn't a lot of people there, but they were really into it. But the next time we came, and it was sold out at the Pump—and it was absolutely crazy. Because we were embraced there, it made a big difference."

Headstones guitarist Trent Carr agrees: "We came to Vancouver when there was a concept of a real West Coast sound. It was a little bit of the Seattle thing that was happening that was coming over the border, but it felt like Vancouver had its own thing, and us coming to play at the Town Pump was a big deal for us."

For homegrown musicians, the Town Pump was just as significant. A litany of Canadian bands including the Scramblers, Age of Electric, Bif Naked, DSK, the Real McKenzies, Econoline Crush, and Roots Roundup regularly packed the room. "The Pump was the crank that turned the spindle as far as Vancouver clubs went," says Matthew Good, who played the Town Pump in the early 1990s and quickly rose to national fame to play large theatres and arenas.

The Valentinos at the Town Pump, 1991. *Photo: Mark Godfrey*

"If you look at the other clubs that fit into things at the time, that's how it worked. Everybody might come up differently in other places, but if you were going to do a night at the Commodore, you had to be able to play multiple nights at the Town Pump first. It was ground zero for everything, and a lot of people cut their teeth there."

Good continues, "It was also a room that taught you how to play, beyond just getting up there and doing it. It offered you this opportunity to learn how to work an audience. The layout was a little odd, with the stage on one wall and bands playing to the opposite wall. You had to walk out from the dressing rooms that were downstairs from the kitchen and go through the crowd to get to the stage. That ten seconds you made your way through was always kind of exciting."

At its height, the Town Pump's audiences, like those at the Commodore Ballroom, were treated to shows by acts either on their way up or on their way down, but in an even more intimate environment. By the early 1990s, the well-worn stage carpet had absorbed the weight of some of the most popular blues, folk, rock, and punk acts to come through the city.

The staff at the club had much to do with its success, and from Tony the doorman to Randy and Sonny the house audio techs to the bar staff, they were recognized more often as part of the Town Pump than some of the bands that played there. "Everybody who worked there were there because they loved the music," says Burrows. "They probably could have worked elsewhere for better money, but they liked being a part of what was happening there. So it had

Art Bergmann playing to a sold-out Town Pump, 1994. *Photo: Kevin Statham*

a completely different vibe than other places—that made a huge difference."

"Because we were open five or six nights a week, everyone got to be pretty organized and worked together well," says former bartender Ryan Grant. "Because of the small amount of staff, customers got to know us in a hurry."

Grant started working at the club in 1991 and is a living repository of stories from shows over the years that included everyone from Soundgarden to Mojo Nixon. "You'd see so many different kinds of music," he says. "You'd see a ska band open for a punk band, or folk and blues acts on the same bill. Music tends to be more compartmentalized now, it seems, but people back then seemed very open to hearing new kinds of music."

For both musicians and patrons, another signature feature of the club was the front lounge near the entrance. For those who wanted a break from the music, or just a chance to socialize, the lounge provided respite from the noise of the stage in the main room. Here, blues guitarists chatted with ska musicians, rockabilly bands hung out with metal-heads, and punk rockers hit on acoustic singer-songwriters. Next to the long oak bar where Wood-ward's executives once congregated for liquid lunches, musicians and patrons would meet, tell stories, bum a smoke or a pint, and hatch plans for upcoming shows and tours.

However, there was a darker aspect to the Town Pump as well. Cocaine and its dealers became regular fixtures in Vancouver clubs of the 1980s. At the

Members of Supergrass in the front lounge of the Town Pump. *Photo: Kevin Statham*

Town Pump, dealers held court on bar stools in the lounge, and the drug became as easy to procure as a cocktail. Drug abuse became a significant problem. It's a chapter of the club's history that most of the Town Pump crew prefer not to discuss on record.

The Town Pump had its ups and downs over the years. Dan and Joe McLean bought the bar in 1988, after some of Allen Achilles's other restaurant investments went under. The Town Pump continued to do well, though the McLeans seriously jeopardized this in June 1991, when they made the bar to a no-smoking venue. Today, it's taken for granted that Vancouver nightclubs do not allow smoking indoors, but in 1991, the decision made headlines around the world as the Town Pump became the only bar in North America that forced its clientele to smoke outside the club

on the street—almost a decade before the bylaw was enacted across the province in 2000. The Town Pump learned quickly that the smokers also tended to be the ones who drank. Bar totals plummeted, and six weeks later, the club fell off the wagon and once again allowed smoking. But there were other changes that were harder to rectify.

In 1995, Bob Burrows noticed the music scene was beginning to shift—and for the Town Pump, it was not for the better. Bands he'd booked before had moved to bigger rooms, and the new acts being signed weren't as good, Burrows recalls. Changing audience tastes and competition from the newly opened Starfish Room didn't help.

It was clear that the Town Pump could not sustain the success it experienced in the early 1990s.

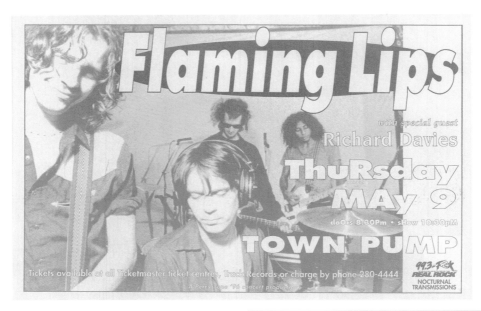

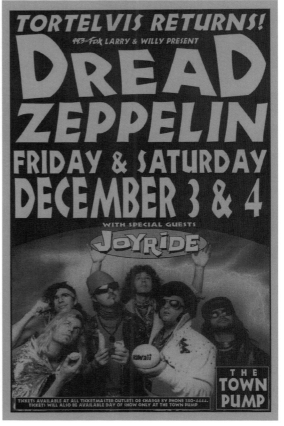

Various posters for the Town Pump. *Credit: SFU Special Collections*

One night in 1997, Burrows realized he had to take a different direction. "I remember walking out of the Town Pump early on a four-band bill that had done poorly," he says. "There were crowds of beautiful women down the street at another club on the corner called the Purple Onion. They were doing great business with DJs. Grunge, of course, had been popular in the 1990s, but one thing with grunge music was that it didn't draw any women. There were some great bands in that genre, but there were a lot that were just awful. I thought to myself with what was happening with the Pump, *This is going nowhere—I gotta do something.*"

Burrows continues, "Local DJ Luke McKeehan was doing rave, house music–style stuff over at Richard's on Richards, and those nights were huge, and we began to think that the only way we were going to save the club was to change the format."

So in 1997, the Town Pump closed. The stage was torn out, and after a $100,000 renovation, the club was rebranded as Sonar. Guitars were out, and DJs were in. Burrows knows the change was unpopular among the old live music crowd, but this pivot saved his business.

"Even with that ton of money we spent renovating, Sonar made a lot of money," Burrows says. "We did big numbers when we opened. If we did $35,000 a week in bar sales at the Town Pump, it was a big deal. We were doing $100,000 a week with Sonar at its height. That's not even the money taken at the door."

But this shift that happened in the late 1990s—not just at the Town Pump but other venues as well—is something that locals say the Vancouver club scene never fully recovered from. A year earlier, in 1996, the Commodore Ballroom closed during a legal battle over its sale that would play out for the next three years, and the venue didn't reopen until 1999. Smaller live music clubs like the Hungry Eye and the Starfish Room closed within a few years of one another during this time, while newer venues like the Brickyard opened, and some small pubs started to offer live music. The damage had been done.

"When the Town Pump closed, it felt like there were plants in proximity that died, if you know what I mean," says Matthew Good. "Other clubs kind of relied on it, in a way. Music was changing too, of course—how people bought and listened to it. The audience of people who really loved bands was diminishing. But as dingy as the place was, [the Town Pump] was a really important hub at one time."

Good and many other musicians who cut their teeth in clubs like the Town Pump look back now a bit nostalgically on those days, even if they have achieved success playing bigger and better venues. "If you came out of those primordial bars, and if you went onto theatres," Good says, "the technology is so different from those days—the sound and experience is so much better. But there's still some part of those rooms that you miss.

"The Town Pump was our Horseshoe Tavern," Good adds, comparing the loss of the room to the legendary Toronto nightclub that still stands on Queen Street. "What would happen in Toronto if the Horseshoe closed? Yeah, there are other places, but a really significant place—a historical place—would be gone."

Sonar enjoyed a ten-year run before it closed, and then reopened for a time as a new dance club called Fabric. It's hard to find anybody who laments the loss of Sonar or Fabric today, but the Town Pump still sticks in the minds of many in the Vancouver music scene. For local musicians and audiences alike, at its best, the Town Pump was a beery centre of activity where crowds were good and there was always a band worth seeing.

The building at 66 Water Street has been vacant for several years now. Perhaps one day a new nightclub will open there—an exciting club again hosting intimate live shows in Vancouver. But it's difficult to imagine such a place would ever match the popularity, notoriety, and success of the Town Pump.

THE PIG AND WHISTLE AND THE HARP'N HEATHER

While the Town Pump was packing in the crowds, behind it, across Blood Alley, sat the Pig and Whistle pub, which hosted an unlikely mix of Vancouver's nightlife—Cordova Street meets *Coronation Street*.

The Pig and Whistle in 1979.
Credit: City of Vancouver Archives CVA 810-140

This vaguely British-style pub had a stage along its south wall, opposite the bar, and a long entrance hall that welcomed all manner of people through its front door: down-on-their-luck Downtown Eastsiders, local musicians stopping in for a beer and sitting in with the band, various Commonwealth expats, local magazine writers, drinkers who'd been kicked out of other bars, and the underaged and the very old. And the whole enterprise was (somehow) managed by Paul and Daphne O'Sullivan.

Vancouver writer and comedian Robert Dayton once summed up the Pig and Whistle most vividly: "The owners were an older couple: Paul, who wore Hawaiian shirts and told dirty jokes, and his wife, Daphne, who had false eyelashes, a wig, and wore pantsuits. She claimed to only be drinking fizzy fruit juice. She would compulsively yell at the customers, a blend of full-time alcoholics and underage girls. Seasonal decorations from all of the holidays lined the walls. Garbage pails situated near the buffet table caught the leaks emanating down from the liver spot–yellow-coloured ceiling. The buffet table was not meant to be eaten from; it was really only there as a liquor licence loophole."

The Pig and Whistle was originally at 315 East Broadway and Scotia Street, in a room that had been known as Maccabee's Hall, and then in the 1930s and '40s, Forrester's Hall—a fraternal society lodge that hosted evening community dances and get-togethers for Mount Pleasant residents. In the early '60s, it was renamed again, as Harmony Hall. With the relaxing of liquor laws in the later '60s, it became one of a number of community halls converted into clubs—or at least granted a liquor licence. It was rechristened again, in 1967, as the Down Under Club, by Paul and Daphne O'Sullivan, who opened it as a space for their fellow Aussie and Kiwi expats in town—Paul being from New Zealand and Daphne from Australia. Although with their affinity for Irish music and culture, and their distinctly Irish last name, they considered themselves Irish as much as they did Australian and New Zealander.

The original Pig and Whistle building at 315 East Broadway at Scotia.
Credit: City of Vancouver Archives CVA CVA 786-56.07

Paul and Daphne O'Sullivan of the Pig and Whistle.
Credit: Vancouver Sun *Archives*

The downstairs pub—accessed via a door that was literally down under the building—was eventually renamed the Pig and Whistle. It featured all manner of guitarist-balladeers playing singalong standards from "Delilah" to "Tiny Bubbles." Upstairs, the O'Sullivans tried to capitalize on the trend of Polynesian-themed tiki bars with the Tahitian Hut, which featured live music by house band the South Seas Islanders. The O'Sullivans managed the place, handling everything from bartending and food to janitorial service—but not necessarily always in that order. If the smell of a luau wasn't exactly in the air, the Tahitian Hut at least provided a good time, with the feisty O'Sullivans as genial enough hosts.

In 1973, they left Mount Pleasant for Granville Street and opened a pub called the Leprechaun across from the Commodore Ballroom, in what had been the Torna A Sorrento, an Italian cabaret and supper club run by Little Italy restaurateur Phillip Seminara, who had been looking to get out of the space for years. "I should have never left Commercial Drive," Seminara said in an interview with the *Vancouver Sun* in 1972. "[On Granville Street] I lost $60,000 in the first three

months. I finally got my money back out of the place, but never again."

It hadn't worked for the Italians, and there was equally no luck for the Irish. The Leprechaun was not a success. After a three-year run, in 1976, the O'Sullivans landed in Gastown and opened a new pub at 15 West Cordova Street. Perhaps hoping for some pop culture recognition, they borrowed the name from the musical television series *The Pig and Whistle* that had been airing on CTV and was set in a fictional pub of the same name.

Daphne O'Sullivan was one of the few female club proprietors in Vancouver—and it was Daphne who ran the pub as her domain, leaving Paul to take a more of back seat role. Perhaps he just deferred to Daphne's larger-than-life personality.

"Daphne was a one-off—she really was," jokes Ray Cartin, a fellow pub owner who had moved to Vancouver from Ireland in 1965. "She liked to think of herself as an accountant. She did all the books, but she usually was drunk as anybody else in there. In her later stages running the bar she wore a wig, and it would be on sideways by the end of the night. She was a beautiful woman in her younger days—she could have given Elizabeth Taylor a run for her money—and Paul was no drag in the looks department either."

"She always stayed so late," continues Cartin. "One night, I drove past and saw the lights on. I went in and found she was the only one there—lying on the floor by herself and passed out. I couldn't get her up! So I put a pillow under her head and a blanket onstage that was used to dampen the band's kick drum, and I turned the lights off and closed the door."

Vancouver owes much of its Irish pub lineage to both Cartin and O'Sullivan.

"When Paul and Daphne were on Broadway, they were sort of the only game in town at the time," Cartin says, but he wasn't far behind. Breaking into the bar business in 1967 with a social group called the Overseas Club, Cartin organized parties and dances at local halls and hotel ballrooms that catered to Irish and British expats and their friends. It was an immediate hit. "We didn't have much money, and had no liquor licence—we got one catering licence for one early event we did, and just kept reusing it, bringing it to each event. Nobody noticed except the liquor inspector one night, who told me his wife loved our events, as it kept her out of the house, so he didn't want to interrupt our business!"

Ray Cartin—a pioneer of Irish pubs in Vancouver. *Credit: Vancouver Sun Archives*

Cartin took the success of the Overseas Club events and, with business partners, opened the Abbey Tavern in Burnaby in 1968 in a space at 5550 Kingsway that had once been a Sambo's restaurant. It, too, was a success, but Cartin was eager to get back into Vancouver proper with a new pub right in the heart of the city.

"In the early 1970s, the word 'Gastown' was beginning to be heard as something new and viable," says Cartin. "It was really just getting started then. [Architect and Gastown building owner] Larry William—who never gets the proper credit for spearheading the new Gastown—saw what I was doing at the Abbey Tavern. He'd been coming there week after week and told me he'd love to have that kind of entertainment in Gastown. So he invited me down to look at some locations he owned."

It didn't take long to decide. Cartin opened the Blarney Stone in June 1972, and it became an even bigger hit than the Abbey. "We paid off the whole mortgage in six months," he recalls proudly. But when his arrangement with his partners changed, he left to start the Harp'n Heather around the corner at 7 Alexander Street. "I was trying to be inclusive," Cartin says, laughing. "I called it the Harp for the Irish, and the Heather for the Scottish. If I could have worked the word 'shalom' into the title and capture another demographic I would have done it."

At the Harp'n Heather, Cartin used all of his prior experience to produce a full bill of Irish-style entertainment with singers, comedians, dancers, and a dance band. Performers ranged from locals to acts imported from Ireland that he booked for six-week-long engagements—with Cartin acting as emcee.

"The city hadn't really seen entertainment like that before," Cartin explains. "In those days, Vancouver could be sometimes a bit pathetic when it came to entertainment for the average guy. Sure, Isy's, the Cave, and the Penthouse were fine for that kind of nightclub show, but there was nothing else happening that wasn't rock 'n' roll. So people came down to see what we were doing, thinking they'd be dancing to Irish music and entertainment all night, when they'd really be dancing to a unique mixture. We had a good stream of locals regularly playing, the band Johnny Hayden and the Blue Notes, comedian Tommy Gilligan—a real showman. There was another guy named Angus MacWhistle—he stripped off to the waist and put on a big tall hat like Abraham Lincoln that covered him to his chest, and he'd painted a mouth on his belly, with his bellybutton being the mouth, and he'd move his belly in and out and walk around to a recording of 'Colonel Bogey March.'"

In the beginning, Cartin tried to audition all the acts himself so that he would know what kind of show he was booking, but as he became so busy with other aspects of the business, he couldn't always screen the performers beforehand.

"One time at the Abbey Tavern, I got a call from a comedian who wanted to come do his show," Cartin recalls. "He said he'd played to great crowds at the legion hall in Newton [in the Lower Mainland]. It was very busy that week and I couldn't find time to audition him, but I figured if he was getting audiences out at other halls, as he said he did, and came well recommended, he must have been good. He was very gentlemanly and friendly on the phone, so I told him to come down on Friday night."

When the man arrived, Cartin saw that he had a cane with him and he was blind. Cartin welcomed him and took him backstage and got ready for the show.

"When his set time came, it was about nine o'clock and we had a full house," remembers Cartin. "We used to dim the lights when the performers came on and hit them with the spotlight so they had the full attention of the room. We were all ready, and I jumped onstage and said, 'Well, folks, you're really going to love this next comedian, he's very funny, let's give him a big hand,' and I introduced him. I was lying, of course. I hadn't had a chance to see him. Well, they gave him a big round of applause, perhaps even applauding more as encouragement when they saw that he was blind—it was a very warm reception. I stood back into the darkness and he went on with his act—and proceeded to tell the most filthy fucking jokes I'd ever heard. The foul language and descriptions—I couldn't believe it! We were sort of a family place, really, and the audience's jaws dropped. I couldn't motion him to get him off the stage because, of course, he was blind and couldn't see me desperately waving at him to stop. So we practically had to stage-hook him off."

After that experience, Cartin tried to curate the entertainment as best he could. And he paid local performers well for the time—forty dollars a night.

The O'Sullivans, however, took a different approach. "Daphne wouldn't pay musicians but just fed them," says Cartin. "She didn't like spending money at all. But the way she booked entertainment—she was like a wolf who lived on the outskirts of town who picked off the odd child."

O'Sullivan found good musicians who were between bands and took care of their food and drink. After hours, the local musicians often stayed for

Advertisements for the Harp'n Heather.
Credit: Vancouver Sun *Archives*

some complimentary rounds long after the public —or at least those that were not close friends of the O'Sullivans—went home. The Pig and Whistle acted as a clubhouse—a sort of home away from home—for like-minded thirsty souls.

Lori De La Fuente first entered the Pig and Whistle in 1981, at age fifteen. She ran away from home in Burnaby, where she had a troubled relationship with her mother, got an apartment in Gastown at the Hotel Europe, and soon became a frequent patron at the Pig. The liquor licence that was grandfathered in for the pub allowed underage patrons to eat there but not legally drink—but this didn't stop De La Fuente.

"I was there all the time," she says. "I looked a little older for my age because I was taller, and Daphne used to let me run a tab—even though I had no money to run one. But I was pretty overconfident in those days, so they just believed me!"

And although most former patrons recall that the food at the Pig and Whistle could in no way be considered fine, or even decent, dining—and it might have just been around to meet the requirements of the liquor licence—De La Fuente says it wasn't that bad. "When you're young and hungry, I suppose you'll eat anything," she offers with a laugh.

"At the end of the night, Daphne would do last call—we used to try to leave. Paul would be asleep at a table. You'd say, 'I gotta go, I'll see you, Daphne.' She'd get up like a bullet, sit you down, and in that Australian accent tell you to 'Shut yer gaggy and have another drink.' The after-hours drinks you didn't have to pay for—she just wanted the company!"

De La Fuente might have been too young to spend late nights at the bar, but she was accepted into the Pig and Whistle family—a family over which Daphne presided like a stern mother. Despite the pub's reputation as a gin-soaked free-for-all, in reality, Daphne ruled with an iron fist. Those who used loud foul language would be escorted out by the scruff of the neck. If you got on Daphne's bad side, she could shut the whole bar down on a whim.

"One night, she was drunk at work and mad at everybody," De La Fuente recalls. "She used to get into these moods—her beehive would start getting unravelled, her eyelashes were holding half-on, and she wagged her finger at me when I ordered another round on my tab and said, 'I've had enough of this, time to pay your tab!' I only had ten dollars on me, so she took it, put it in the till, and came back with a server's apron, and said, 'Get to work, lovey!'"

De La Fuente was only supposed to work enough shifts to pay off her debt, but she ended up staying on as a server for years. "From that work experience I got a great job at Expo 86, and I moved on, but I'm still friends with a lot of people from those days."

Another fifteen-year-old regular who stayed on Daphne's good side (not running a tab) was John Collins. In fall 1983, when he was still attending high school in West Vancouver, Collins and his friends became regular patrons at the Pig and Whistle.

Vancouver singer-songwriter Robert Ford, 1970s.
Credit: Stephen Ford

"The place had been adopted by local mod kids, who were all coming down from the suburbs and milling around that area," says Collins. "Because they let teenage kids in, it became a little bit of a hangout."

He continues, "My friend Bob and I had a mod band called On the Go. It was a little embarrassing, really—an early, teenage band. But we'd come down just to see the Martini Brothers, who were the house band there, who'd rehearse in the afternoons. We were in awe of them."

As wretched as the Pig and Whistle was, the Martini Brothers were an exceptionally talented and tight group. It featured Robert Ford on guitar and vocals, Daphne and John's son Dale O'Sullivan on drums, and a host of rotating players from other local bands. The versatile group was so good they probably deserved to headline at the uptown clubs, where they would have gotten decent pay.

"The Martinis were great," Collins says. "They played R&B, sixties tunes. They'd take requests from us when we were sometimes the only people in there

Left: Paul O'Sullivan, circa 1980s. Right: Daphne O'Sullivan tending bar, circa 1980s. *Credit: Stephen Ford*

some afternoons. They could play all the Who and Kinks songs we loved. They knew them all."

He goes on, "I was so in awe of Rob Ford. He was honestly what I considered the biggest rock star I'd seen. He was a hero to me. He'd play these amazing guitar solos and kind of rock out just for us. He was a really magnetic, fun guy. Just seeing him rehearsing with the band, it was like watching the Rolling Stones rehearse. They were there practising every afternoon."

"Robert was one of those great musicians around then," Ray Cartin recalls. "He'd already had years of experience playing clubs in Los Angeles in his early twenties and was a good-looking guy." Ford's guitar playing garnered respect from everyone from jazz musicians to punk rockers. He also had an irreverent sense of humour that led him to alter lyrics on the fly, adding observations about what was happening in the bar.

Eventually, Collins and his friends summoned the courage to ask if their band could play at the bar, and much to the boys' surprise, the O'Sullivans agreed.

"My mom drove us down with our gear and picked us up again at night," says Collins. "We charged three dollars at the door and, since we'd spread the word so well amongst our friends in the mod scene, three hundred kids came out on a Friday night. The problem was just about everybody was drinking hot chocolate and coffee because they were kids. But it was a big success for us, and we played a few more times in the months afterwards."

The On the Go shows were well attended, but the bar wasn't making any real money off the teenagers who filled the room, so Daphne put an end to the band's run at the Pig and Whistle. "I understood why, but it was pretty fun—it was our little *Quadrophenia* moment," he jokes, referring to the cult movie about 1960s mod culture.

Those times at the Pig and Whistle served John Collins well. He went on to work professionally as a musician and multi-instrumentalist, touring the world as a member of the critically acclaimed bands the New Pornographers and Destroyer, and playing

Vancouver band the Stoaters, led by Robert Ford (far left). The Pig and Whistle became the group's clubhouse, while Ford himself—whether he knew it or not—inspired a number of young musicians. *Credit: Stephen Ford*

on records by the Evaporators and Tegan and Sara. But playing at the Pig and Whistle remains a personal highlight. "I've never had a better time playing anywhere," Collins says.

The Pig and Whistle came to a quiet end in the mid-1990s, and Paul and Daphne O'Sullivan left Vancouver for New Zealand. In that decade, much of Gastown became a series of tourist-trap souvenir stores and unremarkable restaurants. But in recent years, the neighbourhood has filled up with hip gastropubs, modern wine bars, swanky condos, and modern furniture and boutique clothing stores. The district is enjoying a period of cautious prosperity.

Today, Ray Cartin feels mixed emotions when he walks down Water Street to the heart of Gastown at Maple Tree Square. All of these new businesses are for a younger generation to which he feels no immediate connection. It's not *his* Gastown anymore, but it still reminds him of the long nights he spent working to make his small piece of the neighbourhood a place people would want to return to. The flood of memories brings back a smile, but even for someone as good-humoured as him, it also brings back thoughts of how his line of work took a personal toll on him.

"Every publican and nightclub owner will tell you, you don't run a bar and have a good marriage—it ended mine," Cartin says ruefully. "You're never home. The long and late hours aren't for everybody, and it's tough on a family. Eventually, I decided too late I had to move on. So when my lease ended there at the Harp'n Heather, I decided to walk away." Cartin managed the Media Club on Cambie Street for a couple of years in the late 1990s but retired altogether soon after that.

Many of the venues from Cartin and the O'Sullivans' time running bars in Gastown still exist. The Blarney Stone, without much effort or advertising, attracts a new generation of college-age patrons each year. The venue that was the Harp 'n Heather enjoyed a few short years in the late 1980s as the Twilight Zone, then in 2013, took its current form as the Portside Pub. Even a fossilized version of the Down Under Club still exists on Broadway. After the O'Sullivans left, the venue went through a variety of transformations—from the Blue Star Cabaret and Capacabana Cabaret to R.J. Christies and later a rock 'n' roll bar called the Lunatic Fringe. In the '90s, the space became a second-class strip bar with the groaner of a name the Uranus Lounge. The building's two current occupants now offer much less exotic fare: coffee and sushi—Vancouver staples. Today, customers are unlikely to know that this spot was once a bustling Mount Pleasant cabaret, where passersby could hear choruses of "Delilah" echoing into the night.

Sadly, gone, too, is Robert Ford. In the 1980s, Ford formed a Celtic rock band of some local acclaim called the Stoaters, with mandolinist Dennis Crews joining him on lead vocals; his brother, Stephen Ford, on bass; and Dale O'Sullivan on drums. The group went on to headline the Commodore Ballroom and tour across Canada. Although Ford may never have garnered any gold records, he is still remembered fondly in Vancouver by hundreds of local musicians and friends, as well as those across the country and in Europe who saw him perform.

There is no longer a place in Vancouver like the Pig and Whistle. That was another time, another world. Bar operators today would probably fill a space like that with an overabundance of big-screen TVs tuned to sports channels, instead of allowing a ragtag group of musicians to curate something unique—instead of allowing patrons to talk, listen, drink, and let the evening languidly pass. And it is even rarer to find bar owners like Paul and Daphne O'Sullivan in Vancouver now. Today, many local bar managers have taken certified courses in hospitality and interned at spas and ski lodges. Most wouldn't dream of working at—let alone owning—a place like the Pig and Whistle.

The old Pig and Whistle pub is currently a trendy taco restaurant. Gone are the Tudor decor, wood paneling, and nicotine-stained ceiling tiles. Now the bright, breezy restaurant notes its space is inspired by "Southern California design and style." Perhaps a little gentrification is a good thing—at least when it comes to the menu. By all accounts, the food is now far better than what was available at the Pig and Whistle.

86 STREET MUSIC HALL AND THE PLAZA OF NATIONS

The legacy of the 1986 World Exposition on Transportation and Communication in Vancouver, or Expo 86, remains a hotly debated issue among Vancouverites, even more than thirty years later. Some simply recall the event with nostalgia as a summer of family fun, enjoying the pavilions, events, and attractions that came with the five-month-long fair. Others are more inclined to lament how the fair accelerated urban development and led to the abrupt end of Vancouver's nurtured small-town sensibility.

Aside from BC Place and the iconic "golf ball" structure that once housed Expo Centre and is now the Telus World of Science, there are very few physical remains of what was the Expo 86 site: a few low buildings, the old casino, and a parking lot that runs along the undeveloped corner of False Creek. During the fair and into the 1990s, though, one of these buildings held the 86 Street Music Hall.

Formally named the 86th Street Music Hall, though known locally as 86 Street, the club was originally supposed to be one of three nightclubs in the plaza, along with the Flying Club, a 200-seat space that would "give visitors the feeling of sitting above the clouds, eating a meal on the wing of an airplane," and the Waves Cabaret, which planned to have a dance floor positioned extravagantly over a Plexiglas tank full of goldfish—until Vancouver Aquarium officials protested.[58]

As for 86 Street, the planners initially intended to "give visitors a flashback to the '50s and '60s," though the final design reflected nothing of that character, aside from the large framed portraits of rock 'n' roll icons along the walls.

During Expo 86 and the decade that followed,

Poster for Jerry Lee Lewis at 86 Street, 1988.
Credit: Neptoon Records Archives

it featured performances by a long list of big-name mainstream acts, including B.B. King, Jerry Lee Lewis, Loverboy, Bryan Adams, and Colin James. It also hosted the earliest Vancouver performances by the likes of Radiohead, Blur, Alice in Chains, No Doubt, and Rage against the Machine. Even local bands such as Omnibol and Mystery Machine performed

---

[58] Moira Farrow, "Aquarium Chief Offended by Nightclub Idea," *Vancouver Sun*, 16.

Credit: Neptoon Records Archives, 1990

Bryan Adams at the 86th Street Music Hall in 1991.
Photo: Charles Campbell

Credit: Neptoon Records Archives, 1990

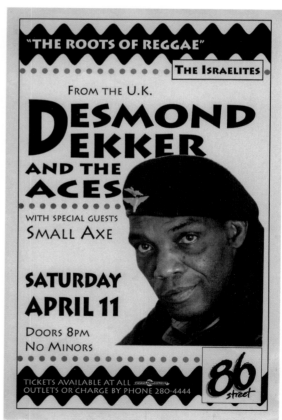

Credit: Neptoon Records Archives, 1992

here. The venue was removed from Gastown, where a number of the other popular live music clubs of the period were, which perhaps contributed to why, as the late Vancouver music writer Greg Potter noted, the venue never endeared itself to bands or local music fans as much as the Town Pump or even the Commodore Ballroom on Granville Street did. In his opinion, 86 Street was "the beginning of the end for Vancouver's golden age of live music." He said the venue was "antiseptic and void of character."[59] English singer Billy Bragg caustically pointed out one

[59] Greg Potter, "Backstage Past," *Vancouver Sun*, January 15, 2000, E4.

David Bowie at the Plaza of Nations, September 6, 1997. *Photo: Kevin Statham*

night onstage that it felt more like a shopping mall than a concert venue.

One night in particular seemed to seal its fate. On June 28, 1989, the legendary New York punk rock band the Ramones's performed at 86 Street. The show had been originally booked for two weeks earlier at the Commodore Ballroom (a venue used to Ramones crowds—indeed, the Commodore hosted the Ramones first Vancouver appearance in 1977) but because of a scheduling snafu had been moved to a new date at 86 Street.

That night, club bouncers threw twenty-eight-year-old Patrick Fraser out of the club's front doors and he landed face first on the pavement. He had to be taken by ambulance to Vancouver General Hospital. The force of the fall not only split open his forehead

but also gave him mild brain damage, and was left with facial scarring.

No charges were laid, but Fraser was awarded $652,400 in damages in a BC Supreme Court trial in 1991. This financial burden spelled the end for the venue, and by 1993, it had closed. Eventually, a new club opened there named the Rage, which was then renamed again, under new management, as the Harbour Event Centre.

A space that was perhaps remembered more fondly than the 86 Street Music Hall was right outside its front doors—the Plaza of Nations. This adjacent outdoor space that was once part of Expo 86's BC Pavilion could comfortably accommodate 4,000 people. Into the early 1990s, it was used as an outdoor concert site for shows by as the likes of the Foo Fighters, the

Left: The night the Ramones performed at the 86 Street Music Hall, June 28, 1989. *Photo: Kevin Statham*

Flavor Flav and Chuck D of Public Enemy at the Rage. *Photo: Kevin Statham*

Radiohead at the Rage, 1996.
Photo: Kevin Statham

The Plaza of Nations was demolished in May 2018.
Photo: Aaron Chapman

White Stripes, David Bowie, Pearl Jam, the Black Eyed Peas, Tool, Bad Religion, Jamiroquai, Lenny Kravitz, the Beach Boys, as well as a host of Canadian acts, including Matthew Good, Nickleback, Bif Naked, Pluto, Gob, Age of Electric, the Odds, and Sons of Freedom. In the late '90s, the site was used for the annual Slam City Jam, which paired skateboard championships with live music events.

By the 2000s, the space was used less and less, and the nearby Edgewater Casino had assumed its management. Noise complaints from the residents in the new condominium towers sprouting up in the area also discouraged live music promoters. But the Plaza of Nations was probably doomed long before this neighbourhood development. It was never an acoustically well-engineered amphitheatre. Its glass roof kept audiences dry, yes, but it had negative effects on the sonic properties of the Plaza—nobody who played there sounded very good.

That roof, which was only meant to last for the ten months of Expo 86, remained sturdy for twenty-one years. In 2007, though, inspectors noticed that the metal bolts that had held the roof together were beginning to rust significantly. With the cost of restoration prohibitive, and the long-term future of the site uncertain, the Plaza of Nations was fenced up and lined with scaffolding, and the roof and stage were finally taken down.

Today, the area is something of a no man's land. The greater plaza area is really only used as a short-cut for sports fans going to and from BC Place and Rogers Arena. Even the casino, once part of the Expo 86 BC Pavilion, is gone and awaiting demolition. Soon, any hint of the 86 Street Music Hall and the Plaza of Nations will be gone, replaced by glassy residential towers.

It's disappointing that Expo 86 did not leave behind a permanent concert venue. BC Place gets used by some of the larger touring acts that are big enough to fill the stadium's 54,000-person capacity, but its size renders it more functional as a sports stadium than as an essential live music space. And while Vancouverites continue to argue about the legacy of Expo 86, the wrecking ball will finally descend on the Plaza of Nations and 86th Street Music Hall site, leaving only dim memories of the performances once held there.

THE CRUEL ELEPHANT / HUNGRY EYE

During the late 1980s and 1990s, at the corner of Granville and Davie Streets, on the south side of the old Hotel California, a huge fifty-foot mural of a midriff-baring blonde in sunglasses stared out onto northbound traffic coming over the Granville Street Bridge. But by this time, the sounds of the Eagles—or any classic rock, for that matter—were getting pushed aside, cruelly, by an Elephant.

The Hotel Martinique at 1176 Granville was, at the time of its construction in 1912, one of the largest hotels on that street, and during the '30s, it was known as one of the better hotels in the neighbourhood. In December 1957, after significant renovations, it reopened as the Blackstone Hotel, but by the '70s, as Granville Street endured a period of decline, the hotel became a trouble spot. Police knew that management had turned a blind eye to drug dealers who worked out of the hotel's beer parlour. City hall wanted to shut the bar down, but with a fresh coat of paint and a new mural of a towering blonde, the hotel was rechristened in the early '80s, just in time for Expo 86. The surrounding neighbourhood, with its pawn shops and sex shops, however, hadn't improved much.

"I walked in there one day and got a job as a hotel bartender," recalls Paul Moes, who started working at the hotel in 1990, when he was in his mid-twenties. "It was a buck-eighty-five a pint. I remember I'd make seventy dollars a night in tips on fifteen-cent tips—you can imagine how busy it was then."

Moes noticed a large vacant room on the north side of the hotel that had once been a restaurant and suggested to management that they turn the space into a jazz bar. They approved his proposal and gave him a small budget to build a stage and fix up the room.

Management was not without its reservations, though. Since the space was not licensed to be a cabaret, and the outdated conservative beer parlour liquor licences from the 1920s and '30s were still in place, dancing would not be allowed. Moes assured them: if any inspectors asked, he'd gladly let them know there would no waltzing or jitterbugging going on in the new place.

From the outset, Moes wanted to open a punk rock club. There hadn't been a room truly devoted to punk rock since the days of the Smilin' Buddha, which closed in 1987. He installed a thick new door between the club and the hotel to help cut down on the noise.

Moes approached a couple of the larger beer companies to help him set up the bar, but they refused to put in new beer lines. "They didn't think it was worth their while—I was barely twenty-six, so they just didn't take me seriously, and it seemed like they wanted me to fail. So I got a couple of independent local breweries instead."

One night, he was with friends kicking around ideas for what to name the new club. They laughed at every suggestion they came up with until Moes suggested the Cruel Elephant, after British painter David Hockney's painting of the same name. "That was the one name we didn't laugh at and felt like it worked," says Moe.

The Cruel Elephant opened in the spring of 1990 and was soon hosting more alternative and art rock bands than other local nightclubs of the time. It was a quick success, but there were still hurdles to overcome. The business licence for the restaurant space called for food to be served if people were drinking, and Moes had no desire to get into that aspect of the hospitality business. "We operated like the old dine and dances, that when you came in you paid for the food and entertainment at once," says Moes. "The law said that you had to at least *intend* to eat. So we figured if anyone asked we just inferred they should say yes, but they never did."

@#*&! and Mary at the Cruel Elephant.
Credit: SFU Special Collections

Moes recounts, "One time, the police came in and said, 'No, no—you've got to have a meat-and-potatoes type of meal available. But I told them the place was vegetarian and that even the name of the bar related to vegetarianism—that the cruelty of the elephant was caused by man, and not by the elephant on its own. The police didn't know what to think. In 1990, a lot of people in general didn't even know what vegetarian food was—they just thought it was food without meat, so we got by with that."

The Cruel Elephant hosted an impressive variety of notable punk and alternative bands, from L7 and Green Day to locals like Nomeansno, Superconductor, and one of singer-songwriter Bif Naked's first bands, Gorilla Gorilla.

"It only lasted about a year and half there," says Moes. "It was getting so full and popular that the owners were getting worried. If anything went wrong in the surrounding neighbourhood that made news, they blamed the punk rockers coming or going from the Cruel Elephant. And even though they were making good money there, they got greedy and wanted me to increase the cover charge a lot. It couldn't continue."

Moes decided it was time to look for a new location. Walking around downtown late one Saturday night he spotted the old John Barley's club in the Stanley

Green Day at the Cruel Elephant on Granville Street, July 1991. *Photo: Kai Korinith*

Hotel building at 23 West Cordova Street. The club had just changed its name to Basin Street, which had previously been an after-hours jazz club run at 163 East Hastings. Gay nightclub operators John Stevenson and Don Whittaker had run both Basin Street and John Barley's; Stevenson was a veteran of Vancouver's gay-friendly establishments, and was one of the principal operators of Champagne Charlie's on Davie Street in the late 1960s, when homosexuality was still illegal in Vancouver. In the 1970s, he'd also been involved in the in the Howe Street lesbian bar Queenie's Truck Stop.

Moes paid Stevenson and Whittaker a visit, and then they came to see what the Cruel Elephant was like on one of the club's final nights at the Granville Street location. They weren't into alternative music,

MONDAYS at JOHN BARLEY'S

| Mar 7 | Face Ditch/ Red Dress $3⁵⁰ | Beat Pagodas/ Mar & Special Guests $3⁵⁰ | Mar 21 |
| Mar 14 | Up Chuck/ Trevor 2000 $3⁰⁰ | Junco Run/ Sausage Republic $3⁵⁰ | Mar 28 |

23 W. Cordova St., 669-1771

The night that Savage Republic was incorrectly billed as Sausage Republic, March 1983. *Credit: Discorder magazine*

NOFX made their Vancouver debut at the Cruel Elephant in 1991. *Credit: Neptoon Records Archives*

and Whittaker sometimes came across as quite conservative—"They were a little odd to deal with," Moes says—but they could see how well his bar was doing. Joining forces to move the business to their location, they agreed Moes could have the take from the door and a percentage of bar sales.

Despite its name—an allusion to the storied road in New Orleans, commemorated in the jazz standard "Basin Street Blues"—the club had no reputation at its current location as a live music venue. The club's gay clientele preferred recorded dance music in the early 1980s, and any live shows incompatible with the regular club nights would occasionally cause some unexpected cross-cultural evenings.

In 1983, post-punk band Savage Republic was booked to play the club (when it was still known as John Barley's). "I remember there was a misprint in

one of the print ads for the show," recalls Live Nation concert promoter Jason Grant, who was the talent buyer at the Commodore in the early 2000s and, in the early '80s, a writer for *Discorder*, the University of British Columbia campus radio magazine. "*Discorder* had printed the band name as *Sausage* Republic rather than Savage Republic, and the night of the show the gay, regular crowd at John Barley's came down expecting a different kind of show."

With Stevenson and Whittaker on board, the new Cruel Elephant on Cordova was born in 1992, and the club continued booking both touring and local punk and alternative acts. These were the days before social media, when more tangible modes of advertising were required to publicize shows: posters and print ads in *Discorder* and weekly newspaper the *Georgia Straight*.

The club's name continued to cause confusion. "I got in one afternoon to open up the club and the first thing I did was listen to the answering machine," recalls Moes. "There was a message from this woman with a regal, educated English accent telling me how awful the name of the bar was and that animals, and elephants in particular, were beautiful creatures. She went on about how misinformed I was, and I should change the name immediately, but she didn't leave a contact number. Listening back to it—I thought, *Man, she sounds like Jane Goodall.* Then I realized it had to be. I played it for a doorman [and another guy] who worked at the club and they said the same thing. We investigated and it turned out she was in town speaking at UBC, and must have stumbled across one of the club ads in *Discorder* and decided to call us up to tell us off!"

The Cruel Elephant on Cordova Street didn't last long but not because of Jane Goodall. According to Moes, both Stevenson and Whittaker felt they could cut him out of the picture, especially with their loose business agreement. "They thought they could just book anything on their own, and they pulled the rug out from under my feet," says Moes.

In 1993, Stevenson and Whittaker dropped the Cruel Elephant name and renamed the bar the Hungry Eye, a tip of the hat to the famous San Francisco nightclub Hungry I. Vancouver's Hungry Eye became a stepping stone for musicians to larger venues like the Town Pump, but it also held its own with an assortment of touring acts, including American artists like Uncle Tupelo, the Didjits, Ben Folds Five; Alberta bands like Chixdiggit and the Primrods; and local bands from the '90s indie rock scene such as Age of Electric, the Bughouse 5,

The Rattled Roosters at the Cruel Elephant, 1992.
Credit: SFU Special Collections

Coal, the Dead cats, Facepuller, Flash Bastard, the Harvesters, the Muscle Bitches, the Smugglers, Terror of Tiny Town, and dozens of others.

It would not be the end of the line for Paul Moes's involvement in the nightclub business, though. In the months prior to leaving the Cordova Street location, he'd found some old turntables that had been part of the John Barley's disco nights and decided to use them to play disco records between sets as a joke. "All of a sudden, you had these punk and skinhead guys doing the 'YMCA' dance," Moes remembers, laughing. When Moes was still running the Cruel Elephant Tuesdays were slow nights, so he started playing the records and bringing in DJs for Disco Nights, which, to his surprise, became a success. "The irony wasn't lost on me. Punk rock happened because of bad 1970s disco, but you take a second listen to some of the music from those days and it was pretty good. So disco created punk, and the punk rock crowd created Disco Night!"

When Moes parted ways with the Cruel Elephant, he took his Disco Night to Drew Burns, operator of the far larger Commodore Ballroom, to see if it could work there.

"Drew asked me how much I wanted to charge at the door," says Moes. "In the movie *Saturday Night Fever*, when they go into the club for the first time, you see a sign on the

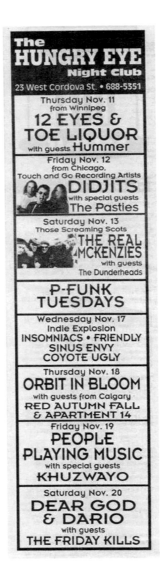

The Hungry Eye's 1993 calendar, which includes a concert by the Real McKenzies, featuring, among others, the author of this book. *Credit:* Georgia Straight

door that says three dollars. So I made it that—three dollars is a barrier to no one. We broke some attendance records with those Disco Nights."

The Hungry Eye closed in 1996. The space later became the Limelight Cabaret, which was then renamed 23 West and featured a number of regular fetish nights. The bar closed for a period before its final incarnation as a club opened by David Duprey, appropriately named the Hindenburg, which closed in 2018. The building, along with the Stanley and New Fountain Hotel, was demolished, except for the facade, in 2019.

Moes now works on local film sets and repairs vintage motorcycles. He looks back favourably upon his years at the Cruel Elephant and, although there are some things he might have done differently, has no regrets.

"I would like to contact Jane Goodall if I could—all these years later," Moes says. "Just to let her know she had the wrong idea about us."

THE BRICKYARD

In the late 1990s, the grungy old Minto's Pub space at 315 Carrall Street changed overnight from a dim bar filled with dozing, down-on-their-luck patrons to a booming rock 'n' roll room when Vancouver needed one most.

The Rainier Hotel was built in 1907 and replaced an earlier hotel called the Balmoral (not to be confused with the Hastings Street Balmoral). By 1913, the Rainier housed not only the hotel but also a taxi dispatcher, café, barbershop, and billiard room. The ground floor space close to the alley was part of the Ranier Hotel throughout the 1930s and was, until the mid-1960s, the Lumberman's Social Club—a private club that stayed there until 1971, when a nightclub called Medicine Man Charlie's took over. In subsequent years, the nightclub went by many names, including Paddy's Cabaret, Dimples Disco, and Bronco's. As a club called In Concert, it became a live music room that hosted such acts as the Powder Blues, Shari Ulrich, David Raven and the Escorts, Snakefinger, and Woody Shaw.

In Concert was short-lived, however, and by the mid-1980s, the bar was rechristened once again as Minto's Pub, a down-and-outers bar full of day drinkers who gathered around its circular bar guzzling cheap beer. A dim and dreary place, it could have easily been mistaken for a Hastings Street beer parlour from decades earlier.

Sandy Kolbeins, a young nightclub entrepreneur with connections in Seattle, took over the club in 1998 and renamed it the Brickyard. He soundproofed the turn-of-the-century room and began

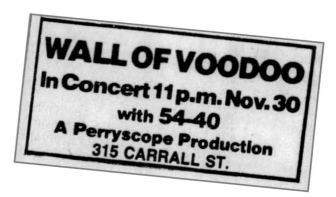

Wall of Voodoo at In Concert, November 30, 1981.
With an early performance by 54-40 as the opening act.
Credit: Vancouver Sun *Archives*

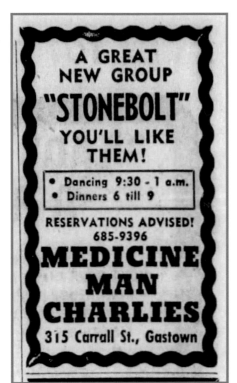

Years before it was the Brickyard, from 1971 to 1973 the space at 315 Carrall Street was a club called Medicine Man Charlie's. *Credit:* Vancouver Sun *Archives*

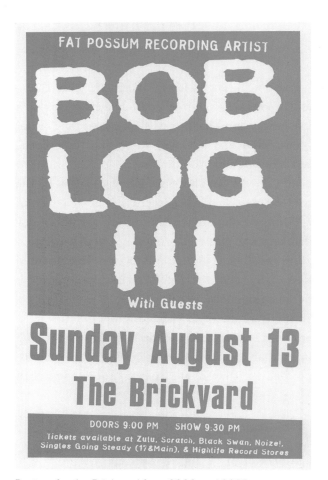

Posters for the Brickyard from 2000 and 2003. *Credit: SFU Special Collections*

booking rock bands. In the wake of both the Town Pump and the Hungry Eye closing, not to mention the Commodore Ballroom still being temporarily shuttered, Kolbeins's new space brought live rock 'n' roll back to Gastown. Although the club hosted some sold-out shows by various punk and rock bands, from Crystal Pistol to Seattle's Murder City Devils, it eventually closed in 2003.

For a short time afterward, the space became the Limerick Junction, an Irish pub that hosted some memorable shows by the likes of touring Celtic rock and folk punk bands like the Town Pants, the Mahones, and the McGillicuddys, as well as local rock 'n' roll acts like Marq DeSouza and Daggermouth, until it closed in 2007.

The Brickyard perhaps never attained the same status as other Gastown live music clubs like the Town Pump, the Savoy, or even the Hungry Eye. Since then, new clubs in the area, like Guilt & Co., have begun to showcase jazz, funk, hip hop, and singer-songwriters, but there is no real loud and proud rock 'n' roll bar in Gastown like the Brickyard, and its closure in 2004 seemed to mark the end of an era for live rock bands playing original music in the neighbourhood. The club was gutted, subdivided, and renovated. Those who now sit in the two side-by-side café/coffee shops that occupy the space have a much quieter experience than when the room flowed freely with loud bands and spilled beer.

CHAPTER TEN

THE END OF THE GOLDEN AGE

The dance floor at Graceland.
Credit: Robert Shea

LUV-A-FAIR

YOU ARE ENTERING
ANOTHER DIMENSION...
...A DIMENSION OF
POWERFUL SOUND
AND AMBIENT
VISUALS...YOU
ARE ENTERING
THE DANCE
VIDEO ZONE

Luvafair

1275 SEYMOUR NON MEMBERS ONLY 685-3288

Advertisement in *Discorder*, 1985. *Credit: Discorder magazine*

The Cave might be the venue most missed by one generation of Vancouverites, but for another generation, it's Luv-a-Fair. The club found its place in the city's nightlife at just the right time. It arrived in the late 1970s, when the culture at large was beginning to veer back toward conservatism after the disruption of the '60s. It was the dawning of the age of Ronald Reagan, Margaret Thatcher, and, locally, the Social Credit provincial government. None of this buttoned-down outlook was to be found at Luv-a-Fair, though, and that's why patrons loved it. But this kind of commentary frames what took place at Luv-a-Fair as high-minded and political—it was not. Like all the best clubs throughout the history of Vancouver, it is simply remembered as a great party.

The building at 1275 Seymour Street had been Gary Taylor's King of Clubs in the mid-1960s, then the Purple Steer, and later, the Garage. Local nightclub operators the Kerasiotis brothers bought the Garage and reopened it as Luv-a-Fair in 1976.[60]

At first, Luv-a-Fair attracted a gay crowd. In the 1970s, the gay nightspots along Davie Street had yet to come, and most of the gay clubs then—such as the Ambassador Hotel pub and the Dufferin Hotel pub—were to be found along Seymour Street, so Luv-a-Fair fit right in.

"It was full of the most eccentric-looking people I'd ever seen before in one place," say Vernard Goud, who first sneaked into Luv-a-Fair as a seventeen-year-old in the early 1980s. "There were punks and drag queens, goths and prostitutes, all dressed up—big hairdos! It was like a Fellini movie, it was so over the top! You couldn't tell if somebody was a guy or a girl—it was wild."

Most of the other nightclubs in Vancouver at the time played Top 40 hits. Luv-a-Fair distinguished itself by playing disco. As the 1970s wore on, though, disco's mainstream popularity had begun to wear out its welcome, and the backlash of the Disco Sucks

Invitation to the grand opening of Luv-a-Fair, June 14, 1976. *Credit:* Vancouver Sun *Archives*

movement had begun—even at Luv-a-Fair. Many regular patrons were tiring of the well-worn disco songs that were two or three years old and wanted something different.

One night in fall 1979, a DJ named Susan Walford was at the club on what would be her last evening working there. She had been one of the DJs who played disco and rarely strayed from her usual playlists. Weary patrons took their complaints to the bar and sometimes to the DJ booth itself, but Walford refused to relent.

"This decision became almost life-threatening," Walford recalls. "Staff members were concerned for my safety and several times came up to the booth and suggested that perhaps if I played one alternative song, the crowd would be appeased."

The crowd even organized a sit-in at the club and refused to dance. It started along one side of the dance floor and worked its way across to the other. Only a few stubborn souls continued to dance to Gloria Gaynor. As Walford remembers it, the protesters gave up and left for other clubs.

[60] Jack Wasserman, *Vancouver Sun*, May 29, 1976, 43.

Although it was known primarily as a dance club, Luv-a-Fair did host a number of legendary live performances by such artists as Nina Hagen, I, Braineater, Divine, Sonic Youth, Nine Inch Nails, and in a memorable 1982 gig, Killing Joke. *Photo: Bev Davies*

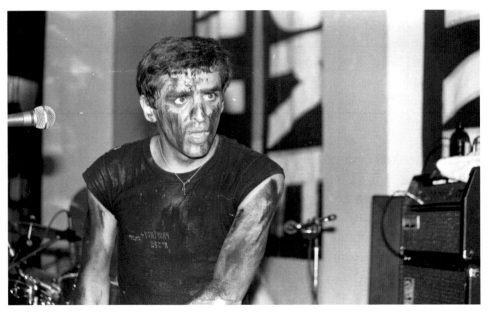

Jaz Coleman of Killing Joke. *Photo: Bev Davies*

But management could see that things were changing. Walford suggests the club had planned to alter its format anyway, but the sit-in at Luv-a-Fair was recognized as a cultural shift not only at that club but also as part of larger trend across the nightclubs in Vancouver. Practically overnight, the DJs who played disco were dismissed, and the sounds of new wave came crashing through the door. This cleared the way in the late 1980s for industrial music bands like Skinny Puppy and Front 242.

Although an impressive array of live acts played Luv-a-Fair, including Killing Joke, Nina Hagen, Wall of Voodoo, Divine, and Nine Inch Nails (who performed here to about 100 people in 1989), the focus of Luv-a-Fair was less about the stage and more about the dance floor.

"There were TVs with video cameras that pointed to the dance floor, or occasionally played videos," Goud recalls. "Add to that the cocktail waiter in roller skates and the black lights—it was a great scene in there."

Luv-a-Fair was the first club in Vancouver to celebrate the role of the DJ. The DJ booth that started out on the floor was soon raised to a dark corner over the stage. Underneath it, a red digital readout displayed the upcoming track. This was a tactic to discourage dancers from pestering the DJ with requests.

"The best DJ in Vancouver was a lady named Kelly Mossley," says David Hawkes, who himself became one of the city's most prominent DJs during his time at Luv-a-Fair. "She taught me how to DJ in an alternative club, and she was one person who was really ahead of the curve more than anybody else in town."

Luv-a-Fair DJs deemed anything playing on the radio to be too mainstream, though everyone on the dance floor might not have noticed the finer details. Some just danced, drank, and pursued other interests. There might not have been any rock 'n' roll, per se, at Luv-a-Fair, but there was a lot of sex and drugs. The men's washroom was notorious for drugs and laissez-faire promiscuity, and since the

Poster for Violent Femmes at Luv-a-Fair, 1985.
Credit: Neptoon Records Archives

whole club was painted black, there were enough dark corners—even with the strobe lights—to disappear into.

Celebrities from Johnny Depp and Ray Liotta to U2 and the Cure were known to drop in at Luv-a-Fair, adding an air of intrigue and glamour to the club.

"The whole point of the club felt like it was an escape from the normal world," says Goud, who occasionally organizes Luv-a-Fair reunion parties at other nightspots. Hawkes agrees: "Luv-a-Fair was built on the open-mindedness of most of the clientele.

MIX

End of the Luv-a-Fair

The demise of the legendary nightclub closes the door on a unique offbeat spirit — and three decades of clandestine sex, drugs and alternative music

KERRY GOLD

Wen the Luv-a-Fair closed its doors for the last time last Saturday, it was the last gasp for generations of giddy club kids who craved something edgy along-

"We would take our bags of quarters and loonies and go down there and have a great time," he recalls. "And for a time there, everything that meant anything to me was intersected at that place — and in that sense, it was definitely an important place for me."

On the outside, it remained a nondescript concrete block of a building, but on the inside, it was a sea of dressed-up kids working hard to affect a look of utter indifference, no matter how intimidated they might be feeling on the inside. Michael Barrick, a goth kid who lived in Nanaimo and would go to Vancouver in the late '80s just for the Luv-a-Fair, remembers the feeling.

Credit: Vancouver Sun Archives

Outside Luv-a-Fair, circa 1980s.
Photo: Gordon McCaw

Black lipstick and dressing like a bat never mattered. At Luv-a-Fair, the 'weirdos' were the suits, and even they weren't bothered by the regulars."

As with clubs from the golden age of the Cave and Isy's, the regulars from Luv-a-Fair eventually got older, started families, and moved on. The club saw its best years when it caught the wave of early alternative dance music and new wave, but by the start of the new millennium, it seemed less relevant. The club closed in 2003, and the building that had served five decades of Vancouver nightclub patrons was demolished. The space is now filled by a thirty-four-storey condo tower called Elan, but it doesn't quite possess the stylishness that word suggests compared to the unique and fondly remembered Luv-a-Fair that once stood there.

RICHARD'S ON RICHARDS

Somewhere about forty feet into the middle of the condo tower on the 1000 block of Richards Street, most likely in a space occupied today by a resident's living room, once sat the stage of what many of Vancouver's live music fans say was the city's greatest nightclub.

The buildings that made up Richard's on Richards were originally two garages for the Leverington Auto Dealership and Sports Car Club throughout the 1960s and '70s. In 1975, after renovations supported by government grants, the building became the David Y.H. Lui Theatre, named for the new owner, a dance impresario. Lui staged performances there for three years, bringing in soprano Dame Joan Sutherland, touring productions of the National Ballet of Canada

Richard's on Richards had previously been a playhouse theatre operated by David Y.H. Lui.
Credit: Vancouver Sun Archives

and the Royal Winnipeg Ballet, and a host of alternative theatre performances. In 1979, it was renamed Spratt's Ark Theatre and continued to present plays. When the theatre closed that same year, it reopened in December 1980 as an unlicensed all-ages rock 'n' roll club called the Laundromat.

In February of the next year, the Laundromat was ground zero for a pivotal sold-out, all-ages festival called Hardcore '81. D.O.A. headlined in support of their new album (which gave the two-night festival its name). Other featured performers were Black Flag and 7 Seconds from the United States, as well as local groups the Bludgeoned Pigs and Insex. The shows were the high-water mark for the local punk scene. In the months that followed, "hardcore" became a new buzzword in the North American punk underground.

The Laundromat's flame burned bright but briefly. The club lasted for less than a year, and it wasn't long before the hardcore acts and leather jackets were replaced by polo shirts and Sperry Topsiders.

Richard's on Richards was opened in September 1981 by brothers John and Ron Teti, with Loverboy's manager, Lou Blair; Bryan Adams's manager, Bruce Allen; and Roger Gibson and Harvey Izen, who once worked together at the Pink Pussycat.

The Teti family had lived in East Vancouver for decades. John Teti attended Vancouver Technical Secondary but left school to work at the Eburne Sawmills in Vancouver's Marpole neighbourhood. He says growing up in East Vancouver helped form his business sense.

"I know people say that the first cocktail bar [in town] was the Panorama Roof at the Hotel Vancouver, but I'm telling you the first ones were between Prior Street and Union in Strathcona," says Teti. "My family ran one right in their home—it might have well just been a bar! The beer parlours closed back

Grand opening of the Laundromat, December 1980.
Credit: Neptoon Records Archives

then between five p.m. and seven p.m., so everybody then went down to Union Street. They never had lots of people in them, maybe only a dozen at a time. But it seemed like every second house in that block was a bootlegger. West side customers in suits and ties would come down to them. They were well known."

Teti's grandfather had run Pini's, an Italian restaurant at 730 Main Street. John, certain he didn't want to remain in the sawmill business, took over the Pini's space with his brother, Ron, and renamed it Puccini's. The restaurant became so popular, they were able to buy the building in 1970 and turn the basement into a jazz lounge they named Hogan's Alley.

"We had Ray Brown, Art Pepper, the L.A. Four, and local guys like Henry Young and Bob Murphy," says Teti. "Great jazz musicians at that time were surprisingly cheap to book. If they made good money, they only made it in Europe." But it wasn't merely the affordable price that attracted Teti. He was a long-time jazz fan and saw shows in clubs around town—including the notorious 1961 appearance by Charles Mingus at the Jazz Cellar when Mingus threw out a football lineman in the audience who had asked for his money back.

The 1970s were good years at Puccini's and Hogan's Alley, so after the Cave closed in 1981, Teti and his business partners began looking for a location where they could open a new club in a modern setting but reminiscent of the Cave. They found the vacant Laundromat space on Richards, signed a lease, and then went to work refurbishing the venue into a nightclub.

"They were tearing out some of the old dark wood fixtures from the old courthouse building on Georgia to turn it into the Vancouver Art Gallery," Teti recalls. "So we took some sections out of that they were going to get rid of—including the judge's bench and witness box—and used pieces to install into the new club."

By Halloween 1981—just a month after opening—Teti and the others knew the club would be a success. "That was the first huge night there, and for years it never stopped after that," Teti says. "It was like a mini Studio 54—it was that era. People wanted to blow off steam in the eighties. They wanted to dance, and they loved the music. We had some great cover bands that we'd bring up from Baltimore or Denver."

Richard's on Richards arrived at a time when Vancouver was taking on a new identity—that of Hollywood North. Movies and TV shows were now regularly being filmed in town, and visiting celebrities looking to cut loose between shoots would often end up at Richard's. Numerous gossipy stories began to circulate. One night, John Candy got onstage to sing with the band. Another night, Howie Mandel had to rescue Tom Selleck from the rows of women wanting to meet him.

"It always had that energy and that buzz there," says Teti. "Alan Thicke used to say to his guests at the end of the show—that they produced here—'We're all going to Richard's on Richards and hang out at the shooter bar ...' You couldn't buy publicity like that."

The Laundromat's most famous concert was D.O.A.'s two-night Hardcore '81 in February of that year. Many consider it a benchmark show in the local punk rock scene.
Photo: Bev Davies

Hardcore '81 poster.
Credit: Neptoon Records Archives

Some loved it, others hated it. But there was no Vancouver club more widely popular in the 1980s than Richard's on Richards. *Credit: Howard Blank*

Richard's on Richards made the meat market at the Body Shop nightclub look like afternoon tea, as the city's rich and beautiful showed up in droves, but depending how they played their cards, they didn't always get in. Outside the club, there were early lineups, and double-parked Ferraris. Inside, Teti claims the club broke national records for the sale of bottles of Dom Pérignon. This was the era of *Miami Vice*–style pastel clothing and cocaine—seemingly mountains of it. Rumours circulated about just how bad that snowstorm was: an unnamed house soundman conveniently dealt grams right from his mixing desk, and a plumber had to come in once a month to clean all the flushed coke straws out of the club's pipes.

"We had those old dishwashers for the glasses in the club that didn't filter out the drinking straws, and they got clogged in the plumbing—and that's

A busy night inside Richard's on Richards, circa 1980s. *Credit: Howard Blank*

Richard's on Richards staff and management, including Roger Gibson, Lou Blair, Bruce Allen, John Teti, and others.
Credit: Howard Blank

what really caused it," clarifies Teti. "Now, were there nights the place was fuelled by people on booze and cocaine? Yeah, it was the eighties. There were a lot of people in that scene then."

For those in the rougher, less monied punk and hard rock scenes in Vancouver, Richard's on Richards was enemy territory back then. As nightclub goers lined up outside, it was not uncommon to hear heckles of disdain from passersby.

Stan Fiddis was a doorman at the club in the early 1980s. He'd grown up in the tough Clark Park area of East Vancouver, where he'd learned to handle himself in neighbourhood dust-ups. "I used to have a thing called the thirty-second read," he says.

"I could see how people would carry themselves as they walked up, and by the time they got to the front door you could tell if they were going to be a problem customer, or cause trouble. You get a master's degree in psychology from working as a doorman at a nightclub—especially one like Richard's on Richards."

Fiddis says he can't count the number of patrons at the club that he had to put into a sleeper hold. He tossed out his fair share of customers—everyone from professional athletes to Johnny Depp. Most patrons were well behaved, and Fiddis had to learn how to deal with the kind of people he'd never met in East Vancouver. The lineups were long enough at

Richard's on Richards that situations arose where the club doormen were handed cash to speed up the admission process. "I made a lot of money taking graft at the door," admits Fiddis. "I don't think Roger liked it, and I'm not sure how John felt. But my thinking was, would you rather have somebody who wants to give me twenty dollars to get in, and who's going to spend a lot more once inside, or somebody who's waiting in line for a couple of hours griping about paying a cover. If he was giving me twenty, he was giving the waitresses more. I didn't think we were stealing from the club, because we'd always make people pay cover, we just put them in the front door."

Fiddis recalls being scared dealing with a customer at Richard's on Richards only once. And it was with an unlikely patron—Tina Turner.

"Tina was in town after a show," Fiddis says. "Her people had called to let us know she wanted to come by. We were keeping an eye out for a limo when all of a sudden three cabs pull up, and it's her and her band! We got her a private table, and they were all having a good time. About an hour later, she decided to leave alone early and asked if I could get her a cab, and if she could go out the back door. I made the arrangements and took her down the back stairs. She was wearing these platform high heels and she slipped and lost her footing on the slippery steps, but I had her by the arm and grabbed her before she fell. She didn't weigh anything—she was so tiny. I thought to myself, *Oh my God, if she'd fallen and hurt herself*—I'd heard her legs were insured for a million dollars each—I'd be blamed for it all and I'd be finished. She said, 'Wow, that was exciting!' She was just fine and laughed it off. She got in her cab and took off."

By the 1990s, Richard's on Richards (or Dick's on Dicks, as it had come to be known), came to mean two things to two different crowds in the city. When the party died down and the yuppies disappeared, the nightclub shifted audiences and the club entered its next chapter, thanks in part to the almost simultane-

ous closures of the Commodore Ballroom, the Town Pump, and the Starfish Room, which all shuttered either temporarily or for good within a year or two.

When the Commodore shut down indefinitely in 1996 (for three years, in the end), and when the Town Pump switched from live music to DJs a year later, Richard's on Richards suddenly found itself to be the premier room in town for live music. At that point, the club endeared itself to a whole new generation of music fans in Vancouver who knew nothing about the club's yuppie years.

Perhaps Richard's never inspired Vancouverites in the same way the Town Pump or even the Starfish Room did. The stigma of the club's yuppie years weighed a little too heavily on the minds of some discerning music fans who found themselves in a venue they wouldn't have dreamed of going to in the 1980s. But those years of champagne-and-cocaine-fuelled excess and superficiality seemed so far away and irrelevant during the '90s and into the new century, given the club hosted such a long list of excellent live shows.

Among the many performers to take the stage at Richard's were Franz Ferdinand, Katy Perry, the Polyphonic Spree, the Jon Spencer Blues Explosion, Lee "Scratch" Perry, Neko Case, Queens of the Stone Age, Nels Cline, Mudhoney, Saint Etienne, Hugh Cornwell, Luther Allison, Gojira, Son Volt, Conor Oberst, and Kate Nash. Killing Joke played a legendary show at the club on Remembrance Day 2003—the band's first Vancouver date in twenty years—where singer Jaz Coleman treated fans after the show to a lecture on conspiracy theories. Then there was the night that Courtney Love notoriously crashed an Evan Dando show by flashing her breasts and demanding to sing a song.

In addition to all the rock bands, hip-hop artists also found a home at the club. "I saw most of the best hip-hop concerts I've ever seen there," says local DJ Martin Ramond. "From Digital Underground throwing popcorn and passing Hennessey around

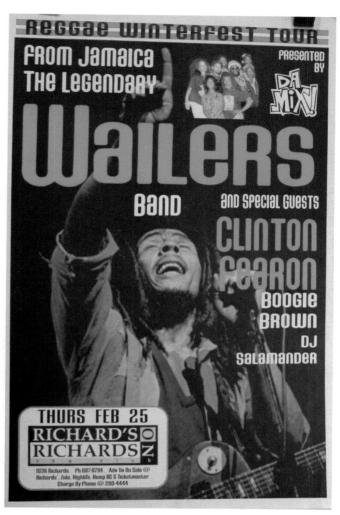

By the late 1990s, Richard's on Richards had dropped its dance club past and become a popular live music venue for a wide variety of touring and local bands.
Credit: Neptoon Records Archives; Killing Joke poster by Rob Edmonds/Evoke Int. Design

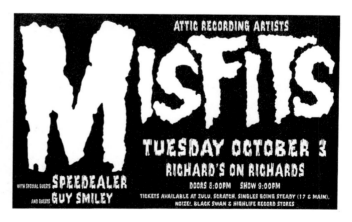

R.E.M. at Richard's on Richards in 2002. *Photo: Kevin Statham*

the crowd to 2 Live Crew and their overweight go-go dancers—hilarious and incredible. Jurassic 5 and the Beat Junkies—at the end of the show, everyone from both crews onstage beat-juggling and freestyling. It was the best hip-hop show this town has ever seen."

"People like Bruce Allen were saying 'tear it down,' but the thing was, the place wasn't for them anymore," says former Town Pump owner Bob Burrows. "They didn't understand. It was a whole new crowd."

With little to no maintenance done to Richard's on Richards—in a building that sat marooned in a sea of rapid downtown development—by the early 2000s, the owners seemed resigned to the fact the club's days were numbered. And when it closed in 2009, the club's glory days were long gone. But this raises the question: When were these glory days exactly? The hedonistic early 1980s, when the club was filled with upwardly mobile pleasure seekers? The musically fertile late '90s and early 2000s, when week after week a stunning assortment of new and exciting performers took the stage? Perhaps the former era established its reputation and the latter era will be its legacy. One thing is certain: during its lifetime, Richard's on Richards served the nightclub needs of a broad spectrum of Vancouver's nocturnal population.

THE STARFISH ROOM

For a few short years around the turn of the new millennium, the Starfish Room at 1055 Homer Street unexpectedly found itself one of the top live music clubs in Vancouver. It didn't last long, but in those short years the club played host to an impressive array of some of the best rock bands of the period, at a time when alternative and post-punk music flourished—if not financially, then at least creatively.

The Starfish Room began as a spot called the Quadra Club, founded in 1923 as a private club for members who paid cheap annual dues. It was a fraternal society in the days when being a member of certain clubs was a way to meet new people and establish new business relationships. The club one belonged to could potentially raise one's status in the community.

The Quadra also provided members with a chance to drink—or at least to drink without the hassles of being interrupted by Vancouver police dry squad raids. With a private club designation, the Quadra was legally permitted to have a reasonable amount of alcohol on the premises to serve to members. Men and women could join the club, and they were not segregated here, unlike in some beer parlours, where there were separate entrances for "Gentlemen" and "Ladies and Escorts."

There was a large number of similar private clubs in Vancouver throughout the 1920s and '30s, such as the Arctic Club and Pacific Athletic Club. Many continued to exist long after liquor licensing rules changed. Vancouver's Railway Club and the now-defunct Marine Club both transitioned from private

The Quadra Club, like the Arctic Club at 724 Pender Street, was a private members' club that served liquor.
Credit: Tom Carter Archives

Tea-time at Reception in the New Quadra Club

THE spirit of comradeship that carried many of its members through the war permeates the Vancouver Quadra Club, which is now housed in one of the city's finest clubhouses. After the war a number of former members of the old Western Club and the University Club joined to form the Quadra Club, named after the Spanish admiral who turned over Spain's possessions in the west to Great Britain. The title is linked with some of the most romantic historic lore of this coast, and the new Quadra Club building, West Hastings street, is designed to carry out the Spanish tradition. There is an air of friendly hospitality about the place, which breathes of interesting personalities belonging to it.

On Saturday afternoon, when the members were formally "at home" in their new quarters, these pictures were taken in the picturesque dining room where tea was served.

LEFT to right: Mr. J. D. Forsyth, Miss Gertrude Beck, Mrs. Forsyth and Mr. and Mrs. P. W. Burbidge; at the back, Mrs. Cyril Tweedale, Rev. W. T. Keeling and Mr. Tweedale.
Below, left to right: Mrs. Frank Barnes, Mr. and Mrs. Bryan Williams, Mr. John Hulbert, Miss Phyllis Tweedale, Mrs. Hugo Ray and Miss Molly Williams.

The Starfish Room had its roots in the Quadra Club, which began in 1923. *Credit:* Vancouver Sun *Archives, January 14, 1930*

members clubs to cabarets. Aside from the occasional light entertainment, the private clubs tended not to feature much in the way of live performance. Theatres, dance halls, and supper clubs remained the venues for shows and big-name acts.

The Quadra Club was named for one of the participants in a curious incident in BC's colonial history. Spanish naval leader Captain Juan Francisco de la Bodega y Quadra crossed paths with Captain George Vancouver of the British navy at Nootka Sound in 1792 while the two were on separate expeditions mapping the British Columbia coast. By all accounts, it was a cordial meeting and the two sea captains respected one another. For the Quadra Club, this encounter came to symbolize friendship between strangers.

In the 1940s, Gordon Towne began his decades-long management of the Quadra Club. Towne organized the club's move in 1942 to a new building at 724 Seymour Street, where it stayed for the next thirty years. He is also credited with giving Vancouver its first piano bar, which featured the legendary local jazz pianist Chris Gage.

It was not always smooth sailing for Towne, though. In 1955, his name surfaced during hearings regarding corruption charges against Chief Constable Walter Mulligan of the Vancouver police. Witnesses claimed to have seen Towne delivering liquor to the chief constable's office at Christmastime in 1953. A seasonal gift of a bottle of good cheer is one thing, but witnesses testified that Towne had brought cases of alcohol to Mulligan's office, proudly announcing that they were "just for the boys." In that same hearing, Towne was also shown to have joined Chief Mulligan's in an effort to discredit reporter Ray Munro, who'd broken the whole story about the corruption problems with the VPD in the *Province* newspaper. Towne claimed that Munro had tried to extort $3,000 from him in exchange for not running Towne's part in the story.

Towne also had a falling out with Ross Filippone of the Penthouse Nightclub when the latter brought African American entertainers the Mills Brothers to the Quadra Club for a night out. Towne seated the group in a private area and later told Filippone that he thought the Quadra Club's regular clientele wouldn't want to eat in the same room as black people. Shocked and insulted, Filippone told him he was not welcome to ever come to the Penthouse again and never forgave him for it.

After a fire at the Seymour Street location, the club moved to its final home at 1055 Homer Street in 1973. Towne retired a year later and died in 1985.

The Quadra hobbled along as a lounge for a few years, until March 1978, when former nightclub comedian Barry Berenbaum—who had performed at Isy's and other clubs around town under the name Barry Dale—re-launched it as the Quadra Theatre Restaurant. Berenbaum had high hopes for the club. In the opening night review of the new establishment, the *Province* wrote that Berenbaum "is convinced that because traditional supper club entertainment has pretty well disappeared in the last decade, it's about time it made a comeback."[61] But aside from a few musical theatre presentations during its first year, the Quadra Theatre Restaurant never really got off the ground. Berenbaum was probably too preoccupied with some of the other events in his life.

In May 1979, Berenbaum was arrested in California by the FBI for bank fraud involving his girlfriend, Margaret Baxter, a teller at a Bank of Nova Scotia branch in Vancouver. The scheme, which involved siphoning $2.8 million from a Calgary oil company's account to a Los Angeles bank, failed when Berenbaum was caught enlisting another man who turned out to be an undercover FBI agent. When Baxter began to have second thoughts, Berenbaum allegedly threatened to have her murdered or kidnap

Man in Bank Theft Plot Gets 3 Years

BY ROBERT RAWITCH
Times Staff Writer

A Canadian salesman, who unsuccessfuly attempted a fraudulent $2.8 million bank wire transfer after reading about a similar $10.2 million theft by computer whiz Stanley Mark Rifkin, was sentenced Monday to three years in prison.

Noting the increase in such attempted wire transfers since Rifkin's actions last year made worldwide headlines, U.S. Dist. Court Judge David W. Williams said he had an obligation in imposing sentence to attempt to deter such crimes.

"Such crimes if completed, and there is a fair chance of it, can bring losses in the millions," Williams told Barry Berenbaum, 49, of Vancouver, B.C.

Berenbaum pleaded guilty Aug. 22 to a conspiracy charge carrying a five-year maximum sentence in exchange for an agreement with the government that federal prosecutors would not recommend more than four years in custody.

Former nightclub-comedian-turned-theatre-impresario Barry Berenbaum took over the Quadra Club in 1978. His plans for the venue had barely gotten off the ground when he was arrested in Los Angeles by the FBI for being involved in a multi-million-dollar bank fraud.
Credit: Los Angeles Times *Archives*

her child. He was later sentenced to three years in a California prison.

The Quadra reopened in 1979 under the management of Suzan Krieger and Heather Farquahar, who ran it as the city's first female-owned lesbian bar. Informally renamed Lulu's, the club featured drag acts and the occasional punk rock show by the likes of D.O.A. and Rabid, and the debut of a new wave band then billed as Ernie Dick and the Pointed Sticks.

In May 1984, the space was reopened as Club Soda, which was run by an ownership group that included Bryan Adams's manager, Bruce Allen; Loverboy's manager, Lou Blair; booking agent Sam Feldman; and nightclub operator Roger Gibson.

Club Soda would become one of the best-known bars in the city, showcasing a variety of hard rock and glam metal bands when this style of music peaked in popularity. Club Soda's rise occurred at the same

[61] Jeani Read, "Supper Club Reopens with Smile, Prayer," *Vancouver Sun*, March 1, 1978, 15.

Chris Robinson of the Black Crowes at Club Soda.
Photo: Kevin Statham

time that Little Mountain Sound Studios in Mount Pleasant became a destination recording studio for a variety of hard rock bands, including Aerosmith, the Cult, and Mötley Crüe. Many of these groups would retreat to Club Soda after winding up recording sessions. Big-name appearances were unannounced, but stories abound of Bon Jovi getting up onstage and jamming, and of hair metal vocalist David Coverdale of Whitesnake having Club Soda staff block off a sizeable VIP section for his cronies.

Rum and Cokes and cocaine flowed freely at the Club Soda in those days—it was the 1980s, after all. The bar was filled with leather jackets, big hair, Drums Only T-shirts, and more cigarette smoke than

the fog machine onstage could ever compete with. By the end of the decade, Club Soda loosened up their booking policy to include punk bands like D.O.A. and Death Sentence. This subtle shift in programming was a harbinger of things to come.

In 1992, Club Soda switched formats and changed its name to the Big Easy. The inside of the club was adorned with swampy decorations and voodoo masks in an attempt to evoke the vibe of a New Orleans dance club. The new establishment was successful when it first opened, but business trailed off quickly. Tastes in music were changing.

"We'd been talking at the office one day that wouldn't it be great to own a bar and have that revenue," says Keith Buckingham, a talent buyer

Queens of the Stone Age
at the Starfish Room in 1998.
Photo: Sprout

for Timbre Concerts in the early 1990s. Owned and operated by Peter McCullcoch, Timbre had been a successful concert promoter in the city since the early 1980s, but promoters rarely owned venues themselves and were usually left to rent places to put on their shows, the cost of which having to be paid out of ticket sales whether the show did well or not.

"We stumbled across the Big Easy, which hadn't been doing well," says Buckingham. "Charlotte Smith, who worked at Timbre, put the idea to her father, Nick. He struck a deal and financed the idea, and we took it over. My friend Bob Whittaker, who managed Mudhoney in Seattle, suggested the name. He had a funny saying that was in the spirit of 'Kid, I'm going to make you a star,' but he said, 'Kid, I'm going to make you a starfish!'"

Despite the increased popularity of alternative music in rock nightclubs in the early 1990s, it wasn't an easy start at the club. The Starfish Room was in direct competition with the Town Pump, and bookers there began to insist that acts who played their club not play at the Starfish Room as well. "I get it, it was just business," says Buckingham. "But it made life at the Starfish Room a little difficult in the early days."

In an effort to get the room going, on Monday nights—usually considered a dead night—the Starfish Room hosted an event called Zoo Boogaloo, which featured local DJs like DJ Czech and DJ Spun-K.

"Those nights were a lifesaver," says Buckingham. "Since it became harder to book bands in the early running, those nights that would do five or six thousand at the bar, it was great to have—kept the place going."

In the late 1990s, Charlotte Smith moved to the UK, and Buckingham left to work at a venue in Los Angeles, and then eventually moved to Portland to be a concert promoter there until he retired. He now lives in Vancouver again.

"I remember some terrific shows at the Starfish—too many to count," says Buckingham. "Jesus Lizard, Girls against Boys, the Jon Spencer Blues Explosion. Guided by Voices were great—at the height of their powers and beer drinking. Singer Bob Pollard used to have a garbage can onstage near him for his empties—they were pretty wild times and great shows."

The Starfish Room ran until 2002, when the owner of the building passed away and the estate sold the property. The club, its parking lot, and other surrounding properties were demolished in 2003 to make way for a twenty-seven-storey condo tower. The new building shares the same 1055 Homer Street address as the old club but offers no hint as to the site's vivid past. These days, Homer Street is much quieter.

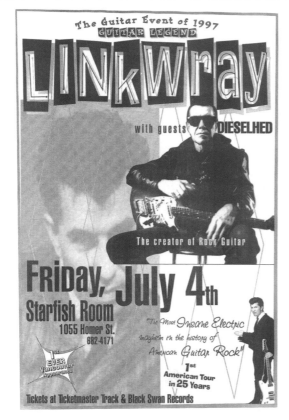

Posters for the Starfish Room.
Credit: Neptoon Records Archives

SATURNO / MARS / ATLANTIS / BOSS

In 1989, local restaurateur Danny Xuan announced the opening of a brand-new nightclub that would be a throwback to the supper clubs of yesteryear. He hired Italian designers to decorate the interior and a former executive chef from the Four Seasons Hotel to run the kitchen, and opened the Saturno Supper Club in 1990 in a large warehouse at 1320 Richards Street that was once used as a movie studio.

Saturno's decor employed all the gaudiness of 1980s style—it could have been a filming location for an episode of *Miami Vice*. The inside was adorned in plush silver and black, and among tables and lounges, rose a floral atrium that featured a live caiman—similar to an alligator—looking rather bored.

Xuan's plan was to offer fine dining and big-name entertainment in his 400-seat club. The steep fifty-dollar cover charge would limit the clientele to only the most affluent patrons—or those willing to spend money to be seen in their company.

The opening night and first few months seemed promising. Soon after, though, the club was only successful on weekends, and it wasn't long before the crowds petered out entirely. Xuan perhaps overestimated how many wealthy Vancouver nightclub goers would be interested in his kind of establishment when there was already a host of other more established places in busier areas of downtown. Perhaps the Saturno's failure was because of the location itself. In 1990, the downtown area south of Yaletown was much different than it is today. Back then, it was still full of car parts shops and machinist warehouses that served the nearby rail yards and industry along the north side of False Creek. The streets surrounding the nightclub had a dark and woebegone feel that didn't encourage foot traffic. Off the corner of Homer and Drake Streets, just a block away from the Saturno, was so-called Boystown—a long-standing pickup zone for young male sex workers that was still busy at night in those years.

The Saturno hosted a few special events, like the *Vancouver Magazine* Fashion Awards in 1991, but by the following year, the club had failed, and much of its contents were auctioned off in a foreclosure in May 1992. It's not known what happened to the caiman.

Other nightclub operators would not be deterred by this location, however. The venue was renamed Mars in 1993, by new investors who promised to spend $3 million to redevelop it. This dance club hosted local and touring DJs that put some of the expensive lights left behind from the Saturno to good use.

Atlantis nightclub, which began its life as the Saturno Supper Club. The club went through several name changes over the years. In the Yaletown South area that was once home to many nightclubs, it was the last of its kind. The neighbourhood is almost completely residential now. *Credit: Wayne Leidenfrost/Vancouver Sun Archives*

The club went through various name and ownership changes in the late 1990s and early 2000s—from Wett Bar to Atlantis to Boss—but aside from a few events during the Vancouver International Jazz Festival, the space wasn't used much for live music. The club instead remained a mainstay of DJs playing Top 40 pop, hip hop, contemporary R&B, and reggae. For a time, Atlantis had one of the city's few oxygen bars, where patrons could pay to inhale scented pure oxygen.

As the Yaletown neighbourhood gentrified and attracted more residents, the club provoked noise complaints. By 2004, the Atlantis nightclub had become such a problem—not only with noise but also with fights breaking out among intoxicated patrons at closing time—that the VPD eventually stationed officers outside the club shortly before closing. Police, however, were not on scene the night of August 24, 2008,

when Yau Aaron Chan, a twenty-five-year-old musician who had previously performed at Atlantis and had spent that evening at the club with friends, was stabbed and killed in an altercation with another man outside the front doors. The assailant fled the scene before police arrived. The murder remains unsolved.

In 2013, the entire 1300 block of Richards Street was rezoned, the club was demolished, and the area was redeveloped as the site of the two large condominium towers that stand there now. Some might suggest that Xuan was a bit premature in setting up a luxury club in Yaletown when he did and the city now has more millionaires to support a club like Saturno.

But that still may not be the case. In September 2018, Drai's Vancouver—an 8,000-square-foot club that included an outdoor patio and indoor pool, where patrons could drink $2,000 bottles of champagne—closed after just over a year.

GRACELAND

"I had the idea that I wanted to open a nightclub for a while," recalls Vince Alvaro, who by his late twenties during the late 1970s was a regular at a variety of Vancouver dance clubs, such as Luv-a-Fair, the Gandy Dancer, and Faces—one of Vancouver's earliest gay-owned and -operated bars. Situated in the ground floor of the Orillia Rooms building at 795 Seymour Street. Faces was an intimate space that quietly became a trend-setting venue for dance music in Vancouver, playing early underground disco and new wave.

In a completely different part of town, on Powell Street, was artist John Anderson's Pumps Gallery, which was part rent party, part dance-and-gallery space. "It was sort of like an Andy Warhol's Factory–type place, where there was some exhibit space and workshops," Alvaro recalls. "They also produced

this multimedia art TV show called *The Gina Show* there, and those places and those parties were a big inspiration for what I wanted to do."

During the late 1970s and early '80s, Alvaro had visited clubs in New York City where he witnessed the kind of scene—populated by people energized by art, music, and fashion—that could surely exist in Vancouver if there were only a club to call its own.

"I didn't think Luv-a-Fair was good enough or big enough, so I went looking around to see what was in that neighbourhood [Downtown South]."

He found a large empty warehouse at 1250 Richards Street that had previously been the home of the Mortifee Munshaw photo-processing lab. Alvaro was immediately taken by the building's industrial interior. Without any immediate residential neighbours to bother, it would make for the perfect nightclub space.

Alvaro signed a lease. The rent was cheap, but getting a liquor licence would be difficult. It was 1983, and the city had a near moratorium on issuing new licences. The first application was turned down, but friendly bureaucrats who were receptive to Alvaro's ideas for a different kind of club urged him to apply again, with more details about what he had in mind.

The British Columbia Social Credit Party was in power in at the time, and although the party was politically conservative and certainly not known for championing alternative culture, Alvaro found the support he needed from an unlikely source.

Graceland owner Vince Alvaro says Social Credit cabinet minister Grace McCarthy had a secret connection to the venue.
Credit: Vancouver Sun Archives

"A very good friend of mine, Calvin Mc-Carthy, was the son of Grace McCarthy," says Alvaro, referring to the prominent Social Credit cabinet minister. "She pulled a few strings, and low and behold, I got the licence. That's where—in part—the name of the club came from: Grace-land. I liked the idea of the name being campy, and we were really going to be the exact opposite of any kind of Elvis music, but at the same time, there was this double meaning that it was a tip of the hat to Grace McCarthy. Very few people knew that at the time, and I can only tell that story now because both Grace and Calvin have passed on. It was a secret for a long time."

Alvaro promptly set to work renovating the club. In an effort to open up the ceiling above the dance floor, the building's second floor was removed entirely. Meanwhile, a new city bylaw enacted in 1985 forced him to make seismic upgrades in order to meet earthquake code requirements. "All of it cost an extra $300,000 in upgrades—this would probably be worth $900,000 today," says Alvaro. "I didn't think it would cost that much to actually open the place, since I wanted to leave it much as it was—with that really industrial look that I loved. While I knew we had to put in the bars and more bathrooms, that upgrade really hit the budget."

To defray some costs, Alvaro held a party in the space on New Year's Eve 1984. "Terry McBride from Nettwerk Records supplied all these bands—Images in Vogue, Family Plot, and some others," say Alvaro. "We had about two thousand people in there that night. There was no heat and everybody was wearing their coats indoors, and it was an illegal event because the inspection hadn't happened. In some of the smaller rooms there had been these holes in the wall where conveyor belts ran through them, so we sold beer through the holes—you couldn't see the bartenders, but you paid through the hole. We figured if the police showed up, we'd be able to hide the bars behind those spaces. The police eventually did show up that night, but they didn't do anything. It was a pretty mild crowd and they let us go, but it helped later because I think word got out that at least people knew we had the space, and it was going to happen."

Alvaro explains, "The idea from the start was to create a club that felt very private. I wanted to keep it very alternative. We were going to do things different. There was little to no signage. The entrance would be in the lane, and we would do no advertising. It would be all word of mouth."

More than three years in the making, Graceland finally opened in October 1986. Alvaro had nearly run out of money, but he didn't have to wait long for his venture to succeed.

"I looked out the back door at eight thirty that night—we were going to open at nine—and I saw a lineup all the way down the lane," says Alvaro. "So we lifted up the garage door, people came up the ramp, and that was it! People loved it. We had two thousand people come through the door that night. Everybody

Projections on the walls and the pulsing beat of house music became the signature sound at Graceland.
Credit: Robert Shea

Graceland's dance floor. *Credit: Robert Shea*

had the same reaction, saying how Graceland was so different from the rest of Vancouver."

Part of Graceland's concept from the beginning was to incorporate artists and art, because Alvaro had been inspired by the New York City clubs decorated by local artists. He commissioned Vancouver artist David Ostrem to create a twenty-five-foot-long and ten-foot-high painting of a landscape on Mars, dotted with small shops. "It was beautiful, and the only really colourful thing that illuminated an otherwise grey room, so you immediately noticed it when you walked in," says Alvaro.

Graceland was always meant to be dark inside, but proper lighting was required to display paintings in such a space. Rather than install banks of lights, Alvaro decided to showcase a number of paintings that had been photographed as slides by projecting them floor to ceiling on the walls. "One week it was Attila Richard Lukacs, the next it was somebody else, and it was constantly changing, so when people came in, they never knew what to expect."

There was also the Lisa Marie gallery, a smaller side room near the entrance where Canadian artists such as Lincoln Clarkes, Paul Wong, Oraf Orafsson, and many others had showings, and with three or four thousand people a week coming through the club, many of the artists enjoyed more exposure at Graceland than they might have in more formal galleries. "It really became popular on its own, and some of the artists started selling their stuff out of there," says Alvaro. The gallery also doubled as a chill-out space where club goers could take a break from the dance floor to catch their breath and talk. But this wasn't the only way Graceland took bolder steps than some art galleries of the period.

"Paul Wong had this video installation exhibit called *Confused*," explains Alvaro. "There was nothing risqué about it—it was just different people interviewed about their sexual encounters in a time before AIDS. It garnered a lot of publicity and controversy. The Vancouver Art Gallery was going to show it but cancelled it at the last minute because they felt it was going to offend the usual gallery audience. I said to Paul, 'Why don't you show it down at the club?' and that's what we did. It was great. The funny thing is, not only has it been shown in the Vancouver Art Gallery since, but now the gallery *owns* it!"

Music at Graceland was primarily provided by DJs, but the club began to work with local concert promoters to book live events as well. In the late 1980s and through the '90s, performers included Jello Biafra, the Red Hot Chili Peppers, Fishbone, D.O.A., Nomeansno, Soundgarden, and the Butthole Surfers. The club also booked appearances by emerging performance artists like John Sex and drag queen acts like Lady Bunny. "You wouldn't normally see those acts in Vancouver," says Alvaro. "Back then, you'd have to go see them in New York or in Europe."

He emphasizes, "It really did become an arts community–oriented club. And in those days, it was very underground. As soon as we saw something advertised in the paper, or heard it on the radio, we'd trash it or we'd want to move on to the new, next thing."

That underground philosophy was also expressed in the DJ music the club was presenting—enter Robert Shea.

Shea DJed once a week at Graceland, playing dance music, mostly from the post-disco era—everything from new wave to early hip hop. He'd been collecting vinyl records of what was then a new genre of music called house, which featured a funky, driving beat like disco but with an industrial edge and often more minimalist, without vocals. Shea started inserting the odd house track into his regular playlists, and when he had accumulated enough records to fill an entire crate, he realized he'd be able to play house for a whole night. Shea and partner, Debbie Jones, became committed to the new music and began to play it regularly at Graceland—though the regular customers may not have been ready for it at first.

"In the beginning at Graceland, in 1986, it was very much a fashion crowd," recalls Shea. "It was

The DJ booth at Graceland could be seen inside a pyramid high up on one wall of the room, while images were projected around it. *Credit: Robert Shea*

Robert Shea heading into the DJ booth at Graceland. *Credit: Robert Shea*

Although Graceland was best known for being a DJ venue, it did host a number of live shows over the years, including the Cramps in 1994 (above) and the Butthole Surfers in 1987. *Photo: Kevin Statham*

trendy and a place to be seen, and the music was arguably a little bit in the background. As Debbie and I would get into things, we saw people react to what we were playing. The fashion crowd never left, but new people came in, really interested in the new music. In fact, there was a period that the people who were coming in were more into the music than they were [there] for the drinks."

Patrons were starting to ask about the music, so Shea began to compile song lists and put them together with calendar listings into a rudimentary magazine that, at first, was little more than a double-sided flyer. But before long, the flyer expanded to include columns written by Graceland bartenders and doormen—and in 1988, *Discotext Magazine* was born. The magazine provided exposure for local DJs as well as the club.

Now that we live in the era of social media, it can be difficult to fully grasp the significant role that music zines played in the 1980s club scene. Today, the same information would be distributed much more easily and widely online. *Discotext* was as an extension of the word-of-mouth principle and watered the roots of what was a locally grown scene. Shea and Jones even began making day trips down to Seattle to drop off copies of *Discotext* and spread the word about Graceland. As a result, the club drew a wave of regular American visitors. Some of the younger American club goers might have simply been drawn to Graceland because the legal drinking age in BC was nineteen, not twenty-one, was the legal drinking age in BC, and the cheaper Canadian dollar didn't hurt either, but whatever the reason, American house music fans were now visiting Graceland.

In the beginning, Graceland's DJs travelled regularly to New York City or London to pick up new records, but house music labels worldwide soon found out about the club through the magazine and began shipping promotional copies of records there. What had previously been a nightclub inspired by tastemakers in New York and Europe suddenly became a club with an international profile of its own.

As with any genre of underground music, the first wave of house music was over not long after it began. By the early 1990s, changes in the audience were evident. University students were now heading to Graceland as the beginning of rave culture spread through bars and nightclubs around town. By the end of the decade, other clubs rebranded, dropping live music, ripping out their stages, and turning to DJs to provide the entertainment. But success was not guaranteed. Although many of the clubs were busy, bar sales, which kept venues afloat, were dwindling. More and more, patrons came to clubs to dance all night but not drink. Ecstasy was the new fuel for the dance floor. By 2002, clubs were closing. At the same time, electronic music was becoming more mainstream, and within a few years, dance music would establish itself on radio and television and at large corporate music festivals.

Those early years of house music are still considered a pioneering era, though, with Graceland acting as a founding church for electronica in Vancouver, and *Discotext* its bible. In 2014, Shea compiled all thirty-one issues of *Discotext* and published them as an anthology.

As for Graceland, it closed in 1998 and reopened under the name Palladium. The new operators were the Kerasiotis brothers, experienced owners and operators of various bars and clubs around Vancouver.

Though not as storied as Graceland, Palladium did attain its own grim infamy when local gang leader Bindy Johal was shot and killed there on a busy night in the middle of the dance floor by an unknown assailant. In a scene that wasn't much different from the shooting at Club Zanzibar twenty-seven years earlier, nobody in the confusion got a good look at who did it.

Those who were involved with Graceland have fond memories of the club—especially during those early years. "It was a fabulous venue," says Shea. "A big place, with a great sound system. There's definitely a group of people in Vancouver who got their first taste of what it would be like to DJ, playing underground house and techno music, and who went on to DJ in other clubs. It all happened at Graceland."

Shea has his reservations about the current state of electronic dance music (more commonly referred to as EDM), now that the genre has its own stadium-filling superstars like deadmau5, Skrillex, and Tiësto, and what began as a small independent scene is now a huge multi-million-dollar industry.

"It's odd. When I listen to EDM today, a lot of it is the same as it was twenty-five years ago," says Shea. "It still has a lot of pulse, but so much of it feels formulaic by comparison. I think some of the music of that genre today could use the same shakeup and change that we found with music when we first were getting started with house and techno." As a veteran, Shea can't help but notice, too, how drastically the tools of the trade have changed. "Nobody DJing today necessarily plays vinyl—so many just have compressed MP3 audio files on hard drives and are mixing on their laptops. It's a totally different world!"

The 1200 block of Richards Street in downtown Vancouver is much quieter today. The booming, urgent bass that beckoned dancers and nightclub goers in the 1980s and '90s is an increasingly distant memory, as are all the clubs that were once there.

Curiously, the large condo development that occupied the space where Graceland once stood is named the Grace. This delights Vince Alvaro. "That a condo building is named after Graceland, which was secretly named after Grace McCarthy—and that's the only remaining physical legacy there!" he says. "She still has got something named after her. I'm sure she'd be happy."

THE MARINE CLUB

The sign above the front door might have been a bit of an exaggeration: "The World Famous Marine Club." Perhaps in some bygone era, the sailors who founded the club would venture abroad and sing its praises, spreading legends and lore about the venue in exotic ports around the world, but inside, this little social club on the second floor of a nondescript building on the 500 block of Homer Street was hardly anything to write home about. Nevertheless, there was something special about the Marine Club that made it a favourite nightspot among Vancouverites who preferred something a little more offbeat.

Entering the Marine Club was a bit like stepping into a Prohibition-era speakeasy. Patrons had to press a small discreet buzzer to be let in by an unseen doorman. This procedure was a hold-over from the days when the Marine Club (like the Railway Club a few blocks away before it) was a private club.

The Marine Club, which opened in 1956 and was demolished in 2013. *Credit: Glenn Baglo/Vancouver Sun Archives*

During World War II, that block of Homer Street was lined mostly with private homes, but in 1956, the Marine Club opened as a private social club for the merchant seamen who worked at the Vancouver waterfront a short stumbling distance down the slope of Homer.

By the mid-1980s, local punk rockers and art students had discovered the bar and the cheap drinks on offer there and adopted the club as an unconventional hangout of their own.

In a way, what *endeared* the Marine Club to its regulars had more to do with what it wasn't than what it was. For many, the kinds of crowds that flocked to popular Vancouver nightspots like the Roxy and BaBalu were to be avoided. The nightclubs along Granville Street had developed problems of overcrowding and fighting, and where there had once been a mix of ages and people, it was now suddenly dominated by suburban nineteen-year-olds getting drunk for the first time.

Meanwhile, the good ol' Marine Club remained charmingly adrift in another era. It was the kind of a place to find down-and-out dames and palookas, the kind of bar that Charles Bukowski might 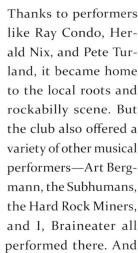 have written about. Thanks to performers like Ray Condo, Herald Nix, and Pete Turland, it became home to the local roots and rockabilly scene. But the club also offered a variety of other musical performers—Art Bergmann, the Subhumans, the Hard Rock Miners, and I, Braineater all performed there. And it hosted many book and magazine launches and comedy shows over the years. But it was Frank Lewis, the one-man house band on the organ, whose encyclopedic knowledge of B-rate, B-side pop songs (Andy Williams's "House of Bamboo" was a favourite), that made the Marine Club so special.

The music, the cheap beer and dirty martinis, the mix of young people and long-time patrons as old as the notorious jar of pickled eggs that sat on top of the bar—all made the Marine Club a place you just couldn't find anywhere else.

AN EVENING OF OLD SCHOOL
WITH THE
SUBHUMANS
TIX AT THE DOOR
SATURDAY SEPTEMBER 18TH
MARINE CLUB
573 HOMER INFO 683 1720

Poster for the Subhumans at the Marine Club.
Credit: Neptoon Records Archives

When Lewis passed away, some of the old guard started showing up less and less. The younger crowd who used to consider the Marine Club to be their local watering hole began to move farther east in hopes of cheaper rent, and the bar just seemed to get emptier every night.

Every sailor deserves a good send-off, but when the Marine Club finally closed in 2007, there were no grand farewells. It simply shut down, with bankruptcy notices taped to the front door. Perhaps by that point Vancouverites had simply gotten used to so many of the city's small clubs, live music rooms, and lesser-known offbeat watering holes disappearing, arguably as a result of Vancouver's rapid growth over the previous decade.

The Marine Club building remained vacant for a few years until it was demolished in 2013. For now, a gravel parking lot stands in its place. The land is owned by BC Hydro, which owns a number of lots in the area. This makes the Marine Club somewhat of an exception when it comes to downtown Vancouver's lost venues: it wasn't replaced by a condo tower.

Buried beneath Homer Street, where the Marine Club once stood, are a bunch of electrical cables that feed nearby substations. This renders the site unsuitable for significant development. The local rockabilly crowd no longer parks their vintage cars out front. Instead, the spots are taken by upwardly mobile modern folk who stop to recharge their electric cars at the stations curbside. They are as good a symbol as any to mark the end of an era.

Vancouverites might not regard the death of the humble Marine Club as a major turning point in the city's cultural history, but it is perhaps symbolic of the drastic twenty-first-century changes that have seen higher property values and significant rental increases push working- and middle-class people out of the city. As one of the oldest clubs to close during this period, the Marine Club weathered a variety of cultural shifts in the city as best it could. So, too, did the bar absorb the shock of demographic shifts. Everyone from hardscrabble sailors to hardcore punks slaked their thirst there, but in the end, these shifts were too much for the Marine Club and it sank.

The Marine Club was not part of a chain of bars and nightclubs. There was no attractive young woman to greet you at the door and take you to your table. There were no signature cocktails or tapas menus. There was no stylish decor or curated atmosphere. The entertainment most evenings was someone you might never have heard of. Yes, there were other unassuming dive bars in the city, especially in the East End, but the fall of the Marine Club, after the loss of so many other nightclubs, felt like the final blow. It was the last bar of its era and one more piece of old Vancouver that disappeared overnight while the city slept.

CHAPTER ELEVEN

LAST CALL

Not only have the nightclubs in Vancouver changed over the years but also the night itself. In the early 1970s, the city swapped the old incandescent street lamps (left) for new mercury vapour ones (right) that had a different tone and colour. Briefly, in 1974, the difference between the two could be seen, like at the Fir Street off-ramp from the Granville Bridge. *Credit: Angus McIntyre*

LAST CALL

Granville Street, 900 block.
Credit: Milos Tosic

Perhaps the biggest change to the Vancouver night-club landscape in the past twenty years or so was the plan that was devised in the late 1990s to create the entertainment district along Granville Street downtown. The only problem was that, by the time it was established, few considered it to be very entertaining.

The idea had been thought up with good enough intentions—other cities had well-known zones or streets with an array of venues and restaurants that at their best attracted both locals and tourists alike. For years, many in Vancouver had thought the city deserved an area where new, modern nightclubs fit in with established venues—and Granville Street, with its pre-existing mixed history as a nighttime hangout spot, became the obvious choice.

But the sheer preponderance of bars pushed into one area created a situation for which the city was not adequately prepared. Although long-time venues like the Orpheum, the Vogue, and the Commodore attracted people of varying ages who wanted to attend live concerts, the new dance clubs seemed to draw only patrons in their early twenties solely interested in getting drunk and picking up. Almost as soon as the district was realized, the police were beset with problems of public intoxication and fighting. The atmosphere evoked the chaos of a fraternity party, but it wasn't just sloppy young clubbers who had become a concern.

In the last couple of decades, the issue that has become the biggest problem in Vancouver nightclubs is the security and safety within the clubs themselves. Gangsters had been hanging out in nightclubs for many decades—and not just Vancouver—but in more recent years, both clubs and police had failed to adapt to dealing with a new breed of troublemaking patrons that emerged.

By the early 2000s, the kind of gangsters who frequented the clubs had changed. The days of the old rounders who hung around Isy's and the Penthouse were long gone. Even the Hells Angels criminal bikers, who had become a presence around Vancouver nightclubs in the 1980s and '90s, weren't the primary problem anymore.

"Twenty years ago, the way police had been dealing with nightclubs wasn't really sufficient," says retired Vancouver police sergeant Curtis Robinson. "Back then, the situation for police was simply to patrol the nightclub areas, looking for overcrowding or overserving. We'd write tickets for jaywalkers and people urinating in alleyways and on the street, but at the same time, a new generation of gang members were causing escalating problems that nobody had a grip on."

The rise in the 1990s of local notorious South Asian gangsters like the Dosanjh brothers and Bindy Johal, who was shot and killed on the dance floor of the Palladium nightclub in 1998, ceded way to a new crop of very showy, buff, heavily tattooed young men who flashed thousands of dollars in jewellery and drove expensive cars. "All of it translated into dangerous situations, having more and more of these people around and endangering the public when they went to clubs, especially when rivals met one another," says Robinson.

He says a turning point was the shooting at Loft Six at 6 Powell Street in Gastown in 2003, which left three people dead and five injured after a fight broke out among gang members. Less than a year later, across the street at the Purple Onion, in an attempt to break up a fight between members of rival gangs, twenty-three-year-old Rachel Davis was shot and killed.

That was when the relationship between the nightclubs and the police changed, and instead of blaming each other for mishandling the problem of gang violence in bars, they started to work together to find a solution. The result was BarWatch—an anti-gang program that works to not only ban patrons involved with violent crime from nightclubs but also prevent them from being admitted in the first place by scanning ID at the door. The plan took months of consultation among nightclub operators, police, and legal counsel to hone the new program to give nightclubs more control over who could get into their establishments. "We could have bars themselves stay out of the confrontation business," Robinson explains. "Police were much better suited for the job, and the message to the gang members was that we were going on much more of the offensive in dealing with them. If you'd been involved in a shooting, or been involved in violent crime, or were a gang associate, it was easy to become banned for life."

The new aggressive policy slowly resulted in gang members avoiding the Granville strip, and eventually much of Vancouver, which mostly pushed them out to the suburbs. Robinson says once BarWatch was fully implemented, the program showed tangible results, protecting the safety and security of patrons in Vancouver nightclubs by keeping out violent criminal elements. More importantly, the clubs and Vancouver police began to have a different, more cooperative relationship, and it's something both sides wish to continue.

The atmosphere on Granville Street after dark is now noticeably far less volatile than it was ten years ago, but the tenor of the nightlife there is changing further as more pubs have opened in place of clubs. In 2019, the 15,000-square-foot Caprice dance club was transformed into a "barcade" called the Colony Entertainment District —a two-floor pub packed with old-school arcade games, pinball machines, ping-pong tables, and a full bocce field. Other Vancouver neighbourhoods like Gastown and Commercial Drive also now have more distinctive nightlife options, with new pubs and restaurants, and many of these businesses are thriving as an appealing alternative for customers who still prefer to stay away from the crowds on Granville Street.

But it is the city's live music venues that many still see as the missing link, which leads some to say that the best years of Vancouver's live music scene are behind it. "Vancouver nightclubs used to be alive," recalls singer B.J. Cook of her time in local clubs during the 1960s. "Now, Vancouver is the beautiful white girl at the party, with no rhythm, who unfortunately claps on the one and three. What was once a music capital is now a wasteland."

Each generation has a tendency to believe that the entertainment of their era—especially of their youth—was the greatest of all time, and both those who came before and after surely missed out. The older generations tend believe that the best years for music and nightclubs in this city are over, but is that true?

In Vancouver, the live music venues certainly do continue to open and close. One recent trend is for clubs to appear in repurposed movie theatres. A number of Granville Street movie theatres such as the Vogue and the Plaza have become nightclubs and live music venues, but it's happened elsewhere in the city, too. The Rickshaw Theatre at 254 East Hastings Street, which reopened in the old Shaw Theatre in 2009, and the Imperial at 319 Main Street (formerly the Golden Theatre) are both now popular live music venues. Even the Fox Cinema at 2321 Main Street, which was a porn theatre for decades, was gutted and resurrected as the Fox Cabaret, hosting events, live music, and DJs. The Rio Theatre at 1660 East Broadway continues to be a home to both film and live events, much like the imagined future for the Hollywood Theatre in Kitsilano, which closed in 2013. David Hawkes, whose experience in local nightclubs goes back to the old days at Luv-a-Fair, and Sean Mawhinney, who was involved in managing the Starfish Room and is now the building manager of the Commodore Ballroom, will lead a team that plans to reopen the Hollywood as a refurbished cinema and live performance space in late 2019. If only the Ridge Theatre at 3131 Arbutus Street had been so lucky; instead, it was razed to make way for condos. The neon sign that once crowned the theatre is now on the roof of that building and seems to some more of a tombstone to mark what once was, rather than a celebration of the past.

Most interestingly, there are new small, independent venues and clubs like the Clubhouse and the Red Gate operating more underground, as well as after-hours spaces that continue to fly under the radar. But despite the new venues that have appeared, the question remains: Is the golden age of Vancouver nightclubs behind us?

Many believe that the era that was set into motion 100 years ago with the rise of the jazz clubs in the 1920s to the '40s, which developed into the supper clubs of the 1950s and then the rock clubs of the late '60s, which begat the live music venues of the 1970s and '80s, and finally, shifted in the 1990s with the ascent of DJs and dance music is finished, thanks to the same thing that upended the music industry—the internet.

Music and entertainment have never been more available than they are now. Streaming and online digital services have completely changed the way people access music. Curious listeners who might have previously considered going to check out a band playing somewhere nearby now have all the they need to help them decide whether to go or not, as even the newest acts have endless photos, reviews, live clips, and audio samples available on websites and social media.

Many note that, thanks to dwindling record sales, most performers now rely on the revenue from concert touring for their income, but although the artists playing the arenas and large theatres do well, it's still a dog-eat-dog world at the local club level. More crucially, the stakes are different, as many in the music industry no longer see playing in local clubs as the main route to building up a following or garnering more attention.

"Bands used to start out by building popularity at the nightclub level," says Jonathan Simkin, co-founder of Vancouver independent record label 604 Records. "Local radio really was an effective magnet for that. There were so many Vancouver bands, like Matthew Good, Default, Nickelback,

Mother Mother, and Daniel Wesley, who came up in the club scene and had commercial radio stations get behind them and play their singles. But commercial radio has really changed. It's much more corporate and ratings geared. Streaming services like Spotify don't have a local option or focus, and the audiences don't really rally around a city in their listening habits like they used to."

Moreover, although entertainment and music have never been more accessible, the space they occupy in popular culture has changed, too. "I've talked about this with friends in the music business," says Bob Burrows, who booked acts at the Town Pump for years. "People are into something for ten minutes, and then onto something else. Live music doesn't seem to be as crucial as it once was."

Burrows regularly gets together for informal round table lunches with industry veterans and insiders to talk about current trends and swap old stories about if not the good old days, at least the days when it seemed easier to stay in business. The consensus in the group is that people don't go out and drink as much as they used to, and if they do, the competition for their patronage is greater, as many restaurants now fashion themselves as nightclubs.

"People don't go out in the middle of the week like they used to. You don't see that anymore," says John Teti, who co-founded Richard's on Richards. "Lots of places are closed on Mondays, and people go to restaurants even more now. The business overall is still viable, but it's cocooned a bit and gotten smaller for now."

Many agree that it was always a poor practice to rely on liquor sales alone to stay in business, and that today events have to be able to sell tickets in advance. So those central tenets of the business have remained unchanged for nightclub operators.

But for those who run the clubs in Vancouver, more tangible challenges than the global changes in the music business have affected their operations—the cost of living. The boom in Vancouver's real estate market, especially downtown, has made the land once occupied by bars and nightclubs far more valuable as condominiums, which forced the closure of several clubs. Where nightclubs remain, soaring rents drive club operators to function on narrower and narrower margins—even in prime locations like Granville Street. The rent for the vacant space at 1047 Granville Street that once housed the Windmill nightclub is listed at more than $13,000 a month—too high to ever be taken on by someone wanting to run a live music club. The space has remained empty for years. In fact, the buildings of many old nightclubs, like the Shanghai Junk, New Delhi, and Town Pump, still stand vacant, the magic left in them remaining untapped.

"We are faced with the same cost pressures as other small independent businesses in this city," says Mo Tarmohamed, who runs the Rickshaw Theatre. "In my case, my rent has increased by nearly one hundred percent since I took over, as has the property tax. Insurance has gone up over four hundred percent, as fewer and fewer companies are insuring music venues. Add to that the Canadian dollar is now a lot weaker than when I took over. This is especially painful given that all international artists get paid in US dollars."

If the cost of living in Vancouver has made it trickier for local nightclub owners to operate, it's had an even greater impact on nightclub patrons and those who work in them. For performers and musicians, gone are the days when three or four friends could get together and rent a house with a spare room for a music studio or art space. And young people—usually the target audience for bars and nightclubs—now have to work two or three jobs to cover the high cost of rent and can't afford to go out multiple nights a week, like people frequently did in the 1980s and '90s. Millennials are often the target of public derision for, among other things, supposedly not socializing outside of social media, but who can blame them when the cost of regularly

stepping out for the night is so expensive compared to their income?

Considering these factors, how will Vancouver shake the name that has dogged it for almost twenty years—"No Fun City." The term arose in the early 2000s, when downtown nightclub operators successfully lobbied city council officials to extend their hours past long-held two a.m. closing times. These days, the slur is more often invoked regarding the city's lack of live music venues, amount of red tape around civic events, strict liquor regulations, and especially, limited late-night transit options and taxi availability.

It would be ridiculous to say that all the great Vancouver nightclubs are gone, but there's still a sense that we've lost a vital part of the city's nightlife that shouldn't have disappeared so easily.

In 1999, Trader Vic's tiki bar was uprooted from its location next to the Westin Bayshore Hotel in Coal Harbour, placed upon a barge, and shipped to Victoria, where a Vancouver Island businessman planned to feature it at a winery he wanted to open in Central Saanich. Trader Vic's was a chain bar, of course, not a nightclub, but the image of the trademark building sailing slowly out of Burrard Inlet, underneath the Lions Gate Bridge, and away from Vancouver carried a ring of melancholy, as if another pivotal piece of the city's nightlife, however kitschy, were sailing away with it. (The plans to build that winery have so far failed to materialize, and twenty years later, the restaurant remains mothballed, waiting to be resurrected.)

Like walking past a Vancouver condo building named after the legendary nightclub that once stood in its place, there's a sense that the city too often cannibalizes itself. There's a feeling that because Vancouver is growing so quickly, we've let some of our favourite nightspots slip through our fingers. Perhaps in another city, where nightclub operators can afford to purchase their buildings, venues are more likely to stay the distance, but time and again,

Most old Vancouver night-spots have met their demise thanks to the wrecking ball. But in 1999, Trader Vic's was barged out of Burrard Inlet. Few nightclubs in Vancouver have departed the city so serenely. *Credit: Rob Kruyt/ Vancouver Sun Archives*

the threat to a Vancouver club hasn't been a fire or mismanagement but property development. From the saloons and great ballrooms of yesteryear to the supper clubs and dance halls that came after and, finally, the discos and live music spaces that followed, perhaps Vancouver fails to value or properly recognize the history and heritage within the walls of its fabled nightclubs and performance spaces.

Cities cannot be museums or monuments, and growth and development are inevitable, but how much richer would Vancouver's entertainment history be if modern acts could perform on more of its legendary stages, only adding to the history of a venue in the same way the Orpheum and the Commodore remain irreplaceable.

That so many Vancouver clubs that have disappeared in recent history are still talked about so avidly suggests something greater than mere nostalgia is at work. The longing for them seems to go beyond just simple reminiscence of the past and connect to the notion that the city has changed too much from development—particularly over the last two decades—that the loss of these means more than just another business closing. These nightspots made up part of the city's DNA—not just because of the legends of entertainment who performed in them but, more importantly, because of the generations of Vancouverites who spent their nights in them. Although many of these nightclubs might have changed their names or music styles over the

years, they were places that our parents or even grandparents went to before us, that we could also visit and, in that way, share an experience through time. But now only a few such places remain, and the possibility of opening new ones is a struggle.

This loss of shared experience in Vancouver's nightspots disconnects us from the past, and from each other. We would do well to recognize the heritage and history these places hold before any more of them are lost.

What the future holds has in store for Vancouver after dark will be determined in the coming years by the city's new players. The nightclub business is certainly much more corporate than it was in the days of the Cave, or even the Cruel Elephant, but there's still room for the graveyard-shift dreamers, the wildly talented musicians who were never meant for stadiums, and the array of nighttime characters who simply can't imagine working or living in the more regimented lifestyle that daytime hours provide. It's difficult to say who the new Isy Walters or Danny Baceda will be. More than ever, there is more room for women and people of other genders in the world of nightclub management, and the business has never been more culturally diverse. One thing is certain, though, whoever creates the future of the city's cabarets and clubs, as the wild history of Vancouver's entertainment and nightclubs demonstrates, they will have a big reputation to live up to.

ACKNOWLEDGMENTS

A book of this kind is dependent on the help and goodwill of a host of people. First off, thanks once again to my publisher, Arsenal Pulp Press: Brian Lam, Robert Ballantyne, Cynara Geissler, Shirarose Wilensky, and to editor Derek Fairbridge and designer Lisa Eng-Lodge for jumping aboard under tight time constraints and deadlines, which they navigated with such aplomb.

My great thanks to the treasure trove that is Neptoon Records and to proprietor Rob Frith for access to Neptoon's extensive playbill and concert poster collection. Where possible, I have tried to correctly acknowledge the artists and illustrators who produced them.

Historians—academic or cultural—benefit greatly when someone as generous and cooperative as Neptoon Records give access to their collections of rare local ephemera or long-lost material, allowing them to be rediscovered and appreciated. If you have vintage Vancouver concert or nightclub memorabilia that needs a home, do contact Neptoon or your local city archives. This book would have been very difficult to produce without such materials that help the nightlife history of the city come alive.

My deep gratitude to John Mackie and especially librarian Carolyn Soltau at the *Vancouver Sun*, who put up with my multiple emails and requests for photos from their archives, and always go the extra mile to pass along a gem or two they find along the way. May Carolyn take solace in not having to wake up first thing to find another late-night email from me asking if the *Sun* has one more photo of some long-forgotten nightlife figure or watering hole—at least for a little while.

Many thanks to Melanie Hardbattle, archivist at Simon Fraser University Special Collections, for her assistance with the poster collection donated by the late Perry Giguere. The new poster collection encapsulates forty years of Vancouver event history, and there will no doubt be continued discoveries, wonderful poster artwork, and fascination (and fun) to be found among the 30,000-plus posters.

Thanks and appreciation to the Belshaw Gang, especially Lani Russwurm, Jason Vanderhill, and in particular, Tom Carter, for his advice and (more often than not, late-evening) counsel that helped wrangle this project when I needed a lasso. I still hope we'll get to work on a project together somewhere down the road.

Jennifer Rosen read and commented on early drafts, much to the benefit of the final text. It is not the first time she has been of aid in such matters, and she always has my appreciation and gratitude.

A final word of thanks to Bill Allman, Gerry Barad, Squire Barnes, Howard Blank, Gyles Brandreth, the Burnaby Public Library, Peter Chapman, Paris Chong, Robbi Chong, Tommy Chong, Jenn Chycoski, B.J. Cook, Bev Davies, Hugh Dillon, Paul Dixon, Danny Filippone, Forbidden Vancouver, the Honourable Judge Thomas Gove, Colonel Chris Hadfield, Erik Hoffman, everyone at Live Nation British Columbia, Caroline MacGillivray, Guy MacPherson, Sean Mawhinney, Kyla McDonal, Riley O'Connor, David Osborne, Kevin Statham, Kevin Stork, the Vancouver Police Museum, the Vancouver Public Library, Roger Vickers, Richard Walters, and the *Vancouver Courier*.

As I noted in the introduction, this book is by no means a complete encyclopedia of all Vancouver nightclubs; instead, it focuses mainly on venues that had live entertainment, or that I considered to be pivotal—the right place at right time. There are other clubs that arguably could or should be included; perhaps they might be in a future edition or volume. If you think I've missed a worthy nightspot, or you have an interesting anecdote or memory of a nightclub from Vancouver's past, drop me a line.

Have a good night,
Aaron Chapman

REFERENCES

Books

Chong, Tommy. *Cheech and Chong: The Unauthorized Autobiography*. New York: Gallery Books, 2008.

Davis, Chuck. *The Chuck Davis History of Metropolitan Vancouver*. Madeira Park, BC: Harbour Publishing, 2011.

Kruz, Jerry. *The Afterthought: West Coast Rock Posters and Recollections from the '60s*. Victoria: Rocky Mountain Books, 2014.

Macdonald, Bruce. *Vancouver: A Visual History*. Vancouver: Talonbooks, 1992.

Potter, Greg, and Red Robinson. *Backstage Vancouver: A Century of Entertainment Legends*. Madeira Park, BC: Harbour Publishing, 2004.

Richards, Dal, with Jim Taylor. *One More Time!: The Dal Richard's Story*. Madeira Park, BC: Harbour Publishing, 2009.

Ross, Becki. *Burlesque West: Showgirls, Sex, and Sin in Postwar Vancouver*. Toronto: University of Toronto Press, 2009.

Articles

This book quotes heavily from *Vancouver Sun* and *Province* newspaper articles and entertainment sections. Newspaper issues are available on microfiche file at the Vancouver Public Library central branch and online.

Armstrong, John. "Too Much, Too Often." *Vancouver Sun*, June 8, 1991.

Asante, Nadine. "And Down Comes Finishing School." *Vancouver Sun*, June 18, 1965.

Boyd, Denny. "The Curtain Drops on Marco Polo." *Vancouver Sun*, January 27, 1982.

———. Recurring column. *Vancouver Sun*, March 8, 1968.

Dafoe, Christopher. "Improvising a Rover Boys Smoker." *Vancouver Sun*, November 7, 1969.

Elsie, Bud. "Police 'Party' Was Followed by Charges against Cabaret." *Vancouver Sun*, March 27, 1969.

Farrow, Moira. "Aquarium Chief Offended by Nightclub Idea." *Vancouver Sun*, January 28, 1986.

Fletcher, Bill. "Town Pump Pair Find Right Market." *Vancouver Sun*, April 1, 1971.

Fotheringham, Allan. Recurring column. *Vancouver Sun*, January 19, 1971.

———. Recurring column. *Vancouver Sun*, November 10, 1971.

Harrison, Tom. "Thunders but No Lightning." *Province*, May 7, 1981.

Lawrence, Grant. "Kitsilano's Legendary Soft Rock Café Remembered." *Westender*, July 5, 2017.

Mackie, John. "This Day in History: 1964." *Vancouver Sun*, November 16, 2012.

MacLeod, Brian. "Daisies in Full Bloom on Opening Night." *Vancouver Sun*, September 5, 1969.

Maitland, Andrea. "Near-Riot by Punk Rockers Wipes the Smile off Buddha." *Vancouver Sun*, November 2, 1979.

Merridew, Alan, and Andy Ross. "Who Will Be Sitting in the Mayor's Chair." *Vancouver Sun*, October 24, 1978.

Millin, Leslie. "Dream Comes True—Live Recording Success Mark." *Ottawa Journal*, April 10, 1965.

Parton, Lorne. *Province*, March 19, 1971.

Potter, Greg. "Backstage Past." *Vancouver Sun*, January 15, 2000.

Potts, Barney. "Pots and Pans." *Province*, May 29, 1965.

Province. Household Facilities and Equipment, Table 25: Telephones, Radios, Television Receivers. September 1955.

———. *Household Facilities and Equipment*, Table 29: Black and White TV Sets. April 1975.

Province. "What's Rock 'n' Roll Drink? ... Milk." May 27, 1963.

Read, Jeani. "Supper Club Reopens with Smile, Prayer." *Vancouver Sun*, March 1, 1978.

Richards, Jack. "Howie—How He Grew." *Vancouver Sun*, January 18, 1963.

Roitman, Martin S. "Not Obscene." *Vancouver Sun*, January 28, 1971.

Smith, Bob. "Creative Combo Keeps It Quiet." *Vancouver Sun*, October 31, 1984.

Vancouver Daily World. "The Concert Hall."
April 13, 1897.
———. "Music Hall Question." April 20, 1897.
Vancouver Sun. "Cave Will Present Another Fine
Show." October 14, 1939.
———. "Chain-Swinging Hoodlums Wreck Granville
Night Club." March 20, 1964.
———. "The Clubman." December 22, 1972.
———. "Drum-Roll Murder Suspect Still Eludes
Police." November 10, 1971.
———. "Jack Wasserman Tells Us about Club Men."
April 5, 1963.
———. "Morals Counts Face Quartette." March 2, 1951.
———. "Reward Offered for Nightclub Killer."
November 18, 1971.
———. "Shipyard Worker Stabbed to Death in Night
Club Brawl Saturday." November 2, 1942.
———. "Witnesses Testify of Inn Brawl." November
6, 1942.
———. "Zanzibar Boss Wins Acquittal." February
2, 1978.
Victoria Daily Times. "Swallowed Hardware."
January 5, 1901.
Wasserman, Jack. "The Beat Walkers." *Vancouver Sun,*
November 15, 1962.
———. "Hoot Toots." Vancouver Sun, July 2, 1963.
———. "The Town around Us," *Vancouver Sun,*
December 5, 1964.
———. Recurring column. *Vancouver Sun,*
March 10, 1966.
———. Recurring column. *Vancouver Sun,*
May 29, 1976.
West, Robbi. "George Vickers: Cabaret Owner."
Vancouver Sun, September 9, 1966.
Wilkes-Barre Record. "Go-Go Girls Must Cover Upper
Torsos." September 20, 1966.
Wiseman, Les. "Rear Window." *Vancouver Sun,*
April 2000.

Television
"Cave Nightclub Demolition." *BCTV News Hour.*
Global TV-BC. July 24, 1981. Tape #404.

Interviews with the Author
Allen, Bruce. June 6, 2014.
Alvaro, Vincent. June 15, 2019.
Armstrong, John. June 28, 2019.
Blank, Howard. July 15, 2019.
Bower, Ralph. June 19, 2018.
Buchanan, Ray. June 14, 2019.
Burrows, Bob. February 11, 2019.
Byrnes, Jim. January 11, 2019.
Carter, Tom. April 15, 2019.
Cartin, Ray. April 27, 2019.
Chisholm, David. May 29, 2019.
Chong, Tommy. May 28, 2019.
Collins, John. April 22, 2019.
Cook, B.J. May 3, 2019.
Cruikshank, Richard, and Jerry Kruz. March 21, 2019.
Crump, Ronnie and Robert. March 15, 2018.
Davies, Bev. May 26, 2019.
De La Fuente, Lori. May 5, 2019.
Fiddis, Stan. April 15, 2019.
Filippone, Danny. November 23, 2018.
Filippone, Ross. February 6, 2007.
Gold, Jake. March 1, 2019.
Good, Matthew. July 2, 2019.
Gordon, Michael. November 21, 2018.
Goud, Vernard. October 15, 2018.
Grant, Jason. May 27, 2019.
Grant, Ryan. March 15, 2019.
Hawkes, David. May 11, 2019.
Headstones (Hugh Dillon, Trent Carr, Tim White).
November 24, 2019.
Hopkins, Brett "Limo." July 26, 2019.
Lee-Nova, Gary. June 27, 2019.
Marchant, Vera. May 6, 2018.

Martin, Steve. July 22, 2015.
McDonald, Grant. May 1, 2019.
McKeown, Kevin Dale. May 3, 2019.
Mills, Dennis. July 21, 2013.
Mills, Rick. September 10, 2015.
Moes, Paul. June 30, 2019.
Newton, Steve. April 15, 2019.
Petterson, Bob. May 8, 2019.
Robinson, Curtis. April 10, 2019.
Robinson, Red. December 14, 2018.
Shea, Robert. April 7, 2019.
Sigmund, Ziggy. May 7, 2018.

Simkin, Jonathan. February 14, 2019.
Taylor, Gary. January 5, 2019.
Teti, John. February 13, 2019.
Tringham, Blaine. June 11, 2019.
Vickers, Roger. April 27, 2019.
Walker, Vincent. November 21, 2018.
Walters, Richard. August 24, 2015;
    September 27, 2016.
Warner, Mel. February 12, 2019.
Young, Henry. July 12, 2019.
Young, Norman. May 30, 2018.

INDEX

Photo: Mike Derakhshan

AARON CHAPMAN is a writer, historian, and musician. He is the author of three previous books published by Arsenal Pulp Press: *The Last Gang in Town*, the story of Vancouver's Clark Park Gang and the Canadian Historical Association's Clio Prize winner in 2017; *Liquor, Lust, and the Law*, the story of Vancouver's Penthouse nightclub, now available in a second edition; and *Live at the Commodore*, a history of Vancouver's Commodore Ballroom that won the Bill Duthie Booksellers' Choice Award, awarded by the BC Book Prizes, in 2015. He has toured as a musician throughout Canada, the United States, Europe, and more than his fair share of Vancouver nightclubs. Chapman has been a contributor to the *Vancouver Courier*, the *Georgia Straight*, and CBC Radio. A graduate of the University of British Columbia, he is also a member of Heritage Vancouver and the Point Roberts Historical Society.

aaronchapman.net